From the Ashes of Sobibor

FROM THE ASHES
OF SOBIBOR

A Story of Survival

THOMAS TOIVI BLATT

Foreword by Christopher R. Browning

NORTHWESTERN UNIVERSITY PRESS
Evanston, Illinois

Northwestern University Press
www.nupress.northwestern.edu

Printed in the United States of America

15 14 13 12 11

ISBN 978-0-8101-1302-2

Library of Congress Cataloging-in-Publication Data

Blatt, Thomas Toivi, 1927–
    From the ashes of Sobibor : a story of survival / Thomas Toivi
Blatt ; foreword by Christopher R. Browning.
        p. cm. — (Jewish lives)
    Includes bibliographical references.
    ISBN 0-8101-1302-3 (paper : alk. paper)
        1. Blatt, Thomas Toivi, 1927– . 2. Jews—Poland—Biography.
    3. Holocaust, Jewish (1939–1945)—Poland—Personal narratives. 4.
    Sobibór (Concentration camp). 5. World War, 1939–1945—Jewish
    resistance—Poland—Sobibór. I. Title. II. Series.
    DS135.P63B547 1997
    940.53'18'092—dc21   97-5455
                                                                 CIP

For all those left behind . . .

The fifth commandment, "Thou shall not kill," is not God's commandment at all: it is a Jewish invention.

—Statement of the high Nazi official Stahle after the protest, on December 4, 1940, by the evangelical priest Sautter against the criminal acts of euthanasia

The worst of everything was nothing in comparison with the reality. To survive Sobibor does not mean living.

—Hersz Cukerman, Sobibor survivor

Contents

❀

Acknowledgments

Shorter excerpts of my story have appeared in several publications. The story of Farmer Bojarski's attempt to kill me appeared in the Polish magazine *Swiat* (May 1953) and in the *Santa Barbara* (California) *News & Review* ("No Time for Tears," December 1977). My interview with Karl Frenzel appeared in various forms in the German magazine *Stern* ("Der Morder und Sein Zeuge," March 1984), the Israeli newspaper *Haaretz* (27 April 1984), and *Jewish Currents* ("Blood and Ashes," December 1978). My testimony about Sobibor, taken in 1945, is on record at the Jewish Historical Institute in Warsaw; my testimony is also contained in the files of the trials of Sobibor Nazis, which can be found in the Central Documentation Center in Ludwigsburg, Germany.

My diary describing the Sobibor revolt was used in the 1987 CBS documentary "Escape from Sobibor," a Chrysler Showcase Presentation, which is also available on video. *From the Ashes of Sobibor* is the full and detailed account of my early years, starting in the town of Izbica and continuing until my liberation by the Red Army in 1944.

I wish to recognize and honor the following gentiles who helped me to survive during a dangerous time in my life: Michał Sudoł (Ukrainian), Julian Pódgorski (Pole), Jan Sztajndel (Pole), Heniek Królikowski (Pole), Niusia Królikowska (Pole), Michał Petla (Pole), Jozefa Kowalczyk (Pole), and the unknown woman I met while escaping Sobibor. To them I would like to say: In a world gone awry, you remained my hope.

Writing this book took me over forty years. It would never have been finished without the help, patience, and insistence of my former wife, Dena. She spent countless hours editing my manuscript, squeezing from my memory stories I thought unimportant, but which she felt were necessary to record. I would like to give her all the credit she deserves as a true partner in writing this memorial.

I also wish to thank my friend Joseph Voss for his helpful advice in straightening out some of the details.

❖

Foreword

Poland was both the demographic and geographic center of the Holocaust. Over half the victims of the Holocaust were Polish Jews. Moreover, as the Nazi regime constructed on Polish soil the major extermination camps, which were the final destination of Jews deported from south, central, and western Europe, Poland became the graveyard for most of European Jewry as well. The district of Lublin in south-central Poland had a prewar Jewish population of 250,000, and was fated to become the site of no fewer than three of the six major extermination camps—Bełzec, Sobibor, and Majdanek.

A voice from the very heart of the Holocaust in Poland, Thomas Blatt recounts the extraordinary odyssey of one young survivor from the time of the German occupation in September 1939 to the liberation by the Red Army in 1944: first as a resident of the heavily Jewish town of Izbica in the district of Lublin; then as a deportee to, "work Jew" at, and escapee from the extermination camp Sobibor; and finally as hunted prey hiding from his relentless pursuers. A brief review of the course of events in the district of Lublin during the Nazi occupation will demonstrate that Blatt was at the very epicenter of the Holocaust—a rare and articulate witness to some of the most savage events of human history.

Prior to the German invasion of Poland on September 1, 1939, Hitler reached an agreement with Stalin for the partition of that country. Initially, the district of Lublin was to be part of Stalin's share of the spoils, destined for occupation by the Red Army. In late September 1939, however, an adjustment was made to the partition agreement. Lublin, and with it Blatt's hometown of Izbica, fell to German rather than Soviet occupation.

Thus began the upheaval and destruction of Polish Jewry. Several hundred thousand Jews fled eastward from the German to the Soviet zone to escape Nazi persecution. Many other Jews, particularly in the Lublin district, were rounded up and driven over the demarcation line by Nazi army and police units. At the same time, uprooted Jews from the west poured into the Lublin district, as Nazi "demographic engineers" ruthlessly tried to implement a policy of what is now called ethnic cleansing.

The western regions of Poland were annexed to the Third Reich as "incorporated territories." The Nazis wanted the land but not the inhabitants. Thus, except for the small German minority, the bulk of the population—both Poles and Jews—were to be expelled into central Poland. This was a region under a German colonial regime designated as the General Government. Within the General Government, one region in particular—the district of Lublin—was to become a "Jewish reservation." Thus, throughout the winter of 1939–40, trainloads of Polish and Jewish expellees were dumped into the General Government, with Lublin the particular destination of most Jewish expellees. Following the ethnic cleansing of the incorporated territories, the "Lublin reservation" was to receive Jewish deportees from Germany and other parts of the General Government as well.

The prospect of concentrating the Jews of Europe in a "Lublin reservation" provided much satisfaction to Nazi officials. As Artur Seyss-Inquart, a leading Austrian Nazi and the future ruler of German-occupied Netherlands, quoted a local Nazi official upon returning from an insepction tour of Lublin, "This territory with its extreme marshy nature can . . . serve as the Jewish reservation, the implementation of which could lead to a severe decimation of the Jews."[1] The head of the General Government, Hans Frank, also initially exhorted his officials to expel their Jews to Lublin: "Make short work of the Jews. What a pleasure, finally for once to be able to tackle the Jewish race physically."[2]

By the spring of 1940, however, many Nazi leaders began to have second thoughts about the consequences of ethnic cleansing in the incorporated territories. Hermann Göring realized a depopulated region could not be quickly harnessed to the war economy. Frank and his officials were overwhelmed by the flood of expellees and belatedly realized that the General Government could not become a "model colony" if it were fated to be the demographic dumping ground of the Third Reich. The pace of ethnic cleansing slowed, and the idea of a Jewish reservation in Lublin was abandoned in the spring of 1940.

Local German officials in Poland, who had concentrated their Jews in urban centers in anticipation of expelling them to Lublin, were now stuck. Their response was to create large sealed ghettos—what amounted to urban internment camps—for their unwanted Jews. As the Lublin district had been designated to receive rather than expel its Jews, the concentration and ghettoization process there did not unfold as it did in Łódź or Warsaw, where the ghettos of Jews concentrated from the surrounding areas were sealed in May and November 1940, respectively. In the Lublin district, Jews were not rounded up in the small towns and rural areas and concentrated in the city of Lublin, the district capital. Instead, many Jews were expelled from the capital city to provincial towns like Izbica before the Lublin ghetto of some 40,000 remaining Jews was sealed in the spring of 1941. In most of these provincial towns with their swelling populations of Jewish refugees, sealed ghettos were not constructed.

If the provincial Jews of the Lublin district were not interned in sealed ghettos, where widespread starvation and epidemics became commonplace, they nonetheless suffered from the same endless stream of discriminatory regulations, expropriation of property, and forced-labor roundups inflicted on all Polish Jews in the early years of the German occupation. But much worse was still to come.

In the spring of 1941, Hitler exhorted his military, party, and economic leaders to prepare for a "war of destruction" against the Soviet Union—a war for the territorial conquest of *Lebensraum,* an ideological crusade against the homeland of communism and an assault upon the demographic center of world Jewry. Operation Barbarossa was launched on June 22, 1941, and the German invaders experienced heady success in the first weeks. With seeming victory in sight, a euphoric Hitler launched a campaign of systematic annihilation against Soviet Jewry in mid-July. By early October, he had approved the extension of this mass-murder campaign—the "Final Solution to the Jewish Question"—to the rest of European Jewry under Nazi control.

Mass execution through firing squad was the method of murder employed on Soviet territory, but it was not suitable for the mass murder of European Jewry. Deportation to camps equipped with poison gas facilities—already tested in the killing of over 70,000 mentally handicapped persons in Germany—was to be the alternative method of execution. Construction of the first two extermination camps, Chełmno near Łódź and Bełżec near Lublin, began in the fall of 1941.

The murder of local Jews in the gas vans of Chełmno began in early December 1941, and deportations from the Łódź ghetto to Chełmno began in January 1942. By mid-March 1942, the extermination camp at Bełżec, equipped with a stationary gas chamber instead of mobile gas vans, was ready to receive deportations. On March 16, the Lublin ghetto was surrounded, and the ghetto-clearing campaign began. Over the next month, nearly 40,000 Jews from the ghetto were either shot on the spot during the brutal roundups or deported to Bełżec and gassed upon arrival.

In the midst of the liquidation of the Lublin ghetto, Josef Goebbels wrote in his diary on March 27, 1942:

> Beginning with Lublin, the Jews in the General Government are now being evacuated eastward. The procedure is a pretty barbaric one and not to be described here more definitely. Not much will remain of the Jews. . . . Fortunately, a whole series of possibilities presents itself for us in wartime that would be denied us in peacetime. We shall have to profit by this. The ghettos that will be emptied in the cities of the General Government will now be refilled with Jews thrown out of the Reich. This process is to be repeated from time to time.[3]

The process described by Goebbels was precisely what befell Izbica. Even as the Germans concentrated on liquidating the large ghetto in Lublin, nearby towns in the district as well as in the neighboring district of Galicia to the east were also struck. On March 24, some 2,200 Jews—nearly half the Jewish population—were deported from Izbica to Bełżec. A second deportation action was carried out in Izbica on April 8. The space vacated by the deportees was quickly filled with Jews deported from the west—three trainloads each from Germany and Czechoslovakia. Izbica had become what the Germans called a "transit ghetto," in effect a holding station for Jews awaiting their turn for the final trip to the gas chambers.

By mid-April the limited facilities of the extermination camp at

Bełzec had been overwhelmed. Within a month, 48,000 Jews from the district of Lublin and 36,000 from the district of Galicia had been killed and buried there. The limited capacity of the three small gas chambers in a single wood-frame building as well as the body disposal procedures were taxed beyond the breaking point. Franz Stangl, the future commandant at Sobibor and then Treblinka, recalled the horrifying scene that he witnessed during his visit to Bełzec in April 1942. "The man I was talking to said that one of the pits had overflowed. They had put too many corpses in it and putrefaction had progressed too fast, so that the liquid underneath had pushed the bodies on top up and over and the corpses had rolled down the hill. I saw some of them—oh God, it was awful."⁴ Thus in mid-April the deportations from Lublin and Galicia to Bełzec were halted, the wooden building housing the three small gas chambers was torn down, and a new, larger stone building with six gas chambers was constructed.

But the mass-murder campaign was not delayed for long. Even as Bełzec was closed for the expansion of its gassing facilities, a new extermination camp in the Lublin district, under construction since mid-March, was opened at Sobibor in early May. The deportation campaign in the district was resumed, and by mid-June more than 50,000 Jews from the district had perished there. In this second wave of deportations, Izbica was struck again on May 15.

When Bełzec reopened in late May 1942, it was reserved for deportations from the districts of Galicia and Kraków but not Lublin. Beginning in late June, all rail transport was temporarily reserved for the military. When Jewish transports were resumed in July, the crucial rail line to Sobibor was closed for repairs until October. As a result, except for occasional shooting actions and a brief flurry of deportations from the northern Lublin district to Treblinka in late August, the Jews of the Lublin district experienced a brief respite.

When the rail line to Sobibor reopened and Treblinka also became available to receive deportations following the liquidation of the Warsaw ghetto, the murderous assault upon Lublin Jewry reached its climax in October and November of 1942 in a third wave of deportations. One Jewish community after another was systematically liquidated. On the "black day" of October 15, 1942, the bulk of Izbica Jewry was rounded up for deportation. As train space was insufficient, a bloodbath ensued, with some five hundred Jews shot on the spot. According to different sources, between six and ten thousand Jews were deported to Sobibor that day. On November 2, Izbica was struck again. Fewer than one thousand Jews remained.

Izbica was then designated as one of the eight remnant ghettos that would be allowed to exist in the Lublin district through the winter, though yet another action struck the town in January. Finally, on April 28, 1943, the last Jews of Izbica were rounded up and deported to the extermination camp at Sobibor. Thomas Blatt and his family were among them.

In 1942 the German ghetto clearers were fairly successful in paralyzing their victims. Each deportation was always to be the last. If everyone remained quiet, the surviving Jews would be allowed to go on working. If there was any trouble, the entire ghetto would be liquidated instantly. Such deception was effective as long as the ultimate German goal of total annihilation remained unbelievable. Why, after all, would the Germans be so irrational as to kill off the skilled Jewish laborers so useful to the German war effort? Given the disparity in power between the Germans and their victims, and the credible threat of collective retaliation for any obstruction of the deportation process, resistance did not seem rational. Hiding during the roundups and making oneself valuable to the German economy at other times seemed to be the most sensible response for most Jews in Poland in the disastrous year of 1942.

By 1943 the evidence of the Nazis' ultimate goal was undeniable, the threat of collective retaliation lost its meaning, and Jewish response began to change. The resumption of deportations from the Warsaw ghetto in January 1943 met with resistance, and the Germans retreated. The final German attack on the ghetto in April encountered tenacious and prolonged resistance. In July the inmates of the Treblinka extermination camp staged an uprising and breakout. In August the Germans encountered resistance in liquidating the remnant of the Białystok ghetto. The Sobibor uprising and breakout in October 1943, in which Blatt was a participant, was thus part of a wider trend in altered Jewish response in Poland.

The German reaction in the Lublin district was devastating. For Heinrich Himmler the remaining Jewish labor camps were a looming danger, but they could not be liquidated in stages without triggering the kind of desperate resistance and escape that had occurred in Treblinka and Sobibor. In early November 1943, therefore, Himmler summoned SS and police units from all over Poland to converge on Lublin for Operation Harvest Festival, or *Erntefest*. On November 3 and 4, Himmler's mobilized forces descended upon the major work camps in Lublin (especially Majdanek), Poniatowa, and Trawniki, and massacred some 42,000 "work Jews" in the single largest German killing action of the Final Solution. The smoke from the burning bodies of the Jews murdered in Majdanek hung like a pall over the city of Lublin for a week. The district of Lublin was then declared *Judenfrei,* or "free of Jews."

Thereafter, the only Jews to remain alive in the Lublin district were those, like Thomas Blatt, who waged a unflagging struggle to survive in hiding. It was a harrowing experience of constant vulnerability and unremitting danger. When the Red Army reached Lublin in July 1944, there were very few survivors in hiding left to rescue. Thomas Blatt was one of them. What follows is his extraordinary story of survival through five years of Nazi occupation.

CHRISTOPHER R. BROWNING
PACIFIC LUTHERAN UNIVERSITY
TACOMA, WASHINGTON

✤

Preface

On September 1, 1939, when I was twelve years old, World War II exploded when Germany invaded Poland. Two weeks later Poland surrendered, and a country of over thirty million people found itself in the grip of Fascism. The persecution of Jews gradually intensified and ultimately escalated into mass transports to specially built extermination camps.

I have always felt the need to write, and even while in elementary school I kept a diary. When war came this habit intensified, and as the atrocities began I kept writing. Later I realized that I was probably writing for others who might not survive the whirlwind. During this time, I periodically gave pages of my diary to Christian friends for safekeeping.

Fate did not spare me from the terrible experiences to which a Jew was subjected in Nazi-occupied Poland. I went from the ghetto to jail, then to the infamous death camp Sobibor,[1] where I became a fighter during its revolt and an escapee from its inevitable death sentence. Soon after, I found myself a hunted animal in the forest, and finally joined the Polish Underground until the liberation.

My diary pages were often lost, then reconstructed, only to be lost again. After the war I was able to recover about 40 percent of my original writings. In 1952 I produced a manuscript based on my notes and offered the material to the Communist publishing company in Poland. They wanted to publish the book, but *their* way, which would have compromised many of the essential facts. Since I did not agree to this, the manuscript had to be put away for another six years.

In 1958, as a new immigrant to Israel, I gave my manuscript to a well-known survivor of Auschwitz for his comments. After three weeks, the only words he said were: "You have a tremendous imagination. I've never heard of Sobibor and especially not of Jews revolting there." I was whipped many times by the SS in the Sobibor death camp, but I never felt so sharp a pain as I did when I heard those words. If he, an Auschwitz survivor, did not believe me, who would? And so another twenty years passed.[2]

When the television miniseries *Holocaust* was released in 1978, people started to write more about those times. Some excerpts from my diary were published in magazines and newspapers, and some material was incorporated into *Escape from Sobibor* by Richard Rashke (Boston: Houghton Mifflin, 1982), which was later made into the 1987 documentary of the same name. My complete book, however, remained unpublished.

While reading over my story recently, I asked myself several questions: What use would my book be, since so much has already been written about the Holocaust? What else could I add? Who would be interested? I concluded that not only would the few survivors of my generation be interested in the story, but succeeding generations would consider it a valuable document.

I have read what I call "positive" books on the Holocaust—in spite of their accounts of human cruelty and suffering, a message always shines through their pages, telling about courage, selflessness, great faith, and the survival of the human spirit. My story has no dominant message; it is the story of a Jewish teenager just trying to survive.

At long last I have completed my story of human suffering and endurance, a story that sounds unbelievable at times, even to me, although every word is true.

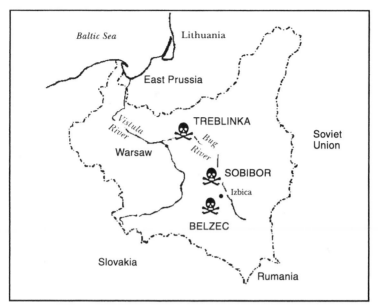

LOCATION OF THE "OPERATION REINHARD" INSTALLATIONS
IN OCCUPIED POLAND

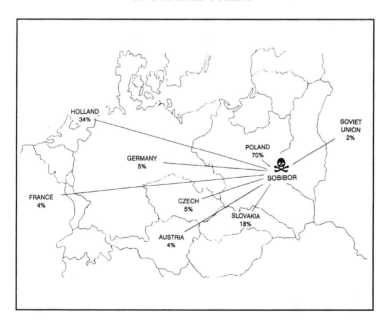

DEPORTATIONS OF EUROPEAN JEWS TO SOBIBOR

SOBIBOR

*As remembered by SS Sergeant Erich Bauer
and survivor Thomas Blatt*

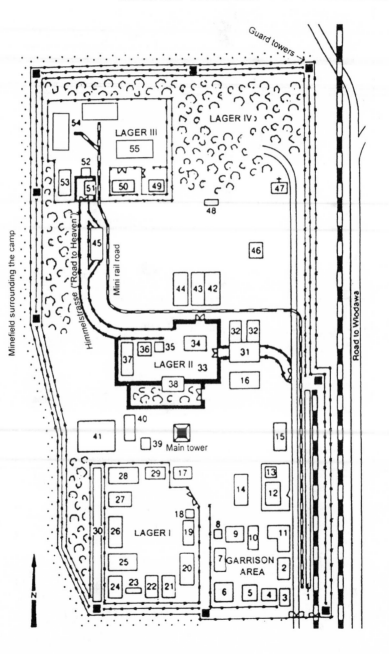

Garrison Compound

1. Unloading platform
2. Dentist office for SS and jail for Ukrainian guards
3. Guard house
4. SS clothing storeroom
5. SS quarters — the Swallow's Nest
6. SS quarters
7. Laundry
8. Well
9. Showers and barbershop for SS
10. Garage
11. SS kitchen and canteen
12. Commandant's headquarters — the Merry Flea
13. Armory
14. Barracks for Ukrainian guards
15. Barracks for Ukrainian guards
16. Barracks for Ukrainian guards
17. Bakery

Lager I

18. Dispensary
19. Tailor shop for SS
20. Shoemaker and saddler for SS
21. Mechanic shop
22. Carpenter shop
23. Latrine
24. Painters' shop
25. Barracks for male prisoners
26. Barracks for male prisoners
27. Prisoners' kitchen
28. Barracks for female prisoners
29. Shoemaker shop for Ukrainian guards
30. Water ditch

Lager II

31. Barracks where new arrivals deposited hand luggage and purses
32. Barracks for sorting hand luggage
33. Undressing yard
34. Food warehouse and porch where SS gave welcoming speech
35. Kiosk where SS collected money and jewelery
36. Electrical generator
37. Stable and barns
38. Administration building and storeroom for valuables
39. SS ironing room
40. Shoe warehouse
41. Garden
42. Barracks for sorting clothes and suitcases
43. Barracks for sorting clothes and suitcases
44. Warehouse for sorted clothes
45. Barracks where women's hair was cut
46. Incinerator
47. "Lazarett" (former chapel) used in the beginning to kill immobile Jews
48. Latrine

Lager III

49. Barracks for Jewish workers
50. Barracks for Jewish workers, kitchen and "dentist" workshop
51. Gas chambers
52. Engine room for gas chambers
53. Enclosed yard
54. Graves
55. Open-air crematorium

From the Ashes of Sobibor

The Beginning

Facing Reality

The gate opened, revealing what seemed to be a beautiful village. Before us lay a black paved road lined with flower beds. On our left stood a neat, colorful house surrounded by immaculate lawns, lovely trees, and flowers. The mass of humanity surged forward. We could see signposts, figures beautifully carved in wood: a waiter holding a dish, a barber with a razor. Could such a place be a death factory? Impossible! Perhaps it really was a work camp, just as the Germans had said.

But I knew better. Even as I passed the green cottage with the idyllic name Swallow's Nest over the door, I knew I was here to die. But why? I was only fifteen years old. What terrible thing had I done to deserve this? I took stock of the situation. Barbed wire and Ukrainian guards with rifles surrounded us. It was hopeless. There was no chance of escape. As I walked with my mother, I turned and looked at her. She looked pale and weary, and for the first time I noticed deep wrinkles at the sides of her mouth. Though she was only forty-six years old, the four years of dehumanizing ghetto life had aged her and drained her strength. She didn't seem to care about life anymore.

This was it. We were going to be killed in the gas chambers, or electrocuted, as some of us thought. These were our last steps in life. The sun was still high in the sky, birds were singing. It was such a beautiful spring day—April 28, 1943. I didn't want to die.

"Halt! Men, right! Women, children, left!" the SS man shouted. A few boys my age remained with their mothers. My ten-year-old brother left my father and went to my mother, whose hand I still held. Did I have a chance? I had to decide . . . I reached over and hastily kissed my mother's cheek.

I wanted to say something, aware that we were parting forever.

But for reasons I still cannot understand, out of the blue I said to my mother, "And you didn't let me drink all the milk yesterday. You wanted to save some for today."

Slowly and sadly she turned to look at me. "This is what you think about at such a moment?"

To this day the scene comes back to haunt me, and I have regretted my strange remark, which turned out to be my very last words to her. I would give anything to be able to recreate that moment, to change it, to hug her and tell her I love her, but by 1943 it was as if we were robots, moving like expressionless shadows. I never cried. I was past crying. Even if I could have expressed myself, there was no time. I walked toward my father in the men's group.

A heavyset German carrying a club strode in front of our formation and asked what trades we knew. Even now there was a ray of hope, a bone thrown to the doomed! People began to push toward the front, yelling: "I'm a shoemaker!" "I'm a tailor!" "I'm a carpenter!" "I'm a baker!" One's life could be saved by giving the right answer. I knew I could not qualify as any specialist. I looked small and thin and much younger than my age.

There was nothing I could say, but I, too, pushed toward the front hoping to be noticed. I fixed my eyes intently on the SS man and repeated silently in my head, "God, let him take ME, take ME, take ME!"

Suddenly our eyes met, and I knew this was the decisive moment. I had reached him! He pointed to me and said, "Komm raus, du Kleiner [Come out, little one]." I was temporarily saved.

The commotion of those people pleading in vain was too much for the SS man. He grabbed a club and swung it right and left, blindly and indiscriminately. My father buckled under the blows. I was in anguish, unable to help him. In the confusion I lost sight of him. Finally about forty men stood aside, selected for various trades. The rest (about two hundred) were led away and slowly disappeared from view. They were going to the gas chambers and my father was one of them, but the reality of that didn't touch me then.

While our selected group was being herded away, I heard screams in the distance and occasionally a gunshot. Then suddenly it was quiet, only the heavy rumbling of an engine could be heard.

"Juden laufen! [Jews, run!]" yelled the SS. We hurried under the whip and the threat of the machine gun to a barbed-wire enclosure. It

AUTHOR'S PARENTS

all happened so fast that we didn't have time to think. "Herein [Get in]." We found ourselves in a yard surrounded by plain wooden barracks.

A neatly dressed prisoner approached. "I'm Kurt," he said. "Give me your name and birthdate." One after the other he entered us into a ledger.

"What kind of place is this?" someone asked.

"You will work," he said, adding quickly, "and now you will go to your barrack. Follow me."

The interior of the barrack was very clean. About one-fifth of the building was sectioned off by a thin wall with a door—the Kapos'[1] quarters, as I found out later. In the center of the larger area stood a big wooden table with two benches, and against the walls were three tiers of platforms reaching from floor to ceiling. These were our living quarters.

"Choose your space," Kurt said.

There was a mad scramble. I immediately headed for the far corner of the top platform and climbed up. The spaces allocated were very narrow, only two feet wide, with the bedding already in place as if someone had just left. Sure enough, under my pillow I found socks, bread, cigarettes, pictures, and scraps of paper with scribbling in a strange language. Someone had apparently been sleeping here. I couldn't think further. I wasn't yet ready to grasp the possibility that I was alive because this someone was now dead.

From my bunk I could see outside through a space where the roof met the wall. An SS man suddenly appeared in the yard. "You, you, and you," he shouted. He picked at random fifteen of the newcomers who were standing about and led them away. I climbed down from my bunk and went into the yard. There were smoke and flames in the distance, and a strange sweet smell in the air. I didn't let myself understand.

Pretty soon the men returned. They appeared to be in a state of deep shock and depression. They had been forced to pick up from a fenced yard the still-warm clothes of the people from our transport and bring them to another place where prisoners sorted them. Some recognized the clothes of their own family members.

I went back inside the barrack and lay down on the bunk again, my thoughts wandering. Not for a moment did I think about or let myself feel any emotion over the loss of my mother, father, or brother. I seemed to know instinctively that any such self-indulgence would destroy me. Instead I compulsively went over the series of events leading to this unthinkable end. I kept wondering what would have happened had my family gone with the others across the border to the Soviet Union in 1939 as we had planned. Maybe we would have survived. I went over the times and places when we had possibly missed our chance to save ourselves. Would this or that have saved us, or only brought us here sooner? How could we have avoided this terrible situation? Could we have emigrated to another country before the war, before the Nazi horror began? And where to? America? Would they have taken us, even if we had the money? But things weren't so ominous back then. How could we possibly have known what was to come?

Izbica

I was born in Izbica in 1927 and spent my childhood there. The mark it left on me will last forever. For me, it was the center of the world. Before I went to school, I learned of other towns only through my relatives: one of my aunts, Chaja, married and moved to Krasnystaw; my grandmothers were in Zamość and Lublin; and an uncle lived in Warsaw. My cousins emigrated to other countries—two of them, Communists, went to Russia in 1930; another, a Zionist, went to Palestine; and a third, with a flair for entrepreneurship, went to the United States. From their letters, I came to know a little of the outside world.

Izbica was a typical shtetl, near the city of Lublin in southeastern Poland.[2] Catholic farmers lived in the hills surrounding the shtetl, but in Izbica itself there were about 3,600 Jews and two hundred Christians. Most townspeople were poor and lived in wooden flats; only a very few, the wealthy, had brick houses. Three artesian pumps and a few wells supplied water. There was no electricity until the mid-1930s.

The Jews were predominantly Orthodox, but progressive ideas were beginning to take hold. The caftan, beard, earlocks, and skull-cap were beginning to give way to Polish or Western dress.

My family lived in a large *yerishe*[3] built by my great-grandfather. With succeeding generations, the building was gradually subdivided into several tiny living quarters. We were considered well-off.

The building was made of wood and had two floors. Both sides of the hallway were lined with small one- and two-room "apartments." We lived in the first one on the left. We had a kitchen with a wood-burning stove, shelves for dishes, and a bunk for the maid. Josele, one of the few water carriers, brought us our water once a day by bucket, a luxury reserved for the "wealthy." We stored the water in a large tin basin.

Our dining room was furnished with a wooden table, four chairs, a large brown dresser, and a grandfather clock. High on the wall hung a colorful stuffed pheasant, a gift from a hunter, and two pictures depicting scenes from Polish folklore, bought from a poor Polish art student. Behind partition was a tiny den, furnished with a single sofa. The bedroom was small, furnished with a double bed, a nightstand that also served as a medicine cabinet, and a large clay oven to keep us warm in the winter.

Next door lived my Aunt Miriam. Her son, also called Toivi, was my age. Living opposite us was Motel Brinker, a widower who owned a small café, and his daughter. Next to him, in a tiny, dark room with a dirt floor, was Rajzł, who eked out a pitiful living by buying a couple of young geese at a time and fattening them up for sale. Her only son, a young man with tuberculosis, never left his bed. At the end of the hallway were stairs leading to the second floor. There, in two rooms, my Grandmother Hany-Sure used to live with her son, my Uncle Jankel. There were two other rooms on that floor, which we never used.

Everybody knew everybody in Izbica, and people were called mostly by nicknames. One or two words often described perfectly someone's beliefs, social standing and family lineage, or physical attributes. There was Łume (Lame) Chaim and Dziobaty (Chicken Pox) Jojne. Everyone knew that *Zamościer bekker* was Szulim Handwerker, a baker from Zamość. My father was called *Leibele goy,* because he was a so-called freethinker who ate ham and associated closely with Christians.

My schooling contributed to my religious confusion. I attended both the Jewish and the Christian religious classes; I was greatly intrigued by the Bible stories. When I was about seven years old I thought: Maybe they're right . . . maybe my father *is* a goy! He seldom goes to the synagogue, he smokes on Saturday, and HE EATS HAM! True, when he does, he locks the doors and closes the shutters . . . but people know, they know.

One day he held out a piece of ham to me. "Try it, Toivi, try it, it's good!" I did, and it tasted better than any meat I'd ever eaten. But the next day my Aunt Miriam, who had overheard our conversation through the thin walls, called me to her room.

"Toivi, you eat ham . . . tell me." It was a statement, not a question, asking only for confirmation. I had never lied.

"Yes, Aunt Miriam, I have eaten ham."

"You will be punished and go to Hell," she said sternly. "Don't listen to your father. He is not a true Jew."

"But, Aunt, why should I go to Hell? My religion teacher told us to listen to our parents. What did I do wrong?" I was looking for an excuse. But she wasn't moved by my shaky voice and frightened face.

"Toivi," she repeated, "it is forbidden for a Jew to eat pork. It is not kosher, and you will go to Hell for it."

Although many years have passed, I still remember how shocked I was. A sensitive and very imaginative boy, I saw myself in flames with devils all around me. "Oh God, I repent, I repent . . . ," I murmured as I lay down on the sofa. My head buzzed in a never- ending spiraling rhythm.

By the time my mother returned from shopping, I had a high fever.

The doctor was called, and he prescribed medicine for me. I was ill for days, and everyone was good to me. My mother even gave me her precious watch to play with. At last my Aunt Miriam appeared.

"Aunt Miriam, I'm afraid."

"What are you afraid of?"

"I'm afraid that I'll go to Hell."

"Toivi, are you worrying?" She looked at me for a long while, connecting events, then she said, "Toivi, you must obey the Jewish law, but God is merciful, and God willing, when you are thirteen and have your bar mitzvah a new life will start for you. All your old sins will be forgiven."

A ray of hope shone on my soul. But for a long time afterward I worried about my father's condemned soul. His bar mitzvah was long since over; he had no second chance. As for me, I had a new lease on life. I miraculously became well . . . and having a few years' credit, I went back to eating ham.

They called me "Toivi Hersz Ber's" after my grandfather Hersz Ber. He was strictly Orthodox, very pious, and well respected in the community. When someone who knew my family wanted to describe my shockingly goyish ways, such as not wearing *payas* (earlocks) or skipping *heder* (Hebrew school), they would often say despairingly, "Toivi, if your grandfather Hersz Ber—blessed be he in heaven— could get up from his grave and see you, he would immediately go back voluntarily, in shame." And so days and years passed, torn between my family's secretive tries to break away from tradition and their need to still get along with my ultra-Orthodox relatives, all living under the same roof. I even had *payas* at times.

I believed in and was afraid of God, and tried to follow the rules as well as I could. After washing in the morning I said "Moyde Ani," thanking God for safeguarding my soul while I slept. I washed my hands accordingly, and said my prayers before eating. And yet my father and mother, whose authority I respected, acted differently. They were occasionally invited to Christian homes and ate nonkosher food! When relatives thought that my parents wouldn't celebrate a particular holiday properly, they would simply "kidnap" me, bringing me to their own homes and tables.

I'm still not sure what my belief in God was based on. I simply believed in His universal power, His ability to help and to punish.

However, I had my doubts when the local *beit midrash* (house of learning) burned down. It was His house. He had the power. Nothing was supposed to happen without His will. There were many questions I wanted to ask God. Nevertheless, I believed in Him. Many times, upon returning late from a friend's house, scared of the dark streets and imagining demons, I would repeat the prayer "Shema Yisrael" over and over. With the praise of God on my lips, nothing could hurt me.

We lived peacefully with our Catholic neighbors. True, once in a while anti-Semitic slogans like "Jews to Palestine" and "Don't buy from Jews" appeared in the post office, but no one took them seriously. Catholic and Jewish schoolchildren kept mainly to themselves. About half of the students were Jewish and half Catholic, for though the town was over 95 percent Jewish, the children from all the outlying villages attended the town's elementary school. Inside the classroom there was no visible antagonism.

There was some religiously based excitement, but it happened among the Jews themselves. Once a group of young Jews from the city of Zamość arrived unexpectedly in Izbica on the Sabbath—without caps and on bicycles. This was too much for Izbica; they were chased out under a hail of stones by their Orthodox brethren.

On the Sabbath everything came to a halt in accordance with Jewish law. There was no school for Jewish students. The whole town would be unusually quiet and in a holiday mood. The Jews would walk to the synagogue with an air of dignity and holiness. The men dressed in black caftans, wearing skullcaps or hats and carrying their prayer shawls in embroidered bags. The women dressed in long skirts, wigs, and kerchiefs, and the children walked alongside like miniature adults. Little did we know that these peaceful Saturdays in Izbica would soon be only memories.

The Beginning

The Nazi terror began when the Germans attacked Poland in September 1939. "Mobilization!" screamed the posters. And in the marketplace the town crier issued the first air-raid instructions.

Two days later the first bombs fell on our town. They did no damage, but our family, wanting to be more secure, left for the forest village of Pańska Dolina, about twelve miles away. When we arrived, the forest was shaking from explosions. The Germans were bombarding Polish army groups taking shelter there.

A few days later the Polish army began to retreat, burying weapons and ammunition in the forest to lighten their load. Immediately some Polish civilians arrived and dug them up.

At the edge of the forest a young lieutenant was making a speech to a group of tired and dirty soldiers. He spoke with sorrow of this most trying moment, recalling how they fought the Germans and were ready to sacrifice their lives for their beloved country. He told the soldiers that they had been stabbed in the back by the Communists, now allies of the Nazis, and that Soviet armies were invading Poland from the East. And although he had been informed that their division had surrendered to the Germans, they would fight their last battle. Now the lieutenant ordered them to defend this village until the last bullet, the last grenade. The soldiers sang "Rota," an anti-German anthem, and moved into the shadows of the forest. Constant gunfire from the west announced the Germans' approach.

We did not know what to do. Some Jews suggested escaping eastward, but others felt that the Germans were also human beings capable of compassion and would not harm civilians. Some moved on to cross the Bug River and meet the Soviets. We returned to Izbica.

Back in Izbica I found out that German soldiers had been there and left, and now the Soviets were coming. I was disappointed. My brother Hersz ran up to me and said that there were still two German soldiers at the Handwerkers' bakery, buying bread. The war is almost coming to an end, I thought, and I cannot miss my chance to see a German. It took only a couple of minutes to get to the bakery, and soon I saw the two soldiers in strange dark green uniforms packing fresh bread into their bicycle bags. I stopped nearby and listened. I could have sworn they were speaking Yiddish. Although some words seemed strange, I understood their conversation. They threw me a candy, for which I said in Yiddish, "A sheinem dank." They laughed and corrected me, "Danke schön." Then they left our town.

It was a dreary, drizzly day when the Russians approached Izbica. A "Red Militia" was organized by local Communists, whose leader was a former cobbler, a Jew named Abram Wajs.

Around noon, our family lunch was interrupted by the noise of engines. From our balcony I could see heavy Soviet tanks followed by trucks full of soldiers. They moved across a stretch of muddy ground alongside the main street, thereby avoiding the antitank mines. As some Polish soldiers and officers were still in the town, the local Communists, together with the Russian soldiers, set off immediately to disarm them.

One couldn't distinguish between Red Army officers and enlisted men, since they didn't wear any insignia and all of them had on long, gray, frayed coats. They behaved decently toward civilians. Some soldiers slept in trucks parked alongside the tanks in the marketplace; others slept on straw in the movie theater. None ventured into private homes.

A few days later my Uncle Shmuel Staw told us that the Red Army was going to withdraw. Rumors circulated that the Germans had signed a nonaggression pact with the Soviets and divided Poland between themselves. In accordance with the agreement, the Red Army would retreat behind a line along the Bug River.

So the Nazis were coming again! Impossible! Uncle Staw had to be wrong! I got dressed and went to see for myself. He wasn't wrong after all—the Soviets were pulling out. Tailing after them were some Jewish horse carts. Jews were fleeing, taking their few humble possessions with them.

I roamed around all day long. When I returned in the evening I could hear my parents having a heated discussion in the next room. My mother was very emotional, trying to persuade my father to leave Izbica.

"Leibele, listen to me, I can speak Russian. We'll get along. Anything is better than suffering persecution by the Nazis. I've heard about the anti-Semitic measures in Germany. They could do the same thing here."

But my father stubbornly kept repeating, "I won't go into exile with small children. I was born here, and here I will die. Besides," he said, "before the Russians came, there were Germans here in Izbica, and there were no atrocities."

Much later, when we had to face the crematoriums, it was said that if the Germans had staged a pogrom and killed a number of Jews upon entering Izbica, it would have been a blessing for us. All the remaining Jews would have gone to the Soviet side.

Six Jews were in fact killed during the first German occupation of the town, among them our neighbor, the butcher Brajtman. But the Jewish population blamed this on chaotic frontline conditions, and again hope played its role. We always hoped things would return to normal. Now our only escape route was closing.

The Soviets had left, but the Germans had not yet arrived. Our town was for a time a no-man's-land. Gangs of local Polish hooligans began to menace the Jewish population. It didn't take much to inspire them. Large colored posters were everywhere—on the streets, in the depot, and in the mayor's office. Jews were depicted as dishonest. One picture showed dead rats being added to ground meat for sale; another showed a big louse climbing from the collar of a Jew onto a Christian Pole, spreading typhus. Others depicted Jews as murderers, sucking blood from innocent Christian children, supposedly for making Passover matzo. The Germans' anti-Semitic propaganda spread like a virus.

We never talked about or even mentioned the posters. This kind of propaganda was merely a part of our lives. There was nothing we could do about it. Yet sometimes I would look at those posters and think: Do my Polish neighbors really believe this propaganda? Before the war, although relations may have been strained, Christians and Jews still socialized, worked, and studied together. Now we didn't know whom to trust.

Around six o'clock one evening, right after supper, the walls shook from a terrific explosion. We heard a piercing cry, followed by a long, deep silence. The next day there were rumors that two local teenagers, Maniek Królikowski and Jacek Malec, had thrown a grenade into a group of Jews standing in the street. A number of people were injured, among them a woman who died after several weeks of terrible suffering. It was obviously an act of revenge on the band of Jewish Communists who had collaborated with the Soviets.

Afraid of future acts of violence in this no-man's-land, the towns-people sent a delegation, headed by my Aunt Miriam, to Krasnystaw, the district capital, asking the Germans to come in and restore law and order. A so-called *Ortskommandatur der Wehrmacht* (local military command) was quickly set up in Izbica, and then it was relatively quiet.

During the first few weeks of occupation, life went on as usual.

The Germans set up a field hospital next to the train station for lightly wounded Wehrmacht soldiers. I wandered about town freely, and was very curious to see the Germans at close range and chat with them.

The next day, without my father's knowledge, when the Jewish elders assigned a group of Jews to clean the Germans' barracks, I joined them. Two of us cleaned the floors and took out the trash. Time passed. When evening came, the barracks filled with soldiers returning from a stroll in the park. They seemed nice, and I asked one for a cigarette.

"Ach du kleiner, du rauchst? [Oh, you little one, you smoke?]"

I explained it was for my father, who was a heavy smoker.

"Do you have a sister by chance?"

I was a shy boy, but knowledgeable in essential matters. I immediately grasped the possibilities. "Oh, yes. She's eighteen," I answered. I wasn't sure if he knew that we were Jewish.

"Here," he said. A whole pack of cigarettes wound up in my hand. "Ask her if she can come and do the cleaning tomorrow."

I told him I would talk to her. The pressure to introduce my nonexistent sister continued several more days and produced another two packs of cigarettes. During that time, I came to know Willy. He was twenty, only eight years older than I was, and bashful in a way. The next time he asked about my sister, while handing me two more packs of cigarettes, I knew I had no choice.

"Herr Corporal, I want to tell you something."

"Say it, Tom."

"Will you hit me if you don't like it?"

"Why should I?"

"Good. Here, I give you back these two packs, and I'll pay you for the others."

"What do you mean, Tom?"

"We're all Jewish here. Would you like to meet a Jewish girl? It's dangerous, you know."

Willy shook his head. "You're not Jewish, are you?"

"Yes, I am."

I waited silently. Intuitively, I felt that this German wouldn't beat me, but still, when he kept staring at me, my heart pounded.

"Tomek, take the cigarettes, and here is some chocolate for your sister." He went about his work and never mentioned her again. A short time later he left for the front, and I never saw him again.

In the beginning, the Jews were left pretty much at peace. Only the Wehrmacht units were in town, no SS, and the soldiers even did some unofficial trading with the residents. Then suddenly, one day, the son of Lejzor Sieczky was killed. He was our neighbor. The German military police shot him on the street merely for sport. It was the first deliberate murder in Izbica, and it came as a great shock to all of us. We realized that Jews were no longer under the protection of the law.

Soon notices were posted around town:

"Curfew is imposed on all Jews between the hours of 5:00 P.M. and 7:00 A.M."

"White armbands, ten centimeters wide and bearing a blue Star of David, are to be worn on the right arm, just above the elbow, by all Jews from age six."

"No Jew is allowed to leave his place of residence without a special pass issued by the German authorities."

"Jews are forbidden to travel by train."

"Jews are not allowed to pursue any trade."

For infringement of any of these rules, death was the only penalty. The Jewish population was thus isolated from the rest of the community. Most Jewish merchants who had previously dealt with Polish peasants gave up their trade; those who didn't risked their lives.

The only big industry in town was the government-owned factory that produced a special type of bricks used for military fortifications. Jews had never been allowed to work there, even before the war. The three existing flour mills had provided jobs for many Jews, but now only Christians were allowed to work there.

Before the war most Jews had made a living in small trades and crafts. Their little stores lined the main street. My father had a liquor store. The Polish government had given him his license as a reward for his voluntary frontline activities in Marshal Piłsudski's Polish Liberation Legions in 1918–19. Now he, along with other Jewish shopkeepers, was forced to close down.

To put food on the table, he managed to arrange with Mr. Frydman, a Warsaw manufacturer, to be a supplier of wood for his shoetree factory. Mr. Frydman, although a Jew, was for a while exempt from the anti-Jewish laws because he was an American citizen. In later years he, his wife, and his children perished. My father would meet Mr. Frydman secretly. If caught, he would have been shot. Many others, less fortunate, went hungry. No longer did Jews come each Wednesday to the market in the shtetl square to socialize, buy what they needed, and sell their produce and wares to gentiles. Now Jews had to go secretly to the villages to buy food.

The cultural life of Izbica had been rich and varied. Now the amateur theater in which my father sometimes acted was closed, as was the movie theater and library. However, many political and religious associations flourished, meeting quietly in homes. And the *beit midrashim* continued to draw Jews to prayer and study.

Public schools, of course, were closed to us. But our Jewish Bible teachers taught us secretly in their homes, and we kept up our studies. Yakov Yitzhak Lewand was the Rebbe, or teacher, and the classes were held in his kitchen. I remember the darkened room, sitting with eight or ten other boys, aged seven to thirteen, around an old wooden table, each with his prayer book in front of him.

It was extremely boring. The sun was shining, and there was so much I could do outside. I felt caged. Over and over, I repeated mechanically after the Rebbe paragraph after paragraph in Hebrew, a language I didn't understand. When one of us yawned, the Rebbe would stick his not-too-clean wooden pointer in the student's wide-open mouth, thus keeping him awake.

Strangely enough, before the war the public school had classes in religious studies for Catholics and Jews. The books were in Polish, which I understood, of course, and the pictures were interesting. But in *heder* I simply repeated automatically what I had memorized so perfectly. My father never checked my studies, but he knew. Once he said, "Toivi, you won't even know how to say Kaddish for me when the time comes." He was right, and I'm sorry now.

I was a bit ashamed when my schoolmates advanced in their studies to Gemara and Rashi while I was still struggling with my beginner's book. Once, while vacationing at my grandmother's place in Zamość, I was put to the real test: my grandmother asked me to read the prayer book. I easily repeated all the verses I had memorized, and everyone was very proud of me. Later, when my grandfather took me to the synagogue, I was afraid that the few memorized verses would not be enough, but I soon discovered that I need only imitate the other Jews praying. I shook vigorously back and forth like everyone else, intoning "amen" every so often while I waited impatiently for the end of the services.

As for public school, I didn't miss it. I didn't particularly like school, but I loved to read. It was the discovery of new worlds that I loved. When a book was especially interesting, I read until late at night. After being forced to go to bed, I often pretended I needed to use the night pot. I would go into the kitchen and turn on the light. Suddenly, hundreds of cockroaches would flee in different directions. Only the first minute was scary. Soon the floor would be empty, and I'd sit on the pot and read for hours. In the morning it would be practically impossible to get me out of bed. I created my own library, gathering books from friends, and I always had plenty to read.

We heard a lot about the Gestapo. They had not yet arrived in our town, but the stories of torture and beatings made our blood run cold.

A new wave of illegal emigration to the east began. The border was not strongly guarded, and one could get to the Soviet side of the Bug River, only thirty miles away, fairly easily.

Again, my mother pleaded with my father to leave, and this time he acceded. He bought a horse and a cart with Szulim Handwerker. Just then, however, some refugees from the first wave to the east came trickling back. They complained of administrative chaos in the Soviet territory and harsh living conditions there as refugees.

My father changed his mind once more. He sold the horse and cart just as quickly as he bought them a few days earlier. We stayed in Izbica, and our fate was sealed.

At that time, all matters concerning Jews in Izbica were handled by the German *Landrat* (district office) in Krasnystaw. One day the Landrat informed the Jewish elders that, as a result of the removal of Jews from the German territories, a transport of Jewish expellees would arrive from the region of Poznań, a former Polish territory now annexed to the Third Reich. Preparations to receive them began. They would be billeted among the local Jewish families. Food was prepared in anticipation.

On December 11, 1939, more than one thousand Jews arrived from

Koło. Given very little notice, and allowed only forty pounds per person, they carried very little with them. Commotion and confusion reigned as a committee dispersed the newcomers among the inhabitants. The Kominkowski and Frenkel families stayed with us.

My circle of friends was within the neighborhood. My best friend was Srulek Handwerker, the baker's son. Together we were mischievous and played practical jokes. Then there were Hersz and Idel Goldgraber, the cobbler's sons, Perec Dorfsman, and a few others. And there was a separate group of girls on the periphery, under the competitive leadership of Srulek's sister, Chawa, a stunning, very blond girl, and Małka Lerner, the butcher's daughter, who was a tall, slender brunette. On holidays and Saturdays we used to go to the edge of the forest and flirt innocently.

It was early 1940. We were just kids, but we had to grow up fast and be of help to our families. Brothers and fathers were being taken away. The Germans had set up labor camps in the vicinity. In the beginning, for the first few months, work in the camps was performed on a voluntary basis. The first to go were naturally the poor, who went, quite simply, to relieve their hunger. As small and as poor as the shtetl was, there were social divisions. The poor were called *grices* (soups), for they were so poor that their meals consisted almost solely of soup. Initially the Germans brought the workers to the sites and back home again at night. Later on, all laborers were forced to remain in the enclosed camps.

Then the terrible news began to reach us. Through smuggled letters and escapees, we learned of sadistic tortures and difficult working conditions. Jews no longer volunteered for the work camps; now the Jewish elders were ordered to prepare a list and forcibly deliver new workers. There was no official differentiation between rich and poor; nevertheless, it was the poor who were delivered to the camps. If a wealthy Jew got an order to go to work, he was able to buy a substitute, who naturally came from among the hungry poor.

The number of work camps grew and conditions worsened. Eventually, however, because of the terrible treatment in the camps, even the very poor and desperate refused to go. It was no longer possible to buy a substitute, and as a result the Jewish elders failed to deliver the required number.

So, in order to fill the camps, the Germans themselves began street roundups. One of the first took place on August 14, 1940. The victims were sent to Bełżec, which at that time was still a work camp.

Everyone hid. Roundups became more frequent. Trucks would come to Izbica in the middle of the day, filled with Germans and black-uniformed Ukrainian collaborators. They would catch Jews in the streets and hold them for a few hours in the marketplace. Whoever had money would buy his way out, or his family would, just like in a medieval slave market. Those who remained went to the camps.

For this sluggish delivery of slave laborers, the German Landrat forced the Jewish community to pay a fine. To protect me from roundups, my father, with his Christian connections, found work for me in a machine shop run by a naturalized Pole of German ancestry, Leopold Platto. A simple, honest man, Platto spoke fluent Yiddish, having worked for years in Goldberg's sawmill.

Transports of Jewish resettlements to Izbica increased. On March 10, 1941, they came from Koło, Konin, and Rzgów. The community kitchen had to be enlarged to handle so many newcomers. Samuel Kohn, a tall, dignified Jew, took on the duty of ladling out soup and hot ersatz coffee (made from roasted corn) twice a day. He and his wife were added to our home, others to other local families, and about four hundred people were lodged in the synagogue. Izbica was not only a ghetto now, but, as we found out later, a holding pen for "resettlement to the East."

War with the Soviet Union: A Turn for the Worse

On June 22, 1941, Germany attacked the Soviet Union. We were shocked. Wasn't there a nonaggression pact? Only a few days earlier Soviet officers were seen in the city of Lublin, and there had been rumors that Germany might permit emigration to the Soviet Union. Had Germany suddenly attacked its own ally?

Within days the Red Army was retreating along its entire front. The news shattered us—it was a radical turnabout. Now Jews who had escaped the Germans and were unable or did not want to go with the retreating Red Army returned to Izbica. The sky hummed with heavy bombers, the highways were jammed with motorized infantry, the trains were crammed with guns and tanks, and everything was moving eastward.

The German victory sign was displayed on every bus and train, as well as office windows, the handiwork of local Nazis and anti-Soviet sympathizers. Soon hundreds of captured Soviet prisoners of war were paraded through the streets.

It was a pitiful scene. Starving and humiliated soldiers, risking being shot, were throwing themselves on pieces of bread and cigarette butts the local Jewish population had strewn on the road in an attempt to help in some way. The Germans were winning.

On December 27, 1941, our roomer Kohn received a letter from his son in Koło. "For over a month now," he wrote, "trainloads of Jews have been suffocated with gas in special vans in a little-known village, Chełmno."[4]

I was present when my parents and Kohn talked about it. The adults considered it a fabricated story, and it made little impression on them. "It's impossible," they said. "It's a fairy tale. Even Germans couldn't do such terrible things! The worst bandit cannot murder this many innocent people! After all, we live in the twentieth century!"

We soon forgot the incident, but unfortunately not for long. First we had to experience life under the Gestapo. For, much to our horror, a permanent Gestapo command finally came to our town. It consisted of two psychopathic murderers: Kurt Engels,[5] a noisy and erratic man whose rank at that time was SS Hauptscharführer, and Ludwig Klemm,[6] a tall, quiet noncommissioned officer who spoke excellent Polish and who faithfully followed the dictates of his feared master, Engels.

The Gestapo set up quarters and soon terrorized the whole area. Engels enjoyed shooting Jews in the early morning hours, before breakfast. A certain smile would come over his face, exposing a gold tooth. Soon the local Christian intelligentsia were sent off to Auschwitz and Majdanek. The teachers Śliwa, Bazylko, Czubaszek, and other prominent Poles disappeared without a trace, never to return.

I was more reckless than brave. I remember I was leaving my friend Srulek's home. It was after the curfew. I knew every shortcut and every corner in my shtetl by heart, and I was sure I could avoid danger. The doors and window shutters of every Jewish home were tightly closed. The curtains were drawn. After curfew hours the shtetl was like a ghost town. Keeping close to the walls, I slowly neared my home.

When I finally stepped on the porch, I felt so secure I played a stupid practical joke. I knocked and, with a stern voice, I mimicked the Germans: "Aufmachen! Gestapo!"

I could picture my parents inside, terrified, and felt sorry immediately.

"It's me, Toivi . . . Open, fast!"

The lock turned and the door moved. My mother was holding her hand over her breast as if to emphasize the pain my joke had caused her.

"Toivi, don't do this anymore, please . . . I thought I would have a heart attack . . ."

But I was proud of myself. I could act like a German. They couldn't tell the difference. I even defied the Germans by staying out after curfew and didn't get caught!

My family moved to a new home. It was a long one-floor apartment building. The structure was about a hundred yards long and had six apartments on each side. Our one-room apartment was in the middle and was the only one that had an extra room converted from part of the attic. In case of a German raid, we built a hiding place in a portion of the attic next to our upper room. All the doors connecting the neighbors' quarters were left unlocked so that people could hide more quickly when it was necessary. The hiding place was the handiwork of an ingenious and trusted Jewish mason who specialized in hideouts. He made a small opening in the wall to the attic adjacent to our room, just large enough to get through. The entrance was camouflaged with a small, light cabinet. A second wall was built inside the attic, enclosing a space of about thirty-five square yards. The sheet-metal roof made it unbearably hot in the summer and freezing cold in the winter, but the hideout remained our best refuge.

One evening after curfew, it was still early and I felt restless. I wanted to go outside.

"Tatte, I am going to see Idel."

"Toivi, you can't. You will get killed someday . . . please," he pleaded.

"Don't worry, I'll make it."

"Toivi, I will sing you some Yiddish songs, all right?"

My father had been a leading actor in the local amateur theater years before. He had a good voice and knew a lot of folk songs. It was a tempting proposition, and I agreed.

The melodies, with their melancholic tones, filled the room: "Mein Shtetele Bełzc," "Oifn Pripetchok," "Bubliczki," "Tumbałałajka," and many others. I could have listened all night, but it was time to go to bed.

Shortly before midnight, a loud knocking awakened us. "Aufmach-en! Aufmachen! Schnell! Gestapo! [Open fast! German Secret Police!]" This was the real thing, no doubt about it. My mother slipped on her housecoat, pushed my father aside, and opened the door.

They walked in briskly. First came a tall soldier with a rifle, who immediately posted himself at the entrance to the bedroom; then the well-known resident *Volksdeutscher*,[7] Jan Schultz, and finally the two Gestapo officers, Engels and Klemm, in civilian clothes. Smiling pleas-antly, Engels suddenly grabbed a large bottle of juice and threw it straight at my brother while we were still lying in bed.

"Raus! Schnell! [Out! Fast!]"

My mother, frightened, begged them not to hurt us. As she was pleading, my brother and I jumped up and ran into the kitchen, terrified. The Nazis were alone now in the bedroom.

Our kitchen was tiny, and our family stood tightly together, keep-ing our distance from the guard posted there. The soldier didn't seem to mind being close to Jews and was conversing quietly with my father. He didn't seem vicious. He allowed me to get a drink of water, and even gave my mother a chair to sit on. From the next room we could hear laughter, sounds of cloth tearing, and breaking glass.

After about an hour the door to the kitchen opened. Schultz pointed to a table in the bedroom. "Pack everything!" he ordered. There on the table lay tea, coffee beans, silverware, crystal, and my father's best suit. The food was put in a sack; the rest we wrapped in paper and put in a wooden box.

"Raus!" they ordered my father. It all happened so quickly. My father went out with the box. There was no chance to say good-bye, no words were spoken, no glance. He was taken away.

My brother and I burst into tears. My mother stood there, help-less. We felt scared and abandoned. I sat in the kitchen and waited. Time went by. Then I heard a gunshot! It was like a stab in the heart. They shot my father! I have no father!

When I went into the other room, my mother and brother were standing as before, in quietness and sorrow. No visible changes. They probably hadn't heard the shot. I tried to appear calm, though I was close to bursting into tears.

Half an hour passed. Again there was a knock on the door. This time the voice spoke Polish. "Open up. It's me, Schultz!" He had forgotten his leather gloves.

I had known Schultz since before the war. I mustered my courage. "Mr. Schultz, what's happened to my father? Will he come back? Please tell me."

"You will see," he said. And he left. He simply doesn't want to tell me the truth, I said to myself.

Time passed, and we still sat in despair. Suddenly I heard quick steps outside. Somebody was running. Metal boot tips on cobblestones echoed in the dark. They stopped on the porch. Then came a delicate knock on the door.

"Who is it?" we asked.

"Tatte!" he said in Yiddish.

"Mamme! It's Tatte!" I yelled uncontrollably. I was bursting with happiness. "It's Tatte!" With trembling hands I lifted the bolts and opened the door. He stood there, haggard and pale. My little brother Hersz leaped at him. Carrying Hersz in his arms, my father sat down heavily. He loosened my brother's grip from around his neck, took him gently off his knees, and turned to my mother.

"Fajgele," he called my mother, "Fajgele, come closer." Now, all of us around him, we were ready to listen to his story. But when he saw our scared faces he changed his mind.

"Kinderlach [children], go to bed. It's late."

"Tatte, I'm not tired, please," I said. "Are you hurt? I heard a shot."

"Yes, Tatte," little Hersz butt in, "I heard it, too. Are you hit?"

It was too much for my mother. Her two children had heard the shot, they knew all the time! They were trying to protect her and each other! Her eyelids blinked a few times, and a few tears began to roll down her cheeks.

"All right, children, you can stay up," my father said, turning again to my mother to tell his story.

"I carried the box on my shoulder, and we stopped in front of Tuchman's house. They checked their list and knocked on the door. When it didn't open, Schultz shot through it, then kicked it in. I waited outside. I could hear beating and screaming inside. Soon Tuchman was dragged out of the house, and we were led to the regional veteri-narian's house, the one the Gestapo uses as their headquarters.

"I left my load there, and they took us to the yard. I was surprised to see about a dozen people we know, already collected. Then Engels made a speech. He said all of us there were known to be respected Jews. We would be the new official *Judenrat* (Jewish Council) in Izbi-ca, and we should consider this an honor. Refusal to cooperate would be punished by death. We were to be responsible only to the Ger-mans and to him in particular. He also said that we were considered hostages. If any harm befell a German or if there was any sabotage, we would be responsible and would be shot."

My father turned to my brother and me, and, noticing the horror in our eyes, again asked us to go to bed. My brother complied, but I refused. I had to know everything. So the story went on.

"Josef Pomp, you know, the old, wealthy fabric dealer? Well, he asked Engels if he could be set free because of his age, and he was set free! So I thought, I'll try too. I raised my hand like in school, and was allowed to speak. 'Mr. Captain,' I said, 'I'm an invalid, a Piłsud-czyk. I fought the Bolsheviks in the First World War.' He looked at me in disbelief. I showed him my invalid card. 'See,' I said, 'it's writ-ten here. I was a voluntary legionnaire. I was wounded in the front line.' Engels looked at me, his face softened, and he said, 'Go home!'

"Fajgele, it's so good to be back home! You can't imagine!" He put his arms around us both, and turned softly to me. "Now go to bed, Toivi."

I reached up around his neck and kissed him. "I was so scared, Tatte," I whispered. "I'm so glad you're safe. Good-night, Tatte."

Life under the Gestapo and SS

A few days later, around ten in the morning, people were running about shouting that Engels and Klemm were killing every Jew in sight. In seconds the streets were silent and empty. Only the two tyrants, the swastika gods, could be seen. Laughing, they forced their way into homes and shot everyone, including babies in cribs, just for sport.

I sneaked over to Platto's machine shop, knowing it would be safer there. Just as I peeked through the window, Engels walked up to the porch of Goldberg's house across from the shop. For some reason my friend, Perec Dorfsman, who lived there, ran down the stairs and into the yard, possibly wanting to hide in the machine shop also. Suddenly he found himself face to face with the Gestapo. He tried to run away, but Engels and Klemm, grinning, had him covered. He was trapped.

"Please, I beg you, don't shoot! Let me live," he pleaded.

There was a pause, then Engels said quietly, "Go home."

Relieved, Perec turned and ran back. As he reached the first step, Engels shot him in the back with a double-barreled hunting rifle. Perec managed to run halfway up the stairs, yet with a second shot, he fell down dead. Similar scenes were repeated in many Jewish homes.

Engels killed thirty-five Jews that day. There was wailing and crying as families mourned their dead. I saw them all in the morgue when I went to see Perec for the last time.

One day a large transport of Jews arrived from Nuremberg, Germany. Izbica was already terribly overcrowded. All the community centers were overflowing. By day the streets were jammed with people; at night, because of the curfew, they filled every corner and corridor of every house. Prices rose. And on top of the hunger and misery, a typhus epidemic broke out.

My brother became sick, and an atmosphere of doom hung over our home. Who would be next? By now our whole family shared one room, and my brother and I slept in the same bed. Because of the typhus I was forbidden to touch him, but I did anyway. Then he would scream, tattling to Mamme about it.

There was no hospital, no medicine. There was nothing we could do. Smoking cigarettes was rumored to ward off typhus, and I began to smoke. We bought the tobacco from Polish farmers, even though dealing with Christians was strictly forbidden.

Because Poland is extremely cold in the winter, fur coats were a necessity. A new order was posted: All Jews were to relinquish their fur coats and collars. The penalty for disobeying was death. Some, being careful of informers, would sell their expensive coats to Poles at bargain prices; others, like ourselves, would give the coats to Poles for safekeeping. Nevertheless, a large number of fur coats reached German storerooms.

Eventually, the Gestapo found out about the Jews' reluctance to hand over their furs, and an immense "contribution," or fine, was instituted. The order came from Engels himself, and the astronomical sum was to be paid to him personally.

Again there was screaming and cursing as the Judenrat ordered Jews to pay. The uproar was brief, however, because payment had to be made immediately. The collector (a member of the Judenrat), accompanied by a Jewish *Ordnungdienst* (policeman), went to each house on his list. Those who had relatives or friends in the Judenrat paid less; others paid more.

Time passed. I worked in the machine shop. Most of the time I ran the hand-cranked lathe. I cranked from early morning until evening. My back hurt terribly, and it was difficult to breathe. Once in a while I was put in charge of renting bikes to the children, and then it was easy. The shop was my only refuge from the Nazis. As it turned out, they would take me from there, too.

On that day, Nazi SS had been rounding up Jews for forced labor in the camps since the early morning. I sneaked away to Platto's machine shop. Srulek, my coworker, was already there.

It was all because of a childish dare. Impulsively, wanting to show off, I turned to Srulek and said, "I don't look Jewish and I'm not afraid. I can go out in the street right now and no one will catch me."

"Oh yeah," he said, "I dare you. Let's see you go to the store and buy candy."

I took him on. I left the workshop and soon was on the main street. The Germans and Ukrainian soldiers were roaming the street, beating caught Jews. Pretending not to care, I reached the grocery store, made my purchase, and was ready to leave when an SS man entered.

He walked right up to me. "Are you a Jew?" he asked me.

I shook my head, trusting my so-called Aryan features.

"Show me your papers," he demanded in an authoritative tone.

"Sir, I'm too young to have any papers."

The German turned to the customers. "Is he a Jew?" he asked coldly.

The Christian employees and all the customers knew me. I held my breath. They shook their heads, disclaiming me. He let me go. I breathed a sigh of relief and walked briskly away.

A few moments later I looked back to see my Catholic schoolmate, Tomasz Kwiecień, talking with the same Nazi and pointing in my direction. I ran, and in a minute I was in the shop, proudly relating my story to my boss. Then the same SS man came in. It was too late to run. He whipped me and ordered me to go with him.

Platto tried to defend me, "He's only a child, let him go."

"I don't care!" the SS man yelled. "The bastard had the guts to lie to me."

He shoved me and led me to the entrance of a narrow street. It was filled with captured Jews, guarded by Nazis. With a strong push, I became one of the prisoners. The street was short; Jews were jammed together, tightly packed. Some were crying, resigned to their fate. Others stood tensely, hoping and praying that relatives would buy them out. I had an awful feeling—the feeling of an animal caught in a cage.

The street was blocked at both ends by Ukrainian guards. At one end the guard knew me; he saw the SS man bring me in. So it must be the other end. It's worth a try, I decided. In seconds I pushed myself through the crowd to the opposite end, not stopping, not even looking for the right moment, not caring about the guards. I boldly walked out.

It worked! They didn't stop me. I wasn't wearing the required Star of David armband. Fair and blue-eyed, I looked just like other Polish youths. I hid in a large sewer pipe and remained there for two or three hours, until the roundup was over. Then I simply walked home. I wasn't concerned about the SS man who had caught me because I knew he had left Izbica with the prisoners. The next day, as usual, I went to work at Platto's machine shop.

Engels had picked a Polish mechanic, Heniek Królikowski, Platto's brother-in-law, to take care of his car and motorcycle. At first he had them fixed in Platto's place, but probably because of Platto's unwillingness to have anything to do with the Gestapo, he asked Heniek to switch the Gestapo business to the workshop just opened by the Volksdeutscher Tadek Solecki.

One evening, as I was passing Solecki's workshop, he asked me to stay overnight and help him fix a motorcycle. I agreed and ran home to tell my parents. My work was washing the disassembled parts with kerosene and helping to reassemble them. It was a nice cool night. I had always loved playing with motors, and I worked until daylight.

In the morning Solecki rewarded me with a few zlotys and a proposition to work regularly in his place. I agreed; I liked the work and, besides, I felt it could be helpful to be in the nest of the local Nazis. Who would suspect a Jew there?

The next day I was the property of Solecki. I worked from morning until evening without pay. When my boss was sober the work was pleasurable, but this was seldom the case. Most of the time he was drunk, and then I became a football. When he asked me for a wrench or a nut, I brought it to him in the style he demanded—the "air way." He would position me with my back to him and would kick me in the rear in the direction of the tool. He would also kick me for no reason at all, simply because I was a Jew. Solecki was a Volksdeutscher, and I would pay dearly if I were to leave the job now.

Meanwhile, because he had helped the Germans, Schultz became mayor of Izbica. The former mayor had been taken to Auschwitz. Schultz exchanged his apartment for a better one and bought an old car, a two-seat Fiat.

Besides Schultz and Solecki, there were others who worked openly with the Germans—Matys, Jan Gut, Rzeźnik, the brothers Krauze, and others whose names I've forgotten. They spread like a cancer: searching, stealing, blackmailing, taking bribes, and all of them, including the Polish police, collaborated with the Gestapo.

It was different before the war when the same police officers would knock on our door, especially on Sabbath evenings. My parents would invite them in. They would be dressed in uniform, but I was never frightened. Usually it was Kamiński, the chief of police, and his deputy Czubaszek. They reminded me of the Polish cartoon "Flip and Flap." The commandant was big and fat, the two ends of his belt barely met; the sweet and courageous Czubaszek was skinny and short, barely taller than his rifle. They knew Mamme's gefilte fish was the best in town. They laid down their rifles in a corner and joined our table. They gulped down a few vodkas with a bit of fish, praised my mother's culinary talent, and left with a stern salute. In return, they would close an eye when my father sometimes kept his store open past the permitted time.

Now our doors were double-locked, and a loud knock from the same people could mean terror and death.

Bełzec: The Death Machine at Work

On the morning of March 24, 1942, our sleepy town was awakened by shots. Another roundup! Frightened Jews quickly dressed, ran, and hid. On the hills encircling Izbica, silhouettes of armed soldiers began to appear. The whole area was surrounded. Bands of uniformed Ukrainian collaborators rushed into Jewish homes. This roundup was different, however. They took every Jew they encountered—children, old men and women, even cripples. They called it an *Akcja* (action).

Our hiding place had a basic flaw: Someone had to stay outside to move the dresser that blocked the entrance back into position. Since I was able to hide myself in the Nazi machine shop, it was my job to move the dresser. After all the others went in, I quickly covered the entrance and ran to work.

From the workshop I could see what was happening outside. Jews caught on the streets and pulled from homes by Nazis were being beaten and pushed toward the marketplace like cattle. The Ukrainians relished their job. Dusk came slowly.

Solecki, formerly an illiterate baker's helper in a Jewish bakery and now a turncoat collaborator, put on a red armband with a black swastika, grabbed a gun, and also ran after the Jews as the Akcja began. He had no more regard for me than for other Jews, but he needed a slave, someone to keep the Gestapo motorcycles and cars shiny and in absolutely perfect condition. Besides working with engines, I ran the shop while he was gone, making small sales and doing bicycle repairs. Therefore, I always had security—not only from him but also from the rest of the local Nazis. That particular evening I had arranged with Solecki to sleep in the shop while the Akcja was in progress.

Locked in the shop, lying on the seat of a Gestapo limousine, I heard the Nazis' curses and the screams of Jews being beaten. It tore at my heart. I worried about my family. What was happening to them? I turned on the radio to drown out the screams, and my fear.

By 1942, the Nazis had overrun much of Europe, and all the radio stations were playing victorious German marches. I tuned in to a Vienna station. I will never forget how the words of the sentimental love song "Lili Marlene" mixed with the blood-curdling screams and cries of the Jews being hunted outside.

In the morning, Solecki opened the shop with a grin on his face. He had had a lucky night: Stolen gold rings gleamed on his fingers.

"Sir," I said, "I want to see how my home is."

"Go, but watch out!" he answered.

The Akcja was essentially finished, but Nazis were still at the marketplace, guarding the thousands of Jews who had been caught. The cattle train that should have come to take the Jews away, supposedly to work in the East, had not arrived on time.

I ran home. Thank God, the hiding place was untouched. I moved the small cabinet and opened the little door. In the dim light I felt eyes directed at me, many pairs of eyes. It was silent; the air was heavy and hot.

"It's over," I said. "It's over."

In a moment the hiding place emptied. The people had strange look on their faces, as if they were cursed. Each had his own worries, but kept silent. When the quota was filled, the remaining Jews had "free" movement in the town. Many would later learn that members of their families had been killed during the Akcja.

I was worried. It was already after curfew, and my father still wasn't home. When he finally came in, I was so relieved.

As he greeted us, I noticed there was a change in his tone of voice and the look in his eyes.

"Children, to bed!"

"Tatte, it's early . . . we never go to bed so early."

"I know," he acknowledged, "but go to the kitchen. I have something to discuss with Mamme."

Many times when we were in bed, he and Mamme would talk quietly in a corner, not wanting us to hear their conversation. But this time it was different. He didn't want to wait. Something was burning inside him, and he had to discuss it right away.

I took my brother and went to the kitchen. There was practically no space there. The brick stove took up most of the room, and two refugees, the Kominkowskis, barely had a spot for their bed. Only a small patch was free, and we sat down on the floor. We had never been asked to leave the room. What was so important now? After a while Father called us in and, as if to make up, he set me on his knees.

"Toivele, I know you like Jewish songs. Should I sing you some?"

He sang my favorites. The Kominkowski sisters joined in. It was pleasant and peaceful, and I forgot my worries.

About nine o'clock in the evening I heard a faint whistle from outside, right below the window. I immediately recognized the tone. It was Jozek Bresler, my new friend. This was our secret cue. But why so late? We would sometimes come home late, but we would seldom leave our homes late. It must be very important. But then again, with Jozek and his crazy ideas, you never knew. His family had been brought to Izbica with a transport from Koło. His father was a dental surgeon. He was an only child, born after twelve years of waiting. He was spoiled, and he knew how to play his game. He was extremely intelligent and had some Christian friends, so he was better informed than most his age. He always seemed to know what was going on.

I went to the kitchen and quietly opened the first of the double doors to the outside. Then I raised the hooks by which the heavier door was closed and slipped out to the tiny balcony. There was Jozek, pressed against the wall so as not to be seen from the main street.

What my parents were trying to hide from me was what he had come to tell me. He poured it out. "Toivi, you know the whole transport of Jews . . . it will never come back. Our friends Fajgele, Awrumele, their father and mother."

When Jozek spoke it always sounded strange somehow. Unlike the Izbica Jews, he knew only Polish. He pronounced the Jewish names with a funny accent, and for a moment I did not understand. "You mean they took them so far away that they won't return?" I asked. For me the next city was already a distant place.

"Stupid!" he almost yelled. "They are murdered. It's true! They are gassed! Jacek [his Christian friend] came and told me everything. His Uncle Ryba works for the railway system. Some Jews paid him to follow the transports. He came back and told them the Jews were not taken very far away, maybe only thirty miles, to a small village, Bełżec. His uncle worked at the station, where he saw transports of thousands of Jews arriving every day from different parts of the country, even from Kraków and Lwów. The train would be directed to a side track where a gate would open, he said, and an area he couldn't see into, surrounded by a barbed-wire fence, would swallow the whole trainload. Then the train would leave empty. Remember Mr. Kohn's letter from Koło? About gassing and burning? It's true then . . . Good-bye."

In the following days, the story was confirmed by others. Jews went to Bełżec by the thousands day after day—men, women, and children. By now the enclosed camp should be overflowing, yet people continued to be brought in, they said, without a stop. In addition, the stench of decomposing bodies filled the whole area.

Some optimists among us still rejected the information as a fantastic lie, arguing, "If the Germans intended to kill Jews, why are they giving them bread for the trip?" Others, although they found the rumors hard to believe, began to devise more hiding places.

There were two types of hideouts. Small hideouts could be found in practically every home. A handy little ditch or hole under the floor could hide two or three people. The panels shielding the tiny entrance were perfectly fit to the design of the floor. Large hideouts were carefully designed to hold ten or more people. They were made in attics like ours, with double walls, tunnels, and so on. The entrances were usually very intricate: you entered through an oven, a show window, the ceiling, a dresser. It was impossible to fathom the many imaginative hideouts. Keeping these secrets from Christian neighbors[8] wasn't an easy task, especially when underground hiding places were being constructed and it was necessary to remove the dug-out dirt.

In addition to our hiding place in the attic, we built another by digging a hole, about four feet deep, under our kitchen floor. We removed soil for close to two weeks. To carry out our task unnoticed, we built a firewood and coal shack close to the outhouse. Whenever we normally went for coal or wood, about three times a day, we took a little soil and secretly threw it into the deep pit of the outhouse.

A typical Akcja would begin suddenly, without warning. At dawn the town would be surrounded. Ukrainian soldiers would lie hidden in the hills and bushes, and along the Wieprz River. In effect, they would establish a cordon around Izbica. A second group of Ukrainian soldiers, together with the SS, would enter the town itself, initiating the Akcja. First they would look for the Judenrat, who would mobilize the Jewish *Ordnungsdienst* (police), and order them to deliver a contingent of people for "resettlement" at a specified time. The Judenrat would prepare—or already had on hand—a list of those chosen for deportaion, and the Ordnungsdienst would pick them up.

The resettlement list would be screened so many times that, in the end, mainly those Jews brought from other places, and the poor or sick, remained on it. But everyone wanted to live. We knew only too well where the cattle cars were going. Everyone hid in terror, including the Judenrat.

I remember one such Akcja. In the beginning, volunteers were offered bread, and some Jews actually still believed the stories of resettlement and assembled in the marketplace. But since not enough Jews assembled voluntarily, the Nazis began a rampage that turned into a full-scale massacre. They broke down doors, ran wildly through rooms, killed the infirm, and drove everyone else, without exception, to the train station. In the end, an overloaded transport departed for Bełżec.

Afterward, it was again safe to go out into the street, and life returned to normal. The morgue had a rich harvest, and the waiting rooms of the two remaining Jewish doctors were full of the wounded who once again had escaped death.

In the early days of the occupation, everyone was forced to relinquish their radios. Those who resisted were executed. Information did reach us in various ways, but not without distortions and rumor. It was impossible to tell which information was true. Rumors of Hitler's downfall and internal difficulties in Germany were especially nurtured; they were repeated constantly with the perpetual hope that tomorrow would bring the end of suffering. Skeptics would say sarcastically that the rumors came from the Y.W.A. Agency.[9] Yet we found a way to receive news from the BBC. How? Well, Mayor Schultz decided that it was again time to exchange his apartment for a better one. A Jew named Yczy Klajner was driven out, and Schultz became our neighbor.

Until that time, we and our neighbors had had easy access to the attic hiding place. Schultz spoiled this by occupying the middle rooms in the building. Yet our hiding place actually became much safer, because it was in his part of the attic, and therefore would not draw attention. Now we also had access to dependable news. As a Nazi, he had a radio, from which we were separated by only a thin plywood door. Against our side of the door stood a heavy dresser.

One evening we heard radio static intermittently, as if someone were trying to tune in stations. We put our ears to the wall. Radio BBC in London was transmitting in Polish. From then on we were able to hear trustworthy news. We even discovered a way to hear the broadcasts when the radio was turned down low. We simple pulled out our bottom dresser drawer and, lying on the floor, put our heads inside the dresser instead.

Not all the communiqués gave us hope. One, from London, informed us that England was not yet fully ready for war. It was already 1942. We were thinking, God, by the time they get ready, we all will have perished.

Sometimes Radio Moscow would broadcast Middle Eastern melodies (because of the similarity of the tunes, we thought they might be Jewish songs). To us they were voices from a world beyond our reach. How bitterly sorry we were that we had passed up the chance to go to Russia. Little did we realize then what it all really meant.

The Jewish population of Izbica shrank considerably. There was an abundance of empty housing, and the synagogue, now a warehouse, was full of confiscated goods from Jewish households.

Soon new transports from distant countries began to arrive. From France came more Polish Jews, formerly immigrants to that country. From Slovakia came people similar in appearance to us, but the Czech Jews from Theresienstadt, Brno, and Pilzen looked different. They did not speak Yiddish, were better dressed, and kept mostly to themselves.

The clever Gestapo officer Engels recognized the potential for sowing intrigue and used it to his advantage. The present Judenrat, comprised entirely of Polish Jews, gained a new faction, made up exclusively of Czech Jews, including a separate Czech Ordnungsdienst. When the next Akcja came, the Czechs were ordered to rid Izbica of the "inferior" Polish Jews. It worked, and for a time, being a foreign Jew saved you from the journey to the gas chambers.

All Those Under Fifteen and Over Fifty-five

It was June 1942. Another Akcja—this one very different from the previous ones. This time the SS marched into the Judenrat building with an ultimatum: "All those under fifteen and over fifty-five must be delivered to the marketplace or they will be shot."

The German and Austrian Jews living in Izbica at that time were undone by their typical German discipline and respect for law and superiors. The Polish Jews had a more realistic appraisal of their situation, and tried to escape their tragic destiny. Most Polish Jews, knowing that "resettlement" meant death, hid somewhere and took their chances. The foreign Jews, on the other hand, didn't believe they were going to an extermination camp, even though they had been warned. It did not enter their minds to disobey authority; they quickly filled the assembly place.

The mental torture of those mothers and fathers was unimaginable. Should a thirty-year-old mother let her five-year-old, crying "Mamme! Mamme!" be taken away? If she protested, they could all be killed, including her frightened sixteen-year-old daughter and fifty-four-year-old ailing mother. Or should she leave both daughter and mother and go to her death with her five-year-old, so he wouldn't be alone and frightened? Should a forty-five-year-old son ask his seventy-five-year-old father—who probably would not survive anyway—to go, for if he didn't all would die? Or should he wait, hoping his father would go by himself? If his father stayed, who would hide him and risk being shot? The choices were horrible. Mothers ran around like crazy, hugging their children, crying, and looking fruitlessly for help or advice from the Judenrat.

Older Jews tried to dye their hair and shaved their beards. It didn't help. Children, older people, and those without families wandered the streets. Hiding places were closed to them; the others were afraid that, if caught, the Germans would take them all.

The transport was due to leave by 2:00 P.M. As the time drew near, lonely figures or groups could be seen going to the marketplace. Some whose families were already dead or gone, and others sent by relatives, walked alone. Some who were not in the specified age group and could have stayed chose to go with their loved ones, the bonds of blood being dearer than life itself.

I saw my Aunt Chaja from Krasnystaw running wildly in the street, screaming, "Oh God, they took my son Toivele! They took my Toivele!" My sweet little six-year-old cousin was gone forever.

I begged Heniek Królikowski, who was fixing a motorcycle in the garage, to accompany me to the marketplace to look for my cousin. He agreed. I didn't dare penetrate the group of collected Jews, so we placed ourselves on the arcade opposite the doomed and observed.

Slowly the marketplace filled with a strange mass of people: at one end there were only children; further on, only the elderly. The most miserable sight was a large group of infants lying on blankets, attended only by a few women. The majority, however, were mothers with children, though not all were their own. The youngsters understood what would happen to them; the horror was clearly seen in their eyes.

It was terrible. The crying of children mixed with the wailing of parents and the devotions the older Jews shouted to God: "Shema Yisrael, Adonai Eloheinu, Adonai Echad!" My little brother could have been among them, but I had hidden him in Solecki's garage. It was impossible for me to find my cousin, and we returned to the garage.

I watched from the sidewalk as the Jews were being led to the boxcars. Children passed by. A shot rang out, then another. I caught a glimpse of one girl, about eight years old, running behind a building. She had run out of the escorted column of Jews. She didn't run far; a Catholic teenager caught her and brought her back. My eyes filled with tears.

When all the Jews had been loaded into the boxcars, there were still a few empty ones, so the Germans and Ukrainians set off again, grabbing whomever they could. Finally the transport was nearly full and ready to depart.

Suddenly, the German Landrat ordered the Czech faction of the Judenrat, who had cooperated until this particular Akcja, to get into the last car of the train. They shut and bolted the doors, and the transport set off for Bełżec, the death camp. Earlier, Abram Blatt (no relation), the elder in the Polish faction of the Judenrat, had bribed the German officials to "resettle" the Czechs. This was his revenge for the Czechs delivering their Polish brothers for shipment to Bełżec weeks before.

Soon rumors reached us of a newly built death factory, one they called Sobibor.

Toward the End

Unexpected news came from the Landrat in Krasnystaw. The Izbica ghetto was considered a productive place for the German war effort. Hope, the proven ingredient of Nazi deception, was at its height. Hurriedly, different establishments were formed: from tailor and cobbler shops to tanneries (everyone knew how fond the Germans were of leather). From now on, we were assured, only unproductive Jews were to be resettled; the rest would live in peace. By making exceptions in the extermination process, the Germans sowed confusion and uncertainty, fostering hope and trapping even those who were ready to resist.

One day in June 1942, after a seemingly quiet period, the Nazis surrounded the town and swooped down upon us. My younger brother was now often with me in the shop. I hid him in a large storage closet and then went home to hide my parents. I could hear people running in the street and the sound of soldiers marching. I camouflaged the entrance to the hiding place and ran out.

I walked through the streets, seemingly relaxed, as usual without my Star of David armband, and finally made it back to the shop. There was a heavy workload. Inside, the Volksdeutscher Schindler was working on his bike, the Ukrainian commandant of the Akcja was changing spark plugs on his motorcycle, and on a bench a few Ukrainians were cleaning their weapons.

One Ukrainian began testing his gun, shooting at the wall behind which my brother was hiding. I couldn't say anything. I couldn't ask him to stop. I waited, holding my breath . . . He shot once, twice—then silence, only ringing in my ears. Trying to be calm and pretending that I needed some bicycle parts, I headed for the storage closet and stepped inside. Thank God, my brother was sitting there, curled up but unhurt.

The mingled sounds of pistol shots, screaming Nazis, and crying Jews reached us from the street outside. Above it, from time to time, the loud voices of the Judenrat officials could be heard: "All Jews, without exception, must go to the marketplace! The selection of the employed will be conducted there. Whoever remains and is later discovered will be shot on the spot!"

The Jews who trusted the Nazi promise of protection for their productivity in workshops laboring for the German army did not try to hide or escape. They were taken first.

So the day passed. In the evening Solecki locked me in the shop and went with the Germans to hunt Jews. As long as I was needed in his shop, he protected me. Then my brother left the closet, and we sat in Gestapo Chief Engels's car. The cries continued throughout the night.

In the morning, as before, I worked and my brother was hidden.

Suddenly, an SS officer entered and demanded, "Any Jews here?" Without a word I pointed to Engels's motorcycle. Welded onto it was the emblem of the SS: a death's-head. That was enough. He left. A few more popped in, but when they saw the motorcycles of the Gestapo out front and their own commandant wandering around the shop, they left without a word.

I overheard the commandant of the Ukrainians asking Solecki to prepare a new tire for Wednesday. I concluded that he might be back in Izbica on Wednesday for yet another Akcja. Half an hour later the current Akcja ended.

Further to confuse the Jews and also to enrich themselves, the German district officials began to deliver new *Bescheinigung*—costly documents designating the bearer to be a specialist necessary for the German war effort, thus protecting him. Many Jews, including my parents and myself, had such documents.

I had spread the word around town that there would most likely be another Akcja on Wednesday, and there was feverish activity. Tuesday evening, Jews were in their hideouts or with Polish friends. The brave ones, having their Bescheinigungs, still moved about in the streets, but you could see in their faces that they had little trust in their protective papers. Tuesday evening I locked my parents and the others in the hiding place. I was lucky to have Solecki's shop to protect me.

My information about Wednesday's Akcja proved correct. It started at dawn. As usual, I was sleeping in the car. Awakened by a faint shot, I ran to the window. The main street was covered in a thick, milky fog. With visibility so poor, everything looked strange, unreal. The figures I saw didn't walk, they appeared to swim in clouds. There was shooting and screaming . . . shooting and screaming . . . I suffered agonies waiting.

After a while the fog lifted completely. Solecki opened the shop. In came the local Volksdeutscher, Krauze, whose motorcycle I took care of.

"Please, Mr. Krauze," I said, "I want to check my home to see if we've been robbed. Will you escort me home?" I wanted to check to make sure the hiding place was secure. I was terribly worried.

He looked at me. "All right," he said. "Let's go."

We set out, taking Zygmund Tuchman, a newly employed helper, with us. We found the door smashed. Ukrainian soldiers were moving about inside. Krauze, as a German, took over and barked an order. The Ukrainians left, but I was still afraid to go to the hiding place because Krauze was present.

I signaled Zygmund to run upstairs to the hideout, and I turned to Krauze to divert his attention. "Let's look in the next room," I said. But he noticed this maneuver. "Let's go up," he said. I tried to talk him out of it, but without success. Krauze was suspicious now, and stubbornly insisted.

Trying to save the situation and counting on his "friendship" with me, I said nervously, "My mother's upstairs. Please, you'll scare her." But Krauze was already on the steps, and we were behind him.

The room was small. The only furniture was a table, bed, and cabinet. He glanced about suspiciously. "Where's your mother?"

The hiding place was untouched. I breathed a sigh of relief. "They must have taken her," I blurted out. This new development worried me. Krauze was smart. He was on to something. His eyes followed the ceiling and walls, then rested on the cabinet. He stepped over to it and was about to move it. I caught him by the hand. "Please, don't. Please," I begged.

"I only want to see," he said quietly.

My heart pounded. He moved the obstacle, and without surprise he uncovered the little door and entered. I peered in, but it was pitch dark. It took a few moments for my eyes to adjust and make out shapes. There was only silence. Slowly Krauze stepped out of the hideout. He looked into my frightened face and said convincingly, "I won't tell, don't worry."

No Jew could believe the word of a Nazi, but we had no choice; we were at his mercy. Where could we go now? Again I masked the entrance and returned to the shop.

At last the Akcja ended. Krauze kept his promise. When I opened the door to the hiding place and let everyone out, they took up a collection to reward him. In the evening, I gave him the money from thankful people.

Other Jews were not so fortunate. They were double-crossed. The Ukrainians didn't even read the protective papers before tearing them to pieces and throwing them in the dirt.

One day all the Jews of Izbica were ordered to stay in their homes.

Looking out from behind the window curtain, I could see many German soldiers on the streets, most of them in black SS uniforms. We were frightened. No one knew the reason for the activity. It lasted until about 4:00 P.M., and then everything went back to normal. The following day we were informed by Polish friends that Himmler himself was visiting the local brick factory, which produced special material for fortifications.

Sometimes the Akcjas virtually decimated the Jewish population, but soon new transports of foreign Jews from Germany, Austria, France, Slovakia, and the Czech protectorate arrived and filled the ghetto to capacity. The old Izbica population was greatly reduced; there wasn't a family that didn't suffer agonies.

In September 1942, all Jews from the small neighboring ghettos of Krasnystaw and Zamość were to be brought to Izbica. Engels ordered the local Judenrat to prepare space for them.

Soon all Jews from Zamość were resettled in Izbica and the city was declared *Judenrein* (Jew-free). The resettlement was a bloody one. The people had been formed into columns and forced to walk the entire twenty-one kilometers. Engels guarded them with a machine gun manned from the roof of a truck. It was a caravan of horrors. He shot to kill those who lagged behind. Riding alongside in horse-drawn wagons were Ukrainian guards, who executed Jews at will and with pleasure. Finally, the remnants of the convoy entered Izbica.

The concentration of Jews from the neighboring ghettos was generally a grim sign of an oncoming Akcja, but some optimistic Jews saw it as a sign that the Nazis had chosen Izbica as a *Judenstadt,* an exemplary Jewish town, which the Germans could show off to the world. These Jews believed they would be allowed to continue living there in peace. Again hope stifled action.

On October 22, 1942, in the morning, Engels called the Judenrat and Ordnungsdienst to his quarters. This was something new. There he announced a deportation order, and made the Judenrat and Ordnungsdienst responsible for a successful Akcja. This time everyone, including the Judenrat and the Jewish militia, had to go directly to the train station, where Engels would personally select who should be exempt from the resettlement. Whoever tried to hide would be shot on the spot.

A few hours later, the town was surrounded by SS soldiers. We suspected this would be the last Akcja and no Jews would be left in Izbica. Never before had the entire Judenrat and their families been included. The news spread in a flash throughout the town.

There was no sense in our hiding, because there was no hope that we would be able to move freely on the street once the Akcja was over. "Judenrein" meant that not one Jew had the right to live in this territory. Now anyone could lawfully kill a Jew or deliver him to the Germans.

We went to the train station, too, because glowing deep in our souls there still remained a tiny flicker of hope that maybe we were going to a work camp. On the other hand, we could count on certain death if we hid and were discovered. We had no choice. Our hiding place was known to Krauze. And, anyway, we couldn't stay in the hiding place longer than a day or two. Even if we weren't discovered, how long could we survive without food and in the freezing cold of winter? The town was surrounded by people waiting to descend on and rob Jewish homes. We stood no chance.

In the beginning only small groups of Jews moved in the direction of the train station. Most were wandering on the streets in seemingly aimless directions. Those were Jews still desperately looking for a way out of their destiny, discreetly attempting to approach their Christian neighbors for help. But even those who would have liked to help were afraid of informants. The penalty for hiding a Jew was death. Rejected, Jews wandered to the outskirts of the town, but there they were met by a ring of SS soldiers with outstretched bayonets. The only way left open was the road to the wagons. There was no escape.

Despite the 2:00 P.M. deadline, the soldiers didn't rush us, for they were busy robbing our deserted homes. Meanwhile, Jews moved in unguarded groups toward the train station, seemingly voluntarily.

It's true that no one was guarding us at this point. But from the very beginning we had been surrounded by an invisible wall made up of anti-Semitic Polish citizens, which, in my opinion, is one of the main reasons why so very few Jews survived. Certainly, there were Poles who risked their own lives and those of their families to help the Jews, but from what I have seen, a great number of Poles actively helped the Nazis persecute the Jews. Poles who wanted to help Jews did so secretly, making it very difficult for any Jew to know who they were and how to contact them.

The fact was that when a Jew took off his Star of David armband

and left the ghetto, the Germans, who knew the Jews only from Nazi propaganda posters as having low foreheads and long curved noses, could not distinguish him from the rest of the population. Therefore, to escape being recognized by the Nazis was a real possibility for the Izbica Jews. The greater problem was the local citizenry. They were particularly good at recognizing Jews; they had lived with us for hundreds of years. Not only adults, but also teenagers and even children, would wait for an occasion when Jews tried to escape; first they would mock, beat, and rob a Jew, then hand him over for a reward of vodka or sugar.

My parents appeared in control of themselves. My mother made the bed, covered it with a new bedspread, then put four candles on the cloth-covered table. She lit them and said a prayer, even though it was not the Sabbath. Then my father gave my brother and me a knapsack filled with food, and we simply left our home.

My mother and father walked in front while my brother and I walked behind, holding hands, just like a family. Passing the Christian cooperative store Łączność, where I once had a confrontation with an SS man, the action of a Polish neighbor saved me. Heniek Królikowski, Engels's mechanic, stood near his home, observing the victims leaving. He noticed me walking and suddenly, courageously, he moved in my direction and, pretending to stroll by, he whispered in Yiddish, a language he knew well, "Toivi, don't be a schmuck. Where are you going? Follow me." And he turned in the direction of his home.

Impulsively, I turned around and followed him. It was before the two o'clock deadline and people were still moving in every direction on the street. I entered his family's bakery, and he hid me in the attic. The time passed slowly. From my hiding place I peeped through the attic's tiny glassless window and could barely see the commotion in the field near the train station. I heard screams coming from that direction. Suddenly there was a burst of machine-gun fire, then another one lasting much longer. I turned my head away in terror.

I was probably sleeping, exhausted from the day's events, when I heard people speaking in Yiddish. I ran to the window. Down the street I could see groups of unguarded Jews returning to the town— some carrying their pitiful belongings, some covered with blood and crying. Making sure there were no SS soldiers around, I snuck out and found to my amazement that there were still Jews alive and about. I ran home, and with great joy found my mother, father, and brother there.

The stories tumbled out. Since there were not enough boxcars, Engels decided to make a selection. Everyone was screaming and crying, pushing to be chosen. There was chaos. Engels became furious. As he rested his machine gun on the shoulder of Judenrat chairman Abram Blatt, he mowed down a group of people and forced the others into the boxcars. They were packed so tightly that some suffocated to death before the train even left town. Those who could not fit in the boxcars, including my family, were told to go home.

I went to the station. An open meadow by the tracks was strewn with about three hundred dead bodies. The setting sun was reflected in streams of fresh blood. Among the dead I recognized Mr. Rubinsztajn from Warsaw, a friend of our family. Nearby lay his gray-haired wife. Even though her lower jaw had been blasted away, I recognized her open eyes, and her dress. I remembered how, not so long ago, I used to feel faint at the sight of blood, not to mention dead bodies. Now, at fifteen, I was immune. Viewing this massacre, I felt only pity for the victims and great fear for myself.

I wandered around my neighborhood. The house where I was born, the *yerishe* that had lasted for a hundred years, was now empty, its windows broken. Wandering through the building, my path was strewn with broken glass. The vandals, wasting no time in searching for hidden money, had torn the pillows and comforters. Feathers were still floating in the air. Gone were my cousins Symcha, Toivi, Rywka, Fajgele . . .

When darkness fell, I was still wandering around the empty houses. A deadly calm lay over this part of town. As I edged toward my home, staying close to the walls, I suddenly heard drunken voices singing a song popular with the new class of unscrupulous, war-enriched Poles. They were celebrating . . .

Drink, drink, drink, brother, drink,
And the war should longer thunder.

The final days were near. It was the end of October 1942. When dusk fell, it was time for the curfew; the streets emptied, doors and shutters were closed. One might think that the town had died. But inside the inhabitants were quietly scheming. They were thinking about how to survive . . . what to do to save at least one member of the family.

For two days a rumor circulated that the remainder of the Jews would be liquidated. It was a tragic situation with no way out. Until that point I had lived with my family. Now, in view of the developing situation, we decided to separate. We saw no other way. We knew that death awaited us. Perhaps if we scattered one of us would survive.

Through a friendly Polish official at the Izbica magistrate, Mr. Paszkowski, my father managed to arrange for me the "Aryan paper," crucifix pendants, and other requirements which would testify that I was a Christian. I was to leave home and steal away to Hungary. My mother was to hide with false papers in Warsaw, and my father and younger brother would look for a hiding place among local Polish friends.

✿

For a Lease on Life

Waldemar Ptaszek Resurrected

It was already six o'clock in the evening, and I still didn't have my Aryan papers. We were to leave at two o'clock in the morning. I had very little time, and my father decided it would be best that I run to the neighboring village, Tarnógora, and pick up the dubious passport to life.

In the darkness I had no trouble getting to the home of Paszkowski, the town clerk. He wasn't there, but his wife handed me the papers. I was now Waldemar Ptaszek, seventeen years old. If anyone were to stop and question me, everything would be in order. I had the papers of a Christian youth who had just died and whose name had not been erased from the books of the living. How ironic, I thought, Waldemar, a pious Catholic, resurrected as a Jew!

Despite the importance of secrecy and the fact that the night's curfew had already begun, I wanted to say good-bye to my friend, Jozek Bresler. I cautiously crept to his home and knocked. His mother opened the door; Jozek stood behind her.

"Jozek, I'm leaving. I'm here to say good-bye," I told him.

"Don't go," he said. "Stay with me. We can escape to the forest."

I would have liked to have stayed with him. But I knew by now that the forest wasn't any safer, and I couldn't change my parents' plans. Sadly, we said good-bye.

When I came home, my mother was sewing small gold coins into the hems of my clothing. My father was looking on, seemingly relaxed, but I knew that his soul was suffering.

I took out the papers. Tense and engrossed, I repeated, mechanically, "Waldemar Ptaszek, born August 20, 1925, district of Krasnystaw, son of Antoni and Maria, whose maiden name was Stankewicz, religion Roman Catholic, living in Tarnógora . . . Waldemar Ptaszek, born . . ."

I was to travel with an organized group of Jews, all equipped with false Aryan papers. Our guide was a Pole, Mr. Gajosz, who was supposed to deliver us to the Hungarian border, where another guide would take us through.

I ate a final meal with my family. Soon it was time to go. I felt a lump in my throat. I was leaving my home and family for the first time, and I knew there was a possibility I would never come back, never see my loved ones again, yet the impact of the whole tragedy somehow didn't quite sink in. We hugged and kissed and said good-bye, nothing more, just good-bye. No tears. A moment later I was outside. Stealthily I crept to Mr. Sznajder's house, our meeting point.

Waiting there was Mr. Rapaport, an iron businessman from Zamość. In overalls, with a long, turned-up mustache, he looked like a typical farmer from one of the villages near Lublin. There was Mr. Rabinowicz from Chełm, my friend Wolf Sznajdmeser, a girl named Langard, and a girl named Winter from Koło. We were six in all.

At the last minute I had the urge to see my parents and brother once more. Pretending I had forgotten something, and despite strong protests, I went back.

I knocked. The door opened and I stepped in. I didn't know what to say. My heart was heavy. I stood for a second in the middle of the room, silently looking at my brother. My father interrupted the silence.

"Toivi," he said, with a shadow of superstition in his tone, "you should not come back now, it's not a good sign. We all love you and we want you to live, and because of it you should leave. There is no question about it. You are fifteen years old, and you are not a child anymore. You know we are Jews sentenced to die. Izbica is dead. If not today, tomorrow they will destroy us. Together we will not survive. You today, tomorrow your mother, myself, and your brother will go our separate ways . . . maybe one way will be the lucky way. Goodbye, son, and may God bless you."

I threw him a last glance, and silently I left.

It was one in the morning, time to get ready for the train. Slowly, one after another, we departed. The date is etched in my memory: October 26, 1942.

It was a cool fall night. We crept from building to building until, reaching the vicinity of the train station, we hid behind the switchman's house and waited. Our guide passed out the tickets, purchased in advance.

The timing was perfect. We could hear the whistle of the steam engine from far away. A few moments later, the train pushed onto the platform. We waited near the last cars, where the light from the station's only lamp did not reach. As the wheels of the train began slowly to roll again, we jumped on. The train gathered speed.

I sat close to Wolf. Our turned-up collars hid our faces. We pretended to be asleep. But my mind raced. Will it work? Will somebody recognize us? Will our guide at least be honest? Or will he kill us someplace near the border, forcing us first to write a letter home that we were safely across, so he could cheat others? We had heard many such tales. Such fearful thoughts bore into my mind like a drill.

Then there was the actual illegal crossing of the border into Hungary, where Jews supposedly fared better. How many dangers were lurking? What would happen if we got caught? The "crimes" I had committed were enormous under Nazi law. I had false documents— the penalty: death. I left the ghetto without German permission— death. I was traveling on a train—death. I didn't wear the Star of David—death. And above all, I was a Jew—death.

At the Zawada station, who should come into our darkened compartment but my former boss, Tadek Solecki! We were terrified. Suppose he recognizes us? We hid our faces in our collars. We were lucky. He got off at the next stop.

Suddenly a kind of subdued anxiety spread among the passengers. They closed the windows; some lit cigarettes. What had happened? Why did the talk turn to whispers? I caught scraps of sentences. "They gas . . . fat for soap." Despite the closed windows, the odor of rotting flesh seeped through.

BEŁZEĊ! Of course! I grew numb with shock. We were passing near one of the rumored death factories! My heart pounding, I looked out the window. There were scarce woods, then, in the distance, I saw flames—now fading, now shooting higher into the sky. This was the destiny I was trying to escape. The smell receded as the train raced on, but I could still see the reflection of fire in the sky.

Between Rawa Ruska and Lwów, I noticed that Rabinowicz approached our Polish guide, Gajosz, and conversed quietly a few times.

At the same time, I heard a peasant woman say, "See that one, over there? I'm sure he's a Jew," tilting her head in Rabinowicz's direction. I felt like fainting.

There was nothing to do but wait. Near Lwów, to my horror, Rabinowicz came to me asking for additional money for our guide. Otherwise the guide threatened to leave us. Seeing that we were in trouble (the woman who had identified Rabinowicz had surely noticed his contact with us), I immediately told him what the peasant woman had said. At the next station we quickly left, mingled with people outside in the darkness of night, and eventually got on another car.

We arrived without incident at daylight in Kleparów, in the outskirts of Lwów. We were afraid to travel through the central train station, where we heard there was strict control and a mass of secret police looking for Jews. We had decided it was safer to go by foot across the whole city to a station in Sknilów, where we would catch another train.

We immediately merged with a group of smugglers, most of them young people who had purchased food from neighboring villages and were returning on the morning train.

Now I realized the mistake my parents had made. I was wearing my best clothes—a new coat, nice woolen pants, and high, shiny leather boots. The contrast with my surroundings was enormous. It was a normal weekday, and nobody was dressed in their best.

We were moving single file now with the other travelers, as roadwork was being done and the path was narrow. Just past the station, a uniformed Ukrainian on a bicycle approached. He looked at us and stopped. Despite my fear I passed him, not heeding his suspicious look.

"Come here," he said in a normal tone, but I knew it could mean the beginning of the end. I wasn't sure his words were directed at me, but no one in our line reacted to his command. Knowing that delay would not improve the situation, I stepped aside and came up to the Ukrainian.

"You are Jewish?"

"No, I'm a Christian. I'm traveling to my aunt's in the village. I could show you identification."

"And what do you have in the backpack?"

"Food," I answered, and prepared to open the backpack, even before he gave the order.

Luckily, he waved his hand and left.

If he hadn't been lazy and had checked my backpack, revealing the extra clothes and food, he would undoubtedly have realized I was a Jew. I wondered at my composure. A few minutes later I caught up to my companions. We walked through the city of Lwów. At one point we saw some young members of the Hitlerjugend beating up a Jew.

To our horror, we passed close to the infamous concentration camp Janów. The camp was right in the middle of town, and as we walked past I couldn't help seeing emaciated Jews working under guard behind barbed-wire fences. I had the same thoughts and feelings as I had had in the train passing Bełżec—I could be one of them! This is the fate they have in store for me! If the Germans only knew that a Jew was passing by . . . For some reason, God must be taking care of me.

After a few hours we arrived at the Sknilów train station. I spent my last Polish currency at the buffet for something to eat, then went to the restroom to wash. It had been a rough day.

I looked in the small corroded mirror, critically judging myself. First, my face. Not too bad . . . light hair, blue eyes. My skin, light . . . some freckles. Only the nose, maybe a little bit too long . . . luckily it doesn't have a hook like the one on the poster hanging in the Izbica station. But my Jewish accent was a problem. At home and with my friends I always spoke Yiddish. I must speak as little as possible now.

Finally, a touchy problem. I couldn't urinate. It was very, very painful. An uncut foreskin was better than any identification papers. Mine had been cut off on the eighth day of my life, according to Jewish custom. For fifteen years I lived with it, and one week before leaving Izbica, I had decided to correct it. Every evening before going to bed I pulled up what was left of my foreskin and tied it with a string so it wouldn't slip back. I hoped it would stretch and stay in place, or at least make the fact that I was circumcised difficult to detect. Instead, my penis became swollen and inflamed.

A childhood memory came to me. I was about three and a half years old. I must have been terribly frightened, for I still remember it vividly even today. I remember the long table, the white tablecloth, the crowded room, the sun shining through the window, and the people, their faces lost in foggy memory. Except for one. That face I will never forget: the face of Dziobaty Jojne. After the shock of seeing my little brother brought to the rabbi and the ritual of circumcision performed, it was he who had grabbed me, picked me up, and pretended to hand me over to the rabbi for the "next operation." I screamed in horror, grabbed his beard, and didn't let go, not even when my father tried to calm me. I remember his red, sweaty face, full of pockmarks, and his bantering smile—and all the while being scared to death.

My introspection ended abruptly. It was time to leave. The train pulled in and we boarded. All went well for a while. Then, just before we came to Stryj, the German conductor, checking tickets, went up to one of the girls in my group. She was looking out the window, possibly to hide her face from the other passengers.

"Your ticket, please."

"I have the ticket," she responded quickly in German. Apparently buried in thought, she had been caught by surprise. When he tried to make conversation with her, as she was a very pretty girl, she suddenly pretended she did not understand, explaining in halting German that she had studied the language in school but could remember only a few words.

She easily convinced the German conductor, but not the Ukrainian peasants traveling with us. Their suspicions were aroused, and they began whispering among themselves. Soon two uniformed Ukrainian policemen whisked her away and the search for other Jews began.

Here I made my greatest mistake. While most of the passengers looked on with interest, excitedly making comments, scared and profusely sweating I buried my face in a newspaper and probably stuck out like a sore thumb. I could feel the whole compartment eyeing me with suspicion. The print danced before my eyes. I turned hot and cold, and my mouth tasted bitter. This is it, I thought, I'm through . . .

"Documents!" called a harsh voice in Ukrainian. In front of me stood a uniformed man. Slowly, heart pounding but with a calm face, I handed him my birth certificate.

"What is your name?"

"Waldemar Ptaszek," I replied, "but they call me Waldek at home."

"Are you a Jew?"

"No."

He looked at my red face and knew I was lying. "We shall see about that, boy. Get up and follow me!" He took me to the lavatory and told me to pull down my pants. He checked, then called his companion for verification. With my pants down, I waited for their medical verdict. They quietly discussed the manipulated evidence. Maybe they were not quite sure if I was circumcised. My weeklong surgical attempt had been in vain: he took me away.

I was led to the end of the corridor where other detained Jews were guarded. The next stop was the city of Stryj. The cars expelled masses of people, and the platform was filled with hustle and bustle, laughter and shouts in the brisk October air. We stood outside the railway security offices and waited. The door opened, and we were led into a large bare room.

Five Ukrainians and one Gestapo man began the interrogation. We were each asked, "Are you a Jew?" Naturally no one confessed, so they ordered us to undress. Then the naked truth came out: we were all circumcised. The next thing I knew I was being punched in the throat again and again until I gasped for air. Some of the Ukrainian Nazi collaborators were taking the opportunity to express their hatred for us.

"Enough!" shouted the cool Gestapo officer. Reluctantly they lowered their fists. They resented being denied the pleasure of beating Jews, and it showed on their faces. If it were not for the Gestapo officer (an exceptional one), I think we would have been crippled by the interrogation. After they searched our clothes carefully, we stood naked against the wall. Our confiscated money and other valuables lay piled on a table.

The door opened with a squeak. In came a Ukrainian guard with Wolf Sznajdmeser in tow. I'd never seen my friend so frightened. His clean, round, perfect "Slavic" face was white, drained of blood. The Ukrainian guard turned laughingly to his comrades.

"The passengers were all gone, and I noticed this boy standing alone on the platform. I never would have suspected that he was a Jew, but when I went up to him and asked him what he was looking for, his accent immediately gave him away."

He broke into laughter imitating Wolf's heavy Jewish accent. The others joined in, thoroughly enjoying the joke. Like us, Wolf was searched, ordered to undress. Again we were ordered to dress and were led to a holding pen.

Prisoner

We sat in a narrow, darkened cell. Above us, at the far end, was a small window with bars. A white object, unrecognizable in the dim light, hung from the bars. After about an hour the lock on the door clicked, the cell opened a bit, and the guard said, "You're lucky the other Gestapo man isn't here. It's his day off. He would have hanged you by the legs and his dog, a big Alsatian, would be gnawing at you alive. But since you're going to die anyway—it's only a matter of time—you would do well to hand over any hidden money you might still have. In exchange I'll give you some good advice."

Rapaport from Zamość opened an eyeglass case, extracted a gold coin from behind the chamois lining, and handed it to the guard, who, after all, looked like an approachable person. Our faces perked up as faint hope rekindled in our hearts. We listened carefully. A scornful smile appeared on the jailer's lips as he delivered his advice. He opened the door wider to let in more light.

"Look," he said, pointing to the little window behind us. "Hanging there on the bars is a pair of underwear. On those long johns a Jew, caught like you are, hung himself yesterday. So I tell you, do the same. Take turns, hang yourselves, and take each other down, down to the last one. It will be an easier death than the one being prepared for you." Our eyes turned to the window. The white object was indeed a pair of long underwear. He closed the cell door.

When he opened the door again two hours later, he was disappointed: no one had taken his advice. We were so used to torment that we did not lose hope in this seemingly hopeless situation. A uniformed official came and took down our names. I gave my true one, since my false birth certificate had been destroyed in the first interrogation. We were told to come out for transfer. Outside the guards readied their pistols, warning us that if we tried to escape they would shoot.

We were led into the street. It was a bright, beautiful day. Everywhere life was blooming. The laughter and talk of free people filled the air; only the presence of the guards separated us.

Stryj was a bustling city. People were everywhere, working or shopping. People passing by, recognizing us as Jews, reacted in various ways. Some stared with wide-open eyes and some laughed at us.

Now and then taunts and curses were directed toward us. A few passed quickly by with downcast eyes as if in sorrow. No one would give us bread or a kind word, for the penalty was death.

At last we came to a large building. As we entered, I saw near the door a sign marked KRIPO (Criminal Police). We were immediately put in a darkened cell. A large platform made of rough boards took up three-quarters of the space. Here we were to eat and sleep. The floor was earthen. A barrel for waste completed our furnishings.

In the evening the guard singled me out to follow him. He handed me a huge pail and led me to a water pump in the hall. I filled the pail with water and carried it to the private room of a KRIPO officer. In thanks, I was given a full dish of their leftovers. Though terribly hungry, I couldn't force myself to touch someone else's food. I was squeamish. I sat down on a broken fruit box with the dish in my hand and looked around the hall. The guard stood close by, hurrying me.

"I can't. I have a stomachache," I blurted out as an excuse. I washed the dish and was taken back to our cell. It didn't take long before I was less particular.

We had been in KRIPO headquarters for five days. We tried to contact the local Judenrat by smuggling messages out. Perhaps they would buy our way out. Rabinowicz, who was in the same cell, supposedly offered the interrogation officer some money to free us. Rabinowicz was, in fact, called outside a few times by KRIPO officers. Wolf and I believed Rabinowicz, and we gave him the valuables we had managed to hide (never before did I suspect that plain clothing held so many hiding places that could stand up to repeated searches).

That night, from the courtyard, we heard loud praying, followed by shooting. Then, in the morning, a boy of about ten was brought in, crying as if his heart would break. We asked why he was crying and between sobs the story came out.

Before the war, a German lived with the boy's family as a boarder, without any incident. When war broke out the German left, but a few days ago he had returned, hoping to appropriate the house and furniture. He accused the boy's parents of prewar discrimination against him. The Gestapo arrested the entire family and brought them here. Last night the Germans took his parents from their cell.

They hadn't returned, and he didn't know what had happened to them. Now we knew why we'd heard gunshots, but we said nothing.

A week later the guard came and told us we were to be transferred again. Apparently the KRIPO section was too small for the number of prisoners that came in daily.

Again they arranged us in a column, cocked the gun, and told us they would shoot without warning if we tried to escape. Again we moved through a stream of free life yet were outside it. It was a humiliating march. Polish and Ukrainian teenagers mocked us and spat on us. Finally we arrived at a large red building complex—the Stryj city prison, a place of suffering for thousands.

A guard rang the bell at the gate. A small barred window opened, and a jail employee exchanged a few words with the guard. The gate opened wide, welcoming us. We moved through a long hallway divided in sections by barred gates. Over and over again the keys rattled, the iron gates swung open and banged shut. Finally they had us face a wall with our hands up.

In time we were called to an office and our names were taken. There were the usual formalities and again a search. This time, however, they were not so thorough. They probably thought that after the Gestapo and KRIPO, there wouldn't be much left in the way of valuables. They took small items such as belts and ties, and escorted us to cell 27.

Our cell already held a few prisoners: two Ukrainians, Michał Sudoł and an old man named Iwan from Struth Niźny; a young, tall, and well-built Czech named Yelinek; the Zelingers, father and son, both photographers from Stryj; and one sick man suspected of having some Jewish blood. All together there were eleven of us.

The cell was clean, with windows facing a much smaller two-story building across a courtyard. Between the two buildings, in the middle of the courtyard, was an artesian well. Next to it was a bell, rung at mealtime. Our cell was furnished with a table, two benches, a barrel for waste, and four straw mattresses stacked in a corner, to be laid out at night. The month of November is normally very cold, but with eleven men sleeping together in such a small area, it was so warm that we stripped to our underwear. And so jail life began. It was the end of 1942.

On the second day we were surprised to be called out one by one by the section guard, a Pole. No one who left came back to the cell. We became nervous. My turn came. The guard took me to a little room and told me to undress. He took my clothes and checked them very carefully. He found a Russian gold coin sewed into the crotch of my pants.

I suspected that the guard was searching us secretly for his own enrichment. "Keep it for yourself," I said. "Bring me bread from time to time in exchange." He shook my hand to seal the bargain and took me to another room where the others, already searched, were waiting. After nearly an hour, he took all of us back to our original cell. We were sure by then that he had acted without authorization, but none of us would complain. We could be severely punished for hiding money.

Days passed. Each morning the same rough yell greeted us from the hallway: "Ready for ROLL CALL!" We would jump from the mattresses and tidy the room. The mattresses were carefully put aside, and the one whose duty it was that day would sweep the floor with paper from the packages sent to the Ukrainian inmates. No brooms were available. We would dress, and when we heard the yell we were ready.

We could hear steps coming closer and the screech of opening cell doors. Then our door opened, and the tall prison warden, Mr. Król, entered with the guard of our section. The head of our cell, Sudoł, screamed "Attention!"; then he turned to the warden to report that all were present. Then the warden greeted everybody with a loud "Good morning, boys."

"Good morning, Mr. Warden," we would answer in unison. He saluted and moved to the next cell. In a few minutes they would give us water to wash with and would take out our waste barrel.

Breakfast was announced by the bell. Through the open door a guard and a prisoner with a tray would ladle out portions. Everyone got a thin slice of bread and some ersatz coffee. As soon as this meal was over, the wait for lunch began. Time moved at an agonizingly slow pace. At last we'd be electrified by news from our watchmen at the window: "Guys, they're washing the cans." That meant it was close to mealtime. Each day we would experience it as though for the first time. Again the bell sounded: lunchtime. Even though it would be an hour before they would come to our cell, we would be standing in line by the door.

We waited tensely. There were three cells before ours. Two, one, and finally we heard the rattle of the bolt and the turn of the key in the lock. The crew was met at the door by a mass of outstretched aluminum bowls. If you were slow, they would purposely try to miss your bowl and burn your hand. To save your hand as well as your stomach, it was essential to move quickly and precisely toward the soup can.

No spoons were given. The soup was slopped. With our fingers we pulled out little pieces of spoiled cabbage; it stank and tasted bitter. On rare occasions we had lentil soup. Then we relished each lentil and rolled it around in our mouths. The soup was supposed to last until suppertime, but it really had to last until the next morning, since "supper" meant ersatz coffee only.

After drinking my coffee in the evening, I gave the grounds to the smokers. They dried them and rolled them up in newspaper, then smoked them like cigarettes. Later, after the nightly roll call, each of us squeezed into his spot on the mattress and was left to his own thoughts. Then I would stare through the bars at the moon shining brightly in the dark sky and think of my home, my parents, my brother, and Izbica. Are they still alive? Where are they? Do they know where I am? I don't think so, I answered myself. I'm left to my own devices. And the worst is that I don't see the end. This Ukrainian, Sudoł, he knows that tomorrow, maybe in a week, a month . . . they will let him out, or maybe he will get a prescribed sentence for his crime. But we Jews? We'll never be free again. Our prison is not only this cell, not only the ghetto, or even Poland . . . it's practically the whole of Europe now. We don't even hope for freedom anymore. All we want is a postponement of our death sentence. I feared suffering, death, and the unknown, not knowing when it would happen, when the murderous demons would come in and kill us. With such thoughts I fell asleep. And so the days and nights passed.

Someone was tapping lightly on the wall. We thought it was Morse code, but none of us knew it. We answered anyway, by tapping also. Then the knocking slowly moved alongside the wall in the direction of the windows to the courtyard. The windows from our cells faced the same way. We were unable to see each other, but we could hear.

"Are you Jews from Izbica?" came a woman's voice.

"Yes. Who asks?"

"Langard."

Now we knew. The girls from our original group went through the same thing we did and were now in the adjoining cell.

Not everyone was hungry. Sudoł received packages from his girl-friend practically every other day; the sick man received soup from the Red Cross;[1] and the Zellingers received parcels from their family still living in the ghetto. But what was most interesting to us was that Rabinowicz, who, like the rest of us from Izbica, had no close family in the area, was also receiving packages. Though Sudoł and the Zellin-gers shared some of their food with us, it was never enough. So you can imagine our happiness when one evening they brought seven loaves of dark bread into our cell.

Each Jew got one loaf, a gift from the Judenrat. We had a bread holiday. I lay down with a feeling of great happiness. I put the bread on my chest, holding it with both hands. Slowly, I bit off little pieces from the full loaf. Each bite was priceless. I must have eaten it even in my sleep, because when I woke up only crumbs were left. My stomach hurt terribly, but for once I felt full. We all hoped the Judenrat would not forget us. A foolish thought. I knew they were busy with more serious matters than feeding a few prisoners.

I wasn't able to solve the riddle of Rabinowicz. Who was helping him? Who was sending him packages, and who was paying for them? He swore by all that is holy that the KRIPO officer double-crossed him and took all his money. Did his daily pious praying help him? It was no longer the age of miracles.

Later, by accident, it all came to light. Zelinger's wife in the ghet-to bribed the guard of our section; through him she sent letters and food parcels to her husband. Rabinowicz had arranged the delivery of food with Zelinger and paid him for the service. Zelinger offered to use his connections to help me buy food. "I'm sorry," I told him, "I don't have any money. I gave most of it to Rabinowicz in the KRIPO jail to buy us out, and the rest was taken by the guard."

Zelinger, an intelligent man, instantly became suspicious and asked us—Rapaport, Wolf, and myself—exactly what we had given

Rabinowicz. Later he compared our currency with what Rabinowicz had given him, and the truth came out. The money we had given Rabinowicz to bribe the KRIPO officer he had hidden for himself, in a not-too-hygienic but very safe place, passing all searches. Rabinowicz, using our trust, had fooled us to get our money, helping himself at our expense. Under our combined pressure he admitted all of it, but what good did it do us now?

We were awakened one night by terrible screams. The prison courtyard was jammed with Jews. Whips were flying and cracking. The SS were barking orders. An Akcja was taking place in the town of Stryj, and the Jews were being collected. It continued until 6:00 P.M. the following day. Then, as I heard later, they were carted away to the cattle trains. The transport must have been overflowing, for a few hundred Jews were left in the courtyard. Soon they were counted and put in the smaller prison building across from us. From then on we saw several Jews brought to this jail each day. Word got to us that they had been caught outside the ghetto without the Star of David, with false papers, or had committed other crimes. Apparently they were being held for a transport to Bełżec.

Time passed, and again late one night we were awakened by bloodcurdling screams. I ran to the window and looked down. A woman was being beaten. SS men were driving Jews out of the smaller building and into the courtyard. Whips were flying indiscriminately.

In the lamplight, the elongated shadows of Jews cowering under the blows must have looked like a scene from Dante's Hell or a film studio "take" of the worst period of the Inquisition. The orgy of violence lasted until dawn.

We were afraid that we, too, would be added to the death transport. We couldn't figure out why our group of eight Jews was being held separately in relative peace.

We got up one morning as usual. We ate breakfast and were waiting for dinner; the luckier ones waited for their packages. About eleven they were delivered. Sudoł was unwrapping bread and threw away the wrappings in a corner. The sharp eyes of Rapaport noticed a scrap of newspaper, and he bent down to pick it up.

As he read it, his face lit up. "Thank God, I survived to this day. I made it!" he exclaimed.

"What are you talking about?" we asked.

Excitedly, he showed us a news article dated December 1942, detailing the Soviet encirclement of General Paulus's army at Stalingrad. For a Nazi paper to admit this, it could only mean that it was very bad for the Germans on the Soviet front. We were jubilant. That piece of newspaper, with its greasy, crumpled words, brought a hint of freedom to our cell. There was hope—the Nazi power might not be invincible!

Alvin Lippman

Time passed. Two more men were added to our cell: a Jewish lawyer from Stryj and a graying German, Alvin Lippman, former commander of the Jewish police in the Zamość ghetto. At the same time, the elder Zelinger was released to the ghetto.

The lawyer, whose name I can't remember, a young man with a tremendous sense of humor, was a fantastic imitator of different musical instruments, so the bored jail guards often came at night after roll call to wake him and ask him to "play." In return, we all benefited by receiving leftover food the following day.

Lippman, however, was quiet, pedantic, particular, and orderly—a typical German. He would get up immediately after roll call, shine his shoes, and button every button. His unfortunate path to Poland was typical of German Jews, with this difference: he was not Jewish and had the chance to stay in Germany if he chose.

The lawyer showed interest in Lippman, and an unimaginable story unfolded. From their conversations it became clear that Lippman was an officer in the German Army. For assisting General Erich von Ludendorff in Hitler's rebellion at the beginning of the Nazi era, he had received an official thank-you letter from the German government and the Nazi Party. In addition, he had top army medals from World War I and the beginning of World War II. He served in the Polish campaign as a captain in the German Army.

When German Jews were relocated to Poland, his Jewish wife and son had been protected by the army as family of a German Army officer. When the Gestapo failed to persuade him to divorce his wife, they managed to make the army discharge him. Without army protection, his family was deported to Poland. Not wishing to leave his wife and son, Lippman was sent with a transport of Jews to Zamość, where he lived with his family in the ghetto and was made commandant of the Jewish police.

He was able to prolong the life of his family for a time, but when they made Zamość Judenrein his influence ended. He tried to save his family but failed; they were all caught. His Jewish wife and children were taken to Sobibor or Bełżec, and Lippman, after being able to prove his German heritage, was set free. After realizing his family was dead and giving up his search, he was again arrested on the train to Germany.

On the advice of the lawyer, Lippman asked for paper and a pen to write directly to the governor of occupied Poland, Dr. Frank, in Kraków. Later, under the lawyer's direction, he listed his military rank and all the medals he received for service for the German Fatherland, and asked the authorities to check his documents in the prison depot.

The letter went through the proper channels. A few days later, at an unusual hour, we heard footsteps and German voices. As the jail was run by Polish and Ukrainian personnel, German was rarely heard, and we became frightened, especially when the steps stopped in front of our cell.

The door opened, and in front of us stood a tall officer with the SS death's-head insignia on his military cap. With him was another man in civilian clothes, probably a Gestapo official.

"Herr Alvin Lippman, present yourself."

"Here," answered the prisoner.

"Please dress yourself and take your belongings."

The tone of voice and the use of the words "Herr" and "please" were unimaginable in addressing a prisoner. While Lippman prepared himself, the officers observed the cell, asking the warden for particulars. When he explained that we had been here for weeks, Aryans as well as Jews, and that this cell was under the jurisdiction of KRIPO, the Gestapo official was furious.

The outcome of this visit didn't take long. A special Gestapo commission arrived. The old Ukrainian was freed. After briefly deliberating, they decided that Yelinek, the Czech, and the sick man were Jews.

Next, all Jews were transferred to the jail across the courtyard, whose occupants so often filled the transports to the death camps. It was our turn now. Apparently KRIPO had either simply forgotten about us, or they were holding us as hostage to get money from the local Judenrat.

One could have called the previous cell heaven, for this one was certainly hell by comparison. About 150 people were jammed into the small cell, some already near insanity. They were now human scraps—too weak to stand, they crawled. Others lay motionless on the floor, or rather the earth, for one could barely recognize boards under the layers of dirt. They had fallen from exhaustion, hunger, wounds, and beatings. The unbearable stench from the "lavatory" (a leaking herring barrel), the babble of half-mad souls, and dead bodies, which lay where they fell, completed the grotesque scene. It was the space of the poor who were unable to pay off the section guard, Nowak, for a better cell.

As I was used to relative cleanliness, I found the filth unbearable. I observed my companions. There were not only Jews here. Standing by the window, a tall Ukrainian peasant prayed ceaselessly. He was one of those Christians who, out of conscience or for money, helped doomed Jews before he was made to share their fate.

We received food only once a day. Nowak would open the door and a prisoner would pour a little soup. We had only a few cups, so we divided into groups of fifteen. When one finished drinking the next one took his turn. Afraid Nowak would say "Enough!" and take the food away, everyone hurried and occasionally spilled it. The soup was always cold, so no one was burned, but many didn't get any food and went hungry.

Everyone received bread, but not his fair share. Nowak simply threw in a sack filled with bread chunks and closed the cell. The "boss" of the cell, a man with a strong physique, a former underworld figure as rumor had it, had powerful fists. With these, and with the help of a select few, he kept order. His cohorts, holding the others back, allowed only one at a time near the boss, who would dip his hand into the sack and take out a piece of bread. Everyone knew that the bread was cut in eight even pieces, and everyone knew what each piece should look like. However, each man got only a fraction of his portion, because the "boss" would break off a big piece of each share and leave it inside the sack. It was of no use to complain. Besides, no one wanted to risk losing the one little piece he managed to get. I was always so very hungry. All I could think of was bread.

Zelinger, My Friend

Now I was separated from Zelinger, who had cared for and looked after me, and I feared my future. Thanks to his connection with the guard, Zelinger had managed to get a better cell at the very beginning, but he didn't forget me, or my friend Wolf. The next evening the door opened, and the guard called out to Wolf and me, "Take your jackets." We were to go to Zelinger, he said. Wolf was standing close to the door and went immediately. But as I was in the opposite corner, I didn't have time enough to push my way through the mass of people. The guard didn't wait and angrily left. At last I got to the door, and in exasperation began hitting it with my hands and head, yelling in frustration. All this got me was a beating with a broom by the section guard. I lay quietly, groaning.

It was already late at night when another guard came for me and led me to the end of the hallway and pushed me into a dimly lit room. At first I could see nothing, but as my eyes became accustomed to the dark, I made out Zelinger nearby. He had bribed the guards to transfer us to a better cell. Thanks to him we were together again. Zelinger had taken a liking to us and took care of us, perhaps because at fifteen and thirteen we were the youngest in the jail.

The new cell was smaller than the old one, but it had two large windows. While there were just as many people, a very different atmosphere prevailed. First of all, there was no hunger and the cell was relatively clean. Wealthier, influential Jews were here. They were helped by their families and sometimes were even able to buy their freedom.

Christian prisoners worked in the courtyard. If we lowered money down through the bars, a basket of food could be pulled up. The guards were bribed not to see it.

The floor was swept a few times a day, despite the size of the room, and to stop the spread of lice, delousing sessions were organized every twenty-four hours. It went like this: A group of prisoners undressed close to the window for better light, then checked their clothing. The lice they caught were thrown into the waste barrel. Then the other groups, in turn, did the same.

In the evening we recited the work of Polish, Jewish, and Russian poets, told happy anecdotes, offered political satires of Hitler, and so on. Among us were people who tried to pull away from the stark reality so that they would not break down from sorrow. And so our time passed.

One day a very strange thing happened. An older Jewish jailmate asked me to retrieve his bread ration, which he had pushed beyond reach on top of the tall brick oven in the cell. He lifted me up, and as I fetched down the bread I noticed several strange paper containers resting on the bricks up there. For while I told no one. Then I went to Zelinger and informed him of what I had seen. This time Zelinger lifted me up and I removed the boxes. To my great surprise and pleasure, I found that they were Russian cigarettes, about a hundred to a carton, most likely left by a prisoner when Stryj was under Soviet occupation. It felt like finding a pot of gold. Not a smoker myself, I sold one carton, gave some to Zelinger, and exchanged others for bread.

Sleeping was the worst thing. There literally wasn't enough room on the floor for all of us. So we took turns, but with difficulty. We lay like sardines in a can. When one turned, all of us woke up.

Despite our efforts at cleanliness, it was not long before an epidemic of typhus broke out in our cell. First one, then another would begin to weave unsteadily, until many were overcome by illness. The typhus outbreak was confirmed by a prisoner doctor. We were afraid to report it, for we knew the Nazis only too well. It was obvious what kind of medicine they would prescribe for us. Therefore, the sick would "stand" on their feet at daily roll call. Crammed together, we could prop each other up, and, being tightly packed, we drew no attention from the guard.

Through the mail we smuggled out, we let the Judenrat know that some of us were now sick and asked for help. The Judenrat probably bribed the Nazis for permission to transfer the sick to the Jewish hospital in the ghetto.

Zelinger received a letter from his wife telling him to report himself as sick. She claimed she knew for certain that the sick would not be shot but would be transferred to the hospital, where it would be easier to gain freedom. With this information Zelinger told me and Wolf to report to the doctor when he came, and assured us that he himself, when out, would not forget us and would take care of us in the hospital.

A few days later, a doctor and his assistant appeared in the company of a prison guard. The sick were informed to report for a transfer to the Jewish hospital. Everyone was so distrustful, however, that apart from those who were prostrate, few revealed their illness. I felt intuitively that I should take the chance.

Thermometers were handed out. I took one thermometer and then hid in a corner. Rubbing it against my shirt, I raised the mercury to 38 degrees Celsius. Wanting to add another degree, I rubbed again. The mercury shot up to the end of the tube. With this I should be in a coma! I had to get the mercury down. I gave it a few good whacks and looked again. To my horror the silvery thread was all broken up. I became panicky. This was my only chance. Finally I managed to bring the mercury down to about 39 degrees without any breaks. I handed it to the doctor. It was all in vain. He looked at me, decided I was well, and motioned me to the side.

Not giving up, I pinched my chest to make the red marks I'd seen on my brother when he had typhus.

"I don't feel well. Look at me," I said to his assistant, while discreetly pushing into his hand my cigarette money, my last twenty zlotys. He hid the money, pushed me into the corridor, and I was among the sick.

It didn't work for Wolf. That was the last time I saw him. Zelinger also didn't pass. The Ukrainian guard was present when taking Zelinger's temperature and wouldn't allow him to join the sick, overruling the Jewish doctor.

Soon the group of sick gathered in the hallway. The doctor signed a release for the guard, and with the assistance of only the Jewish police they led us out. Snow and ice covered the streets. After marching in the freezing cold for some time, we found ourselves in the outskirts of town.

There were moments when I wanted to run, knowing that Zelinger was left in jail and I could no longer count on his promised help. I think my plan would have worked because the Jewish police were up front flirting with the nurses and took little interest in the group, believing us all to be quite ill.

I examined the group around me. There were twenty of us. I studied their faces. Some had eyes hazy with high temperatures; others were so visibly depressed that I doubted their ability to think and act independently. But one looked like he might be willing and able. He was a tall, skinny lad and looked fairly healthy.

His name was Dawid. I started a conversation, asking about the ghetto of Stryj and the layout of the city. He understood and admitted that he, too, was thinking of running away, but talked me out of doing this now. We agreed to escape from the hospital together; afterward he would contact his father in the ghetto and get money and papers.

The "Stolen" Identity

It was January 1943. We were now in an unheated hospital room. There were no beds, only mattresses on the floor. Although this was a civilian hospital, Jewish police sat guard day and night by the door and window of our ward, responsible to the Germans with their lives if anyone escaped.

My friend Dawid tried to contact his father, and we waited. Dawid came to the hospital with the early stages of typhus, but was now suddenly overwhelmed by it. I was mentally prepared for our escape, but I preferred to do it with somebody familiar with the territory. Now I wanted to be in the hospital as long as possible, until Dawid recovered.

I continued to feign illness. When the nurse handed me the thermometer, I repeated the procedure I had used in the jail. I hoped that while waiting I would regain strength lost from starving in prison. But at the same time I was afraid of *really* getting typhus. So rather than sleep in an infected bed, I slept on four chairs set in a row.

The nurses asked me, as a sick but still able person, to help wash and shave the sick. I couldn't tell them the truth, and it didn't look good to always try to get out of work. The worst came after a night inspection when the young doctor forbade me to sleep on the chairs. From then on I had to share a narrow mattress with a patient deathly ill with typhus. Under these conditions it was no wonder I was soon overtaken by the disease and lay helpless with a high fever.

I was ill for about a week. I looked horrible. All I could eat was a little porridge, which was so bad that even those who were recuperating couldn't swallow it. I was able to get water, but only when I successfully begged for it. The personnel were not qualified and worked only in the hope that they would avoid deportation to the camps.

One day the doctor came to my bed on his regular rounds and handed me a letter and package of food from Zelinger! Excitedly, I read that he finally was able to get out of jail with another group and ended up in another hospital.

I was so overcome with emotion, I cried. Zelinger, a total stranger to me, with enough of his own problems, was interested in my well-being and thereby strengthened my will to live. From that day on I occasionally received small food packages.

Then, one day the doctor seemed to avoid me and moved quickly through the line of beds. He was about to leave. A feeling of foreboding swept over me.

"Doctor?" I called out.

He turned around, shook his head, and said in one breath as if unloading a heavy weight, "Today I don't have anything for you. Zelinger is dead. They shot him this morning."

I can't say I was shocked. Nothing shocked me anymore. But I felt as if I had lost another father. Zelinger had been so good to me and had given me the will to live. Feelings of grief quickly gave way to fear and then depression when I discovered the chilling circumstances of his death. The Gestapo had liquidated all the sick prisoners in the other hospital. I was sure that we would not fare any better, and that any day the guards would come for us.

A few days later, on the afternoon of January 29, 1943, the doctor came to our ward. In a nervous voice he instructed all the sick to move to another building in the same hospital compound. It was about eight yards away across the snow-covered yard. Those who had strength walked; the rest were carried by orderlies.

I was very feverish at the time, moved slowly and unsteadily, and I still don't know why I turned back halfway. I was outside and felt frightfully cold; the snow seemed to burn my bare feet. I could barely walk. Something kept urging me to turn back. Some unknown power warned me. Taking advantage of the turmoil around me, I broke away and, very weakly, headed back to our hospital room. It was an instinct that would take charge of me many times in those years.

The room was empty when I returned. In the next room a few nonprisoner patients from the ghetto were groaning. I hid under the bed. I had been there only a few minutes when a Jewish policeman looked in. Trusting a fellow Jew, I crawled out and asked what was going on. He looked startled. He knew I was from the prison ward, since he often kept guard at the door. After making certain that no one was looking for me, he ordered me to go back under the bed, saying that he would let me know when it was all right to come out.

A few minutes later I heard shots and screaming. Then all was quiet. Only then did I realize that the transfer was an execution (the Germans were probably afraid to go into the typhus-infected room and so had ordered the patients to go to the other building to be killed). I waited about an hour, but the guard didn't come back as promised. I decided to escape.

Lifting the mattress I drew out my clothes. Instead of turning them in for disinfecting as required, I had hidden them there with the thought of escape. I managed to dress and slowly got up. Then I realized how weak I actually was. As long as I held onto the back of the chair, I could stand straight. As soon as I let go, my legs buckled underneath me as if they were made of rubber. How far could I go like this? I slid under the bed again.

Late in the evening I heard the door open. It was the doctor. I crawled out to meet him. He looked at me, speechless. Then he took me in his arms, crying, and hugged me. "Toivi, Toivi . . . ," he repeated. "How come you're alive? I can't understand it . . . they counted them before shooting. There had to be twenty, and there were twenty. How could it be?"

With a quick check of the roster, however, the doctor found what he had suspected: one of the patients from the ghetto was missing.

This was a Jewish hospital in the city of Stryj. With each deportation the ghetto had shrunk in size, so that the Jewish hospital came to be outside the ghetto and in the so-called Aryan section of the city. Yet Jews who were ill were still sent there.

The room allocated for prisoners was near the entrance and connected to the rooms of "free" ghetto patients. Guards were continuously posted at all doors and windows. As is commonly known, patients in the crisis stage of typhus often rave, get out of bed, and run away. And so it happened.

A ghetto patient named Lederman, in his delirium, jumped out of bed and tried a few times to pass through our room. There was always a guard at the door to turn him or the others back. This time, however, because of the confusion, no one held Lederman back. He followed the others and substituted for me in death.

The doctor was a good man, but he was afraid that if the story of the "exchange" spread, somebody would inform the Gestapo. At the time of the shooting, most of the personnel had run away in panic. With no one around, he put me in Lederman's bed and reminded me that from then on my name was no longer Blatt, it was Lederman, and that secret was equal to the price of our lives.

So in a matter of a few months I had been reincarnated as two different people—Waldemar Ptaszek, dead from natural causes, and Lederman, executed by the Nazis. With this second stolen identity, I was promoted to regular ghetto patient status and as such was no longer a prisoner.

I lived in constant fear, even though I was no longer a prisoner. Only the doctor and the guard who first saw me under the bed knew I was alive. True, both were Jews, but while the doctor was a good and honest man, the guard proved to be an unscrupulous persecutor.

A few days later, finding me as Lederman, he immediately began to blackmail me. He insisted that I owed him my life and for that he should get something. I explained as well as I could that I didn't have any money, but he wouldn't listen.

As long as I was conscious, I was in fear, but when the typhus reached its crisis, it was all the same to me. I lay with a high fever, almost senseless. Raving in delirium I made the expected mistake.

According to the account given by the doctor, I was a frightful nuisance of a patient. I complained constantly of dirty bedding and demanded other bedding. Consequently, I lay in several places. Whenever the temperature chart was being changed, the nurse would ask me my name. In moments of consciousness I would give the fictitious one. At other times I apparently gave my true one. Turmoil ensued. Obviously something was not in order. The matter was referred to my doctor and he confessed the truth to the nurses, asking at the same time that it be kept secret.

When the delirium passed my appetite increased and I had a terrible thirst. I watched with torment when someone would bring my neighbors compote, lemonade, apples, or other fruit. I had no friends in the area, and I felt that if I didn't help myself, nobody would. I had to live.

I began to steal. At nightfall the nurse on duty would be asleep or would leave her post and go home. Then I would crawl out from under the dirty bedding and drag myself to the floor on my elbows, making my way to the nightstands of fellow patients who were lying in delirious fever, all the while breathing heavily from the effort. Carefully, inch by inch, I quietly opened the drawers of the nightstands. While my hand probed for food, my eyes didn't leave the face of the sick, even for a moment. If there was any movement I was ready to stop and crawl away. I helped myself to whatever I could find until my hunger and thirst were satisfied. In that way, slowly, I got back on my feet.

It wasn't long before a new group of prisoners were brought to the hospital. Rumors again spread that all Jews would be shot. I thought, what a strange death dance!

I had to disappear. But I was still very weak, and that ogre of a Jewish guard threatened to reveal my "Lederman" secret. He pointed out in no uncertain terms that there was simply no joking with him, and I had no right to leave the place until I repaid him for "saving my life." I remained, therefore, trying to figure a way out of my dilemma.

Then, in February, I was simply dismissed from the hospital and ordered to get out. I was in a bind. I was afraid to leave because of the guard's threats, yet I couldn't stay. As a discharged patient I had lost my daily food ration and space to someone else. I began to hide from the doctors and nurses in my ward. Most of the day I wandered in the hallways. At night I slept in the bathroom. I fed myself with patients' leftovers.

The guard understood my situation, but didn't care. He must have thought I had some money hidden somewhere. I was still very weak and thought it might be worthwhile to stay in the hospital a few more days, and yet, just as strongly, I wanted to tear myself away from my persecuting guard and from the nightmare of the rumored executions. It was an impossible situation.

One day the guard was absent. I had a chance to leave! I took a bag of food and stepped over the threshold. It was a frosty winter day. My coat had been taken, and I wore only a thin jacket. It was freezing cold. Where should I go? What should I do? I headed for the ghetto. Soon I heard footsteps behind me. A Jewish policeman I'd never seen before jumped on me, kicked me, and beat me.

"You dirty one! You wanted to run away from us? I'll show you! I know you're from the prison ward!" he yelled, chasing me back to the hospital.

Now I understood that my longtime persecutor, while off duty, had entrusted his victim to a loyal fellow guard, who was faithfully returning me, to my terror, to the prisoners' room, which was filled up once again. Now, I thought, I'm done for sure. So many narrow escapes only to land back where I started? Almost healthy only to be shot? This was bad luck indeed.

Once again I was fortunate. It wasn't long before the doctor noticed me. He knew I had been discharged from the hospital, and even if I hadn't been, he knew I shouldn't be in the prisoner group anymore. Just then, Mr. Sztark, the deputy commander of the Jewish militia in the Stryj ghetto, happened to be visiting, and the doctor (probably his friend) told him about my case. I was called into the doctor's office.

At first I was determined not to admit the truth because of the doctor who helped me. But the same doctor encouraged me to tell the truth. So I confessed that my name was not Lederman but Blatt, and explained how it all came about. I told them about the guard who had beaten me and the guard who had blackmailed me. After a short consultation, they informed me that I had nothing to fear and could safely leave the hospital. Mr. Sztark assured me he would take care of his two subordinates.

Now formally free, I requested the permission to stay a few days longer in the civilian section of the hospital. I also requested the return of my coat, which a hospital employee had taken, thinking I was dead. The doctor complied.

In the hospital, by surprise, I met the Izbica girls who had been in the jail cell next to ours, and they told me their story.

The same Gestapo officers who had come to our prison cell to free Lippman inspected the women's cell soon after. They decided to allow the girls to enter the ghetto for five hundred zlotys a head from the Judenrat. They lived together in a little room and worked in the communal ghetto kitchen. Now they were visiting friends in the hospital.

From that time on, the girls brought me food daily. They also sent my parents a letter informing them I was alive. According to information we received, there were still a few Jews in Izbica, including my family. I waited for a reply. Days passed.

A week later the Gestapo came in the evening and executed the remaining sick prisoners. What strange paths our destinies take. Now nothing could hold me back. In the morning I left once again for the Stryj ghetto.

The Stryj Ghetto

It was early 1943. The ghetto reminded me of a crawling mass of ants. Here were survivors of the notorious pogrom and the ghetto liquidation in Stanslawów on February 23, 1943, and survivors of the February roundups in Boryslaw and Buczacz, where the beastliness of the Ukrainian Nationalists surpassed even that of the Gestapo. Here there were also groups of Jews brought from Chodorów, Mikolajów, and other nearby cities. Strangely, there were still some Jewish coffee shops and restaurants where the wealthy passed their time. There were still those who actually profited, even at this time, and were able to eat and drink well, while the majority were hungry and miserable.

I searched for Zelinger's father, whose address I had received from the Judenrat. Wandering in the labyrinth of little streets, I finally found the right place. The steep stairs were slippery, half-covered with drifted snow. Holding onto the shaky rail, I slowly reached the door and knocked. Zelinger's father stood there, momentarily baffled. Who was this stranger in front of him? I was so changed by my illness.

"Please, come in," he said. I entered a tiny kitchen and walked into another small room, furnished only with a bed and a table.

"Mr. Zelinger, I'm so glad to see you. Your son helped me so much," I said.

Then he recognized me and embraced me. "Please, Toivi, sit down. Where do you live? You could stay here. We don't have our son anymore . . . " He looked like my grandfather—short, with a white beard and kind eyes.

"Yes, stay," encouraged his wife, "please."

I immediately felt close to them and accepted. They gave me a bed in an empty room. Their only big pillow was my coverlet. The nights were very cold for lack of fuel, so the upper half of my body froze, then the lower half, whenever I moved the pillow. Only with my knees bent under my chin was I able to keep warm through the night.

They were extraordinarily good to me, but I felt uncomfortable about their giving so much to me. Every day before I had time to dress myself, the old lady moved a chair next to my bed on which she placed tea, bread, and jam. I begged her not to do it, but she insisted. She had recently lost two children, and to console herself she was treating me as a son. But I couldn't impose forever; I felt that they already had enough difficulties. After a while I moved with a young Czech Jew into one of the many abandoned homes in the ghetto. Not having received an answer from my parents, I wrote again and asked them for money to come home.

On February 28, 1943, I survived a roundup in Stryj. I happened to be in a watchmaker's shop when suddenly there was a commotion in the street. "AKCJA!" I stood confused, helpless, a stranger in this area, exposed to easy capture. But, before I could think, the watchmaker closed his front door, covered the shop window, and twisted a small nail in front of it. Immediately the face of a large clock used for advertising was moved away to reveal a hidden doorway. I found myself descending into a large cellar, where a few Jews were already hiding. Apparently, there were two entrances. We waited in silent suspense.

Suddenly there was fast drumming on the front door. "Jankel, do you hear me? Let me in, Jankel."

No one dared to go out and open the door of the store. It was too late. Another few seconds and the knocking stopped. A Jew coming late to a known hiding place was one of the biggest dangers during an Akcja. With the hiding place camouflaged and the entrance blocked, no one could come in without risking the lives of those already hidden. But a hunted man, running and scared, in his anger and desperation, doesn't think logically. We agonized. Would he betray us for refusing to let him in? There were many such cases. This time we were lucky; he didn't betray us.

The Akcja was over. Now there were two thousand fewer Jews in the ghetto. They were taken to the cremation pits of Sobibor.

On the streets there were visible signs of the tragedy. Commonplace articles lay unclaimed in the gutter. Goose feathers from ripped pillows and comforters floated like snow on the sidewalks, strewn about as the Nazis searched for suspected hidden treasure. I decided to escape from the ghetto. Desperate, I again sent a letter home asking for help.

Late in March, by chance, I ran into Alvin Lippman, my German cellmate. He pulled me into a coffee shop on a narrow ghetto street and his story unfolded.

When they released him from jail, they took him to Gestapo head-quarters, where he was very politely received. He related his life story and was told to put it in writing. He slept in a Gestapo office, and on the second day, after a new interrogation, he received a small sum of money and private living quarters. He was to report back in a week. When he did, they offered him work in Stryj. In this way he became director of the city gas company. But he was still afraid of the Gestapo. Sometimes he ventured secretly to the Jewish ghetto in Stryj. He couldn't tolerate living with the butchers all the time, he said. Possibly he still hoped his wife and children were alive somewhere and he might find them here.

A few days later, by accident, my past tormentor, the Jewish guard from the hospital, spotted me on the street. He blackmailed me again. I told him I had no money, that I ate in the communal kitchen, and in the homes of friends and acquaintances. I showed him where I lived and finally he left me alone.

Still there was no sign from my family. So I approached a Juden-rat official asking for help. Not willing to tell him I wanted money for a train ticket to escape from the ghetto, I said that I was only recently discharged from the hospital and was hungry. I asked for a small loan. It was very naive of me to try, but it couldn't hurt. The official observed me critically for a moment, then went to the next room and soon returned with a paper in his hand. It was a requisition to the hospital to feed me for three weeks. I took the paper without a word. Only rarely, when I was very, very hungry, did I use the requisition. One of the girls from Izbica, who was now living with a senior Jewish militia officer, shared many home-cooked meals with me. Most of the time I wandered the streets of the ghetto, thinking about a way out.

On the surface, the ghetto appeared almost "normal." Surprisingly,

I saw no hunger; the communal kitchen functioned well. Yet it wasn't normal, of course. It was a huge prison: from time to time thousands were brought in, and thousands were also taken away to death camps in a strange game of musical chairs. If caught in an Akcja you were "out." How long would my luck last? I wondered.

During those terrible times, simple intuition never failed me. I was always a late sleeper and hated to get up in the morning, but one day something pushed me out of bed very early and made me head toward the hospital.

In the course of the many deportations the Stryj ghetto had shrunk considerably, and now, although there was still a Jewish hospital, it stood even farther outside the ghetto boundaries than it had weeks before. The only way one was allowed to get there was in the company of the Jewish militia. They were permitted by the Germans to escort groups of sick Jews. But I didn't want to wait for such a group to be assembled. I decided to risk it and go alone.

The ghetto was surrounded by barbed wire, but it wasn't closely guarded by the Germans and Ukrainians. I passed through a hole in the fence, then walked quickly to arrive in time for breakfast. I made it there within half an hour. Showing my convalescent pass, I ate breakfast and then wandered aimlessly. I didn't know what or whom I was looking for, or why. Suddenly I remembered a man from near Izbica I had seen in the hospital. I decided to look for him. Not finding him, I went to the office to inquire.

"What is his illness?" the official asked.

"Tuberculosis," I answered, "and he is from Izbica."

"He isn't a patient anymore. He died."

I left, and a moment later the same official ran after me down the hall calling, "Hey, are you also from Izbica?"

"Yes."

"Do you know a Blatt?"

"My name is Blatt."

"Then come back to the office. Someone is asking for you."

I entered, and there sat a middle-aged woman. I had seen her earlier when I was looking for the man, but she was a stranger to me.

"I am Toivi Blatt," I said. "Are you looking for me?"

She asked for identification. I didn't have any papers except the release from the hospital and the requisition for meals, and both were in the name of Lederman.

I explained that when I left Izbica I only had forged papers. The woman interrogated me. Was I really the son of Leon Blatt? Did I know Izbica? What does it look like? She made me describe my friends and parents. Apparently I passed the test, because she revealed that she was my wet nurse, Ola. My father had sent her to Stryj.

Because my letters always asked for money, first giving the return address of the hospital and later Zelinger's address, my parents felt sure that somebody was trying to swindle money from them. Only my younger brother disagreed with this theory. To ease their conscience they sent a letter to the hospital superintendent asking if I was there now, or had been there before. The hospital checked the records and replied that I had died there.

This strengthened their belief that I was dead. But when one day, unexpectedly, another letter came, they were puzzled. Although they didn't really believe I was alive, they sent a trusted Christian woman to check the ghetto and the hospital in person, and this was Ola, my wet nurse.

She handed me some money and my brother's treasure, a small wristwatch, which in the past he would never have even allowed me to touch. So I could see he didn't doubt for a second that I was still alive. I gave Ola my address and she left.

The money was not enough to get forged Aryan papers, and I parted with the wristwatch the next day when I was spotted by my old tormentor, the Jewish policeman. He noticed my new watch, and without a word he took it off my wrist.

One of Them

A week passed, and unexpectedly one evening, past the curfew, I heard a knock. My Czech friend opened the door and in came Mr. Krauze, the same Volksdeutscher from Izbica who one year earlier had discovered our hiding place and not turned us in.

"Hi, Toivi, I'm here to take you," he said simply.

Seeing my confusion, he told my companion to leave us alone for a while, then he explained further. My father had approached him, explained the problem, and asked for help in returning his son safely to Izbica. After securing from the Landrat a special permit for me to travel by train, he came to help me on my way. Undoubtedly he was paid a hefty sum of money by my father.

Half an hour later, without any problems from the Ukrainian guard, we went out through the ghetto gate and headed for the train station. As usual, it was overflowing with smugglers. Krauze left me in a dark corner while he went to get the tickets. In a minute he was back.

"Toivi, listen to me. The train that will leave in three hours is a regular train. It will stop in every station. It will take the whole night to arrive in Izbica. There are a lot of smugglers and black market speculators on this route, and they could spot you. And who knows if the travel permit will really help. If something happens, I may not be able to help you." He paused and looked at me carefully. "But there is another way, and even if it looks dangerous, it is actually safer. Tear off your Star of David, and let's go on the train reserved for Germans. The train leaves in twenty minutes. It's an express, and in a couple of hours you will be home!"

As daring as it sounded, it really wasn't illogical. If he's willing, why not? In his view, I didn't look Jewish, and traveling with a true Volksdeutscher, a swastika on his lapel, no one would know the truth. It was practically no risk for Krauze: he was a German, and I, traveling with him as a young boy, needed no papers. It actually appeared safer. As we boarded, he whispered, "Remember, if there's any trouble, you're on your own."

It was early 1943. The Eastern Front was already starting to crumble, and many wounded German officers on leave filled the compartments. Krauze cleverly introduced me as a convalescing patient; this explained my paleness, frailty, and poor posture. Now, what kind of German officer would he be if he didn't have the good breeding to make a seat for a pure German youth returning home from the hospital after a difficult illness?

I was given a space between a tall German in the green uniform of the military police and an older German woman, also in uniform. Across from me sat an officer with the regular army and two other officers, whom I recognized as members of the SS by their insignia.

Strangely, months before when I rode in a train full of Poles and

Ukrainians I was scared, but now in the midst of these Germans, real Nazis, I had no such feelings. Being one of "them," I felt safe. I knew from experience that the Germans were seldom able to recognize a Jew in the midst of other people. Krauze, too, seemed relaxed and calmer than in the ghetto or on the way to the station.

Like most Polish Jews, I understood German. The officers talked mostly about their families in Germany, and although they did not actually mention the Allied bombing of German cities, they worried about their children and hoped they were in a safe place. Apparently the woman had been back to Germany more often, so most of the questions were directed to her. But she, too, for some reason, avoided a direct answer, and instead talked about their successes in Tunisia. Interesting, I thought. They were coming from the Eastern Front, yet they didn't talk about it, except for mentioning Goebbels's speech in the Sports Palace, referring to "the quarrel between the Western Powers and the Soviets," insinuating that at any moment the Allies could break up. One officer seemed to be from Essen, for he asked the woman about that city over and over. Finally she brushed him off by saying, "When you get there, you'll see." And there was silence.

About halfway to Izbica, the woman shook me awake and offered tea. Everyone joined in a meal. The SS man opposite me opened his knapsack, filled himself a glass of vodka, and jokingly teased me, pretending to offer me a drink. Later he stroked my head and said he had something better for me. Digging into his luggage, his hand surfaced with a piece of chocolate. I hadn't seen chocolate for years. I had even forgotten how it tasted. I would have refused but I had a part to play.

"This is for you, my son," he said, and handed it to me.

"Danke schön," I answered quietly, drawing no suspicion with the correct German accent.

I said no more. Krauze leaned over and said softly, "Better sleep, don't talk, you're too weak," and I knew what he meant.

As I ate the chocolate I observed the neatly dressed and well-mannered SS officer. I shuddered. He might be a murderer. How would he act if he knew who I really was? He seemed human and kind, but I knew too much to view him that way. When Engels's son and wife came to Izbica to visit him, didn't I see him hugging and kissing the little boy? Yet the same day, the same morning, he had murdered six people, including a boy not much older than his own seven-year-old!

This was my third stolen identity and, I felt, the safest. How I wished I could sit on this train and travel until the end of the war. But soon the train would stop, and I would be just another "Jew boy," hunted, fearful, without the right to live.

As I had six months earlier, I now passed Bełżec. Again the same horrible stench and flames. The Germans showed no interest. Could it be they were unaware of the death camps, coming from the front? I saw no unusual reactions, no understanding looks or conversations about it, but Krauze, who did understand, watched me intently.

My God, I thought, nothing has changed in these six months.[2] Six months! How many days . . . hours? And over there they are burning people . . . Jews, people like ME! Will the fire never stop? Is there no help? . . . No, I mustn't think about it. It will show on my face and somebody will recognize me. And so my thoughts ran. Little did I know that in only a few weeks I'd find myself in a similar hell, and I'd be one of the morticians of my own people.

The train was approaching Izbica. Soon I recognized the brewery and some houses on the outskirts. The train didn't stop. It sped on, with a whistle through road crossings, past the town. I became nervous. Krauze explained in German that the express didn't stop in small places like Izbica but would stop in Krasnystaw, about twelve kilometers away.

Well, I thought, maybe it's better for me to get off in a nearby town where no one knows me. The train slowed down little by little, and with heavy panting it stopped.

"Station Krasnystaw, get off!" the conductor called, holding up his lamp. Here I must be careful. Someone just might recognize me. It was a typical small town in eastern Poland with the train station outside its boundaries. A single building housed the station office and ticket clerk. Open fields lay on either side of the highway and railway.

At this point Krauze wished me luck and went to meet his Nazi friends in town. His role was finished, and I was left to my own devices. Keeping a distance of about a hundred yards from the highway, I headed toward Izbica. German trucks passed, their headlights dimmed due to wartime restrictions. Their lights were too weak to expose me in the night, but I could see them very well, and they kept me oriented to the road.

After walking for about two hours I came upon the first group of houses, then the fence of the brick factory. Further on there was a turn in the road leading straight down to the marketplace. Moving like a shadow between houses, I reached my home. I knocked lightly. Nobody answered. I heard steps.

"Mama! It's me," I called impatiently in Yiddish and in Polish. But instead of a familiar voice I heard an angry bark.

"Who is 'me'? Run while you're in one piece, you Jew!" Someone else was living there. I ran to the house of a friendly Pole, Bazylkowa. She opened the door a crack. Quickly and nervously she explained that my family now lived in Mr. Sznajder's house, the place where my journey to Hungary had begun.

Again I maneuvered from house to house until I found the right one. It was dark, and everyone was sleeping. I pushed my forefinger into a break in the window shutter and, not wanting to scare them, knocked ever so lightly on the glass.

"Who's knocking?" Immediately I recognized my father's voice.

Before I could answer I heard the happy scream of my brother: "It's him! It's Toivi!"

The door opened, and I fell into the arms of my weeping mother. My father stood nearby, trying to hide his tears. Then I turned to my brother. He was so glad to see me he wasn't able to tear himself away from me. He hugged me tightly, crying with happiness. Unfortunately, he didn't forget about his watch. Figuring I didn't need it anymore, he asked for it back.

My mother, wiping her tears, took an envelope from a box and handed it to me. I opened it, and there wrapped in dark velvet was my photograph. Under it was a telegram. In large type it read: "THIS IS TO INFORM YOU THAT TOIVI BLATT DIED JANUARY 29, 1943, IN THE JEWISH HOSPITAL IN THE CITY OF STRYJ. THE JEWISH COUNCIL."

It was a strange feeling, reading about my own death. I looked at my mother. What she must have gone through! My father, who was always a little superstitious, embraced me and said, "Toivi, you will survive the war. When somebody is mistakenly declared dead while he is still alive, it means the opposite. You will live a long and healthy life."

My father's words followed me in the most difficult times during the war, and, I believe, gave me strength to survive.

How happy we felt now that we were a family once more. And

how I wanted to believe, sitting peacefully together in the house, that our agony was over. But though we never spoke of it, I knew in my heart this was only the beginning.

Return to Izbica

We were too excited to sleep, and there was so much to catch up on. We talked through the night. I told them my story and they told me theirs.

Not long after I left for Hungary, on November 1, 1942, Engels killed two members of the Judenrat, Raphael Sznajdmeser and Abram Blatt. It seems he had ordered them to move his furniture from Izbica to Zamość. He awaited their return as night fell, and when they approached he simply shot them. Apparently they knew too much about his private dealings. Besides, with the liquidation of Izbica's Jews almost complete, they had outlived their usefulness.

The last Akcja took place the next day. From then on Izbica would finally be Judenrein; any Jew found at the end of the Akcja was to be shot immediately. To facilitate this "mop-up," the Nazis engaged the help of the local fire department and its chief, Śliwiński, and all were given legal permission to hunt and rob Jews.

The Jews were loaded into one cattle car after another. When no more freight cars were available, the overflow was assembled in the movie theater. They were kept there for several days without a drop of water. Only if they could pay large sums of money would a Pole standing outside give them a drink. Later they were transported by horse carriage to the camp Trawniki, and from there, together with Jews from other towns, to the death camp Sobibor.

Only a small workforce was to remain in Izbica—those already working exclusively for the Germans in the local tannery. Officially there were about twenty-five people, but many others were hiding there secretly. At that time my mother, who possessed Aryan papers, was hiding in Warsaw. My brother was hiding with Bazylkowa, and my father was jailed by Engels.

A month later, Engels removed my father from jail. In imitation of Jesus Christ, my father was forced to crown his head with barbed wire and hang a sign on his chest, saying, "I am King of the Jews." He was forced to walk the streets with the message that Jews could return. The town was now officially a Judenstadt, a place where Jews would be allowed to live.[3]

About two hundred Jews, freezing in the forests in the fiercely cold winter and hunted by bands of peasants, fell into the trap and returned to the ghetto. Thus my mother and my brother came out of hiding and joined my father.

When a large number of Jews assembled, the Germans ordered the formation of a new Judenrat composed of three persons: my father, Mojsze Kornfeld, and Mojsze Blank, manager of the tannery. The tannery building was now the center for the remaining Jewish population, which now numbered about two hundred people.

In the morning I took a look at Izbica. I was shocked that the town had changed so much in six months! Most Jewish homes had been ransacked by gentiles seeking gold and other treasures. Only the houses on the main street remained intact, and they were now occupied by Poles. Close to the Łączność general store, I noticed a few people standing about talking. I approached a man I knew well, a friend of the family.

"Hello, Mr. Pilewski," I said warmly.

"Oh," he said, smiling sarcastically, "you're alive? You could live yet another couple of days."

Naively, I moved on. I saw a store janitor I'd known for years. He greeted me in the same manner. "You're still here? Soon, I hope, the Devil will take you."

I shivered in disbelief. Coming to my senses, I went to what was left of the Jewish section, looking for friends. I picked a house close to the tannery and went in. Inside were a group of teenagers. In bed was the Langard boy, the brother of one of the girls from the Hungary trip fiasco. He was lying motionless, his body all black, even his face. He was found frozen in the forest. There emanated from him the terrible stench of rotting flesh.

Later in the street, I met an acquaintance, Roża, to whom Jozek Bresler had once introduced me. She was an extremely beautiful girl. She greeted me warmly. I went to her room, a tiny space in the middle of the partially dismantled Jewish houses. She had two friends with her, Zisel the saddler and Adolf Herszow, a Jew who had escaped from a POW camp on Lipowa Street in Lublin.

We reminisced and exchanged survival stories. Each of us had horrors to tell. I asked about my friends. All of them, including my first "love," Fajgele Brajtman, the little girl with a crown of braided hair, were gone.

When I was about ten I was in love with Fajgele. I loaned her books, we exchanged glances. This didn't escape the attention of my friends. She became known as "my" girl. I never got even as close as a handshake, but I was proud to have my own girl. It was supposed to be a secret in our group, but my brother found out. Whenever he was angry at me, his favorite revenge was saying loudly, in front of my parents, "Toivi, Fajgele's calling you," making me angry and embarrassed.

I remember the wedding of Fajgele's older sister. Late in the evening when the guests were still dancing, Srulek, who was much more mature than I was, ran up to me and said excitedly, "Come with me to Fajgele's house. Tonight is her sister's wedding night." I didn't quite understand the difference between this and other nights, but he was smarter, so I went along. The house was an old one, like most of the buildings in Izbica, and the wooden shutters were dried out and loose. My face was glued to the shutters as I stared through the cracks. I knew that if Srulek told me to be patient, he knew what he was talking about. Finally, the young bride arrived, looked in the mirror for a while, then sat on the bed, exhausted from the feast. Soon the husband arrived, and sat close to her without a word. We waited for the action to unfold, but there wasn't any. In any case, I didn't see any because her husband simply stood up and shut off the light. The rest was Srulek's imagination.

All day I wandered through houses where life once shone. Now the wind whistled through the demolished doors and smashed windows.

Friday night came. My first Sabbath back home. But, except for the candles, there was no resemblance to previous ones. My parents had long ago dropped any attempt to make it special. Special now meant getting something to eat—anything.

Now various Nazi officials appeared, demanding bribes to leave us in peace. But at least they took only our money. Then, on the afternoon of April 18, 1943, I heard the whirring of motors on a nearby street. Suspecting Germans, we ran to our hiding place. After removing a panel in the wall, we entered a narrow space about two feet wide, that ran the length of the room. We were enclosed by a double wall. We had barely managed to close the entrance when the Germans entered the hallway. Someone had probably pointed out Sznajder's home as a Jewish residence.

Through the cracks of the poorly fitting panels, it was possible to see everything clearly. I was afraid, but still I looked in horror. I thought if they looked and listened more carefully, they would see my terrified eyes and hear the pounding of my heart.

With us were two small children, both around four years old. They were so quiet, heads pressed against their mothers' breasts, and I wondered, did they understand? We were so afraid that they might cough or cry or in some way betray our presence. We waited an eternity.

Meanwhile, the Germans plundered. They were big, barrel-chested men in green rubber coats with metal chest plates hanging on chains from their necks. On them was the word *Feldgendarme,* field police.

As they were about to leave, they came upon a Jew named Kalman Lipsz, who, unaware that Nazis were already there, was running to our hiding place.

"Halt!" they yelled.

He stopped.

"Take off your coat and jacket."

He complied.

"Now hand over your money."

He gave them all he had. They shot him twice, yet he ran through the house, blood flowing from his wounds, yelling and screaming. With labored breath, at last he fell down. The German shot once more, and Lipsz died.

With us in our hiding place was his eight-year-old son. Though the boy didn't actually witness the shooting, he must have recognized his father's voice, but he remained silent. For us a second was a lifetime.

Then for some reason a ten-year-old Jewish boy ran into the same hallway and came face to face with the Nazis.

"Are you a Jew?"

"No, I'm looking for Jews. Can I help you catch some?" The blond Jewish boy looked utterly convincing as a Polish youth. They believed him, and he was saved.

The Germans finally left Sznajder's house, but the massacre continued. We waited. We could see the window opposite our hiding place; the rays from the shining sun fell on our wall. A couple of Polish girls I knew peered through the window. They laughed and joked about the grotesque position of the murdered Jew, Lipsz. A few minutes later they left, still giggling.

Not knowing how long the Nazi rampage would continue, we sat in the hiding place waiting for nightfall. In the evening Symcha Białowicz and another Jew came and removed the dead man. Then we left our hiding place. On that day eight Jews had been killed.

Besides the Nazis, we also had to contend with gentile townspeople who would rob Jews and plunder Jewish homes. One evening around nine o'clock, as my mother and I sat on the sofa, the door opened and several men in civilian suits, brandishing guns, rushed in.

"Hands up! Face the wall!" We complied, and within seconds, threatening to shoot, they had rounded up everyone in the house.

Our neighbor, Chaim Kornfeld, was sick. He stood naked except for a shirt and begged for pity. We were sure they would kill us. They searched us one after another, took our valuables and better clothes, and packed them in knapsacks. Before leaving they took my father into a separate room, beat him, and demanded that he turn over weapons he supposedly had hidden. My father screamed from the blows.

Suddenly the whole house shook from an exploding grenade. The robbers stopped and ran, dropping the stolen goods on the way. I found out later that my brother, coming home late, had noticed one of the men at our door. Since it was past curfew, this aroused his suspicions. He hid behind a corner of the neighbor's house. When he heard Father's screams he grew desperate and ran to the Jews at the tannery. They, in turn, notified the Polish police, who, feeling they should have the monopoly on robbing Jews, moved in to stop the bandits. The grenade was thrown by a bandit standing guard outside to stop the police and to warn his cohorts. After this episode, our family moved to the tannery, where we slept on the floor.

We got word of the Warsaw ghetto uprising. At first we didn't believe it, but Polish black marketeers traveling to and from the capital verified the news that the ghetto Jews were fighting the Germans. They told us about the ghetto being obscured by clouds of smoke from burning houses and German tanks being destroyed by Jewish fighters. And most important, they told us about the first SS men killed and of the retreat of the Nazis attempting to enter the ghetto.

We knew that the uprising was an act of desperation. A handful of people, devoid of hope, doesn't expect to gain its freedom. All they want is to take revenge and die with honor, to fall fighting.

Their courage had an effect on us. Youngsters started to buy weapons secretly from the Poles. I asked my father for money. He said he wouldn't give me any. "It will only provoke them and we will all suffer," he said. "They will find out and kill us."

So I decided to sell a blanket and my jacket to buy a gun. That day I told my father I would sleep in the attic and would take one blanket and a coat. A few days later I sold everything, but I still didn't have enough money, so I took as a partner a boy my own age, Rysiek Gdański, a refugee from Koło. With his money and mine, we had enough. We bought a gun, a six-shooter with four bullets, from a Jew named Pelc. He even gave us a few minutes of instruction in the attic of a deserted house.

We were worried: First the Nazis said that the Jews could remain and would not be disturbed since Izbica was supposed to be a Judenstat. Now the Gestapo ordered the Judenrat to deliver a list of all Izbica Jews. This was suspicious. From then on, every night we posted a guard at the attic window of the tannery to warn the rest of us of any suspicious movement in the area.

The next day, while walking with my father on the street, I told him that we had no choice, it's all the same: we should buy a gun. He didn't answer.

Then I told him, "Remember the coat and blanket? Well, I sold them to buy a revolver. It's here in my pocket."

He reacted with uncharacteristic resignation. Not slowing his pace, he said, "Be careful. You could get us into trouble." This only reinforced my fears.

As I fantasized about the ideal hiding place, food always came to mind. Why must people eat? How happy we would be if that weren't so. Bears are so lucky; they can hibernate and not eat. Why can't Jews do that? I would dig myself into some hole in the forest and I wouldn't put my nose out till the end of the war.

Caught

At dawn on April 28, 1943, I was awakened by a gunshot. An Akcja! It's the end, I thought. I jumped ten feet from the tannery attic where I slept to the earthen-floored hallway. I felt a jolt through my spine and, evidently not hurt, ran to our hiding place.

We had a big hiding place in the tannery; it had been built in the west wall leaning against a hill. By secretly removing the earth at night, we had cleared a good-sized space, enough to hold a hundred people standing jammed together.

It was hot and stuffy and difficult to breathe. We could hear the SS men shouting and shooting. They were searching the tannery grounds. They caught a few Jews who didn't have time to hide, and left. Then the local Poles started their hunting. They were more experienced, and something about the tannery was suspicious: too few Jews had been caught.

We heard voices in Polish. "They must be here . . . must be here." Again the Germans entered the tannery. Somebody explained in broken German that without a doubt Jews were hidden somewhere. They need only look more expertly. They tore down different parts of the walls but they couldn't find us. We could tell that the Germans were again ready to leave. We breathed a sigh of relief.

But just then the locals began tearing down the whole wall indiscriminately. One of them had probably seen the hiding place being made, for they were certain it was there. One after another the wooden panels, dried out from age, were ripped off. Systematically, the blows of the pickaxes came closer and closer to the panel hiding the entrance . . . closer and closer . . . My heart pounded. This was the end.

The panel was ripped and began to give way. Finally, a stream of daylight poured in. In a moment they would uncover us. For a few seconds, light flickered as the panel banged back and forth against the wall. It was as if the panel itself wanted to help us. But the Nazis had already seen the entrance and doubled their efforts. For them it was a game—they would catch a Jew or not catch a Jew; for us it was death.

Wham! The panel broke off. "Raus! Schnell!" screamed the Germans. One after another we came out and assembled in the courtyard. In the confusion, I left one shoe inside the hiding place. I asked a German nearby if I could recover my shoe. He consented, and I went back into the hole. While searching the floor I touched some people cowering in the darkness; they chose not to heed the order to come out. I found my shoe and returned outside. Then the SS threw a grenade inside and the explosion shook the yard.

Standing about was a group of Polish youngsters, evidently pleased with their job, smiling submissively at the Germans. They were waiting for their reward—permission to rob our homes. The Germans shoved us all outside the building. Our Polish neighbors were looking on, some with pity, some with delight. It was spring, and so beautiful outdoors.

"No talking!" the Nazis ordered. We stood, each with his own thoughts. It was windy. The guard was concentrating on lighting his cigarette. I took a chance, slid out from the Jewish group, and mingled with the Polish onlookers standing nearby. No one gave me away. I walked casually to Mr. Smyk's blacksmith shop. Smyk, a friendly Pole but terribly frightened, begged me to leave immediately and run to the village beyond. Just then, I noticed my brother. Apparently he had managed to run away, too. He was about two hundred yards away, heading in the opposite direction.

With no time for thought, I started for the village in the foothills that surrounded Izbica. Strangely, no one intercepted me. I knew that beyond the village, on the hills, was a solid cordon of Ukrainian Nazis. I had to hide for while and wait out the Akcja.

Luck was with me. Running toward me was my Polish schoolmate, Janek Knapczyk.

"Janek," I begged, "help me . . . hide me!"

Janek, though obviously in a hurry, was willing to help a good friend. But he only had time to point the way to his barn and say in one breath, "Sure, run to the barn."

He moved on. I found the barn with no trouble. But the barn door was padlocked. I looked for another way to enter but couldn't.

"Toivi, run away! He's coming!" a voice cried out.

I turned around. A Polish woman was calling to me.

"Who is coming?" I asked.

"Knapczyk is coming, run!" she repeated.

Good. If Knapczyk is coming, he will open the barn for me so I can hide, I thought, but why is the woman so frightened? Why does she tell me to run? I walked toward Janek.

When I looked closer I felt like fainting . . . Knapczyk with a

Nazi! It was too late to retreat. They had seen me. My friend pointed to me and said, "This is the Jew. Take him!"

I couldn't understand. My head spun. Knapczyk . . . I considered him a good friend. We were in the same class each year. We played together and went swimming together, and now he is denouncing me?

I recovered my composure. Still not believing my own eyes, I said, "Janek, you're joking, aren't you? Say that this is a joke."

The Nazi pushed me forward and we walked on. From behind came Knapczyk's farewell shout: "Good-bye! I'll see you on a shelf of soap in a store someday."[4]

Is this what Nazi propaganda had done? Is this the result of anti-Semitic indoctrination—people selling Jews for a few pounds of sugar or a bottle of vodka? I was trembling, in shock, I but quickly recovered, concentrating on survival.

I was led back to town by Knapczyk's Nazi. He probably had expected a grown Jew with money he could steal, and here he only had me, a skinny young boy wearing a ragged shirt. He had rank, and when he noticed a private in the distance, he decided to transfer me over to him. "Come here! Take him," he yelled, pushing me toward the soldier. And he went off looking for better prospects to rob.

As I approached the new Nazi, my brain raced full speed. I wanted to live. What should I do? Noting the puzzled expression on the face of my new guard, I sensed he was somehow confused. Was I one of the boys who points out Jews or was I actually a Jew?

Immediately, confidently, and excitedly I said, "Come, I'll show you where Jewish gold is hidden."

He believed me completely. "Okay, let's go," he answered in Ukrainian. He couldn't resist. Gold was the magic word.

On the way I saw the gangrenous black body of the Langard boy lying in the mud, shot through the head.

I had a plan. I led the Ukrainian to the edge of the town. There, close to the Benesz meadow, stood an old, run-down Jewish flour mill. This building was three stories high and, just like the tannery, one wall was built into the hill. I knew that on the third floor was a door leading straight to the meadow and the hills beyond. Because the steps were in complete ruin, I told the Ukrainian that I would climb up the handrails and be back with the treasure in a minute. He told me to hurry.

At the top I had to struggle for a long time with the rusty door hinges. At first, the Ukrainian asked quietly if I had found the treasure. Later he became suspicious and screamed, "Come down immediately or I'll shoot!"

At last I was able to open the door. I ran through the meadows to the forest. I was free! But not for long. I wasn't able to get through the outer ring of armed Ukrainian guards. One of them caught me and delivered me back to the marketplace.

There were most of the Izbica Jews. Among them I found my parents and brother. I supposed my brother went through a similar experience, but we weren't allowed to talk. We sat on the cobblestones and waited for the end of the Akcja.

Just then a woman was brought in crying and screaming, "Oh, God! I'm innocent. I'm not a Jew. I'm an honest Catholic. People help me! I'm not a Jew. Help!"

The Christians standing around us confirmed she was not a Jew, and she was set free. She will probably remember until the end of her life what it felt like to be a Jew, if only for a few minutes.

I stared at a row of buildings about a hundred feet away, along the marketplace. There used to be Jewish stores in them; now everything was bolted shut. Passing in front of them was my elderly school principal, Mr. Sztajndel, a kind and honest Pole. Because of his German background, he could have qualified long ago as a member of the "super-race" with all the attendant privileges, but he, like Platto, considered himself loyal to Poland and didn't give in to Nazi pressure. This may have been the reason he lost his only son to the ovens of Auschwitz. Perhaps the Nazis thought this a better punishment than simply killing him. Sztajndel was walking toward the main street. While the Poles on the street and behind the curtains watched us as if we were a circus act, his head was demonstratively lowered and turned slightly to one side, away from the marketplace scene. I don't know why at this tragic moment I gave this so much notice, but I felt that this man was feeling for us, that this one man was ashamed for his fellow Germans.

About three o'clock in the afternoon they told us to get up and searched us for weapons. A few Jews with guns had supposedly resisted earlier. My gun was hidden in a bundle of straw in the tannery; I hadn't had time or an opportunity to take it with me. Only my diary and the cable from Stryj about my death were in my shirt pocket. The Ukrainians were quickly searching us, concentrating on stealing valuables for themselves.

Big trucks covered with sturdy canopies stood open and waiting. They shoved us in. There wasn't space on the trucks for all of us, so a few were left in the marketplace. Among them was Rysiek Gdański of Koło, my pistol partner.⁵

The trucks rolled on. A woman by the name of Izbicka was in labor and suffering terribly, screaming from pain. Naively, she had begged the SS to leave her behind because she was obviously going to give birth any moment.

Thirst tormented us. It was very hot inside, and I felt anguish for my father, who was with me; my mother and brother were in another truck. In the faint light that came from outside I could see my father perspiring heavily. I pushed a handkerchief through a hole in the canvas and, when the wind had cooled it a bit, I wiped the sweat from my father's forehead. He nodded weakly, as if to thank me. Mothers were comforting their small children, holding them tightly in their arms. Faint prayers could be heard from the middle of the truck. A few young men discussed their chances of escape. They would throw themselves on the guards if it looked certain we were being taken to Sobibor. Some protested any plans of resistance; resigned to die, they wanted to be together with their loved ones.

The worst curse for Jews of that epoch was their everlasting sense of hope. It anesthetized our will. To the last minute, to the last second, hope was with us and weakened our resistance. Yet at the same time it gave us strength to go on. We were so used to suffering, and we were a people who always hoped for better. I, too, felt there was still hope. Didn't the German allow me to go back for my boot? They might just take us to a concentration camp, a few of which lay on the way.

The canvas canopy had a small hole. One Jew's eye was glued to it, and for us, the rest of the doomed, he was the almighty prophet. Every word he whispered was immediately transmitted to the farthest corner of the dark truck. Everyone needed to know: Where were we going? Are these our last moments of life? We were passing the turnoff to the labor camp Osowa . . . then we passed the Trawniki turnoff. I heard a gasp of sorrow . . . there were no more work camps on the way. So it was to be Sobibor. My heart was beating relentlessly.

I could hear desperate cries, but most were quiet, paralyzed by their visions of suffering and death.

Ahead of us and behind us, in separate army vehicles, rode our guards, armed with machine guns. After another half-hour or so, the trucks slowed down, took a left turn, and stopped. I can still hear the last words in Yiddish coming from the Jew at the hole in the canvas: "Ys Schwarz fyn Ukrainer [It's black with Ukrainians]," a reference to the black uniforms the Ukrainian guards wore. We were overwhelmed by them.

We were ordered out of the trucks. Resistance was impossible now. We were surrounded on three sides by an army of SS and black-uniformed Ukrainians. In front of us, barbed wire and a big gate. Above the gate were large black letters: SS SONDERKOMMANDO.

❀

Sobibor – Hell

Sobibor

Was I awake or still dreaming? I was in a strange place, on a top
bunk in a huge barrack. If I stretched out my arm, I could touch the
rough wooden roof. I looked down: bunks all around, filled with
bedraggled men.

Suddenly terror struck my heart. SOBIBOR!! I was in a death factory . . . I must have slept. From this top bunk I could see, through a
large open space where the slanting roof met the wall, into the yard
and beyond. The afternoon sun was warm and inviting. I could see
another world, a lost world, so close and yet so unreachable.

Across the barbed wire I could see the Sobibor village train station.[1] The stationmaster is probably ticking away dots and dashes on
his telegraph, I mused, meters and meters of narrow white paper
falling to the floor, like in Izbica. I was always excited when my
father took me to see Stanisław the stationmaster. Seeing my fascina-
tion with Morse code, Stanisław gladly gave me old rolls of tape to
take home. I saved them, hoping to decipher them someday. Who
knew what intrigue and suspense could be discovered in the hidden
messages? I fantasized sending a message now: "Help! Help! Save us!"
But there was no one to send it to, no one who cared, no one who
would help.

I stopped daydreaming and observed the countryside. It was spring.
The trees were just beginning to bud. Birds darted in and out of the
branches, chirping. A dog barked. Smoke curled from the chimneys
of a few cottages nestled among the trees. The farmers were going
about their business. Behind the cottages, like a dark wall, stood the
Sobibor forest. I looked farther into the distance, afraid to lower my
gaze, but eventually it was unavoidable. The long line of barbed-wire

fencing and the watchtower made it clear that I was in a cage, like an animal waiting to be slaughtered.

I heard people singing, and I jumped down and went outside. The gate opened wide, and in marched a group of about twenty robust youths. They wore dark blue overalls and fancy caps, with the letter B embroidered within a yellow triangle. The leader held a whip and issued a sharp command in German: "Abteilung . . . Halt!" A few steps forward and the group halted; with the next command, everyone dispersed.

If I hadn't heard them speak Yiddish after they broke ranks, I would have mistaken them for German soldiers. Though I had seen them with my own eyes, I still couldn't believe they were really Jews. I found out later that the B stood for Banhofkommando, train brigade.

Soon the empty square in front of the barrack filled with prisoners from different parts of the camp. I looked for someone to talk to as small groups began forming. The old-timers wanted news from the outside world. How's the front? Who's winning? Are there still some free Jews? Sealed off from the outside world, they didn't even know about the Warsaw ghetto rebellion. They listened with barely restrained emotion to the newcomers' accounts of the uprising, how SS bodies lay in the streets, tanks stood burned out and crippled by Jewish Molotov cocktails. "The lucky Warsaw Jews!" I heard one say enviously.

Suddenly I felt a pull on my sleeve. I turned around and there stood an old friend.

"Jozek!" I called. We fell into each other's arms. They had caught him in the last ghetto Akcja of 1942. When he got to Sobibor he was saved because the Nazis needed a dentist and his father volunteered. Jozek was allowed to work as his father's dental assistant, but his mother went to her death.

We couldn't talk too long; "supper" was waiting. We stood in line before a small kitchen. I got half a cup of ersatz coffee and roughly three slices of bread. Soon it was time for roll call. Columns were formed and the numbers checked by the Kapos. The German SS men were coming. Each Kapo stood at attention alongside his company.

"Attention! Caps off! Face right!" Our faces were frozen in the direction of the oncoming Germans. The Kapos all reported their numbers, and the SS men checked them and ordered us to disperse.

Now we were at "liberty" until 9:45 P.M. I found Jozek. "Tell me something, Jozek. What will I do here? What's this place like?"

His answer was brief and to the point: "It's a death factory. They don't make selections here. The reason they took you and other people from your transport is that a few days earlier they killed seventy-two Dutch Jews for trying to organize an escape. You filled their space."

Knowing that my survival was a direct result of an unsuccessful escape and some kind of tragedy in the camp, I was eager to know the full story. I noticed that Jozek was uncomfortable with my inquires. His answers weren't clear and in a way shameful. I insisted in the name of our friendship that he tell me the full story. This is what he said:

"A group of Polish Jews planned an escape, but their tools, shears, and ropes were accidentally found by Ukrainians. To save their own skin, the escape project was cunningly ascribed by the Polish Jews to the innocent Dutchmen. As a result, all seventy-two Dutch Jews at the camp were executed, except for Max van Dam, an artist, and his two female assistants. They were in the process of finishing portraits for the Nazis.

"Only a few prisoners know the truth. The official version is that a former Dutch naval officer was betrayed as an organizer of an escape. He refused to deliver his co-conspirators, and all were killed."

Before I overcame my shock and disbelief, he went on to describe the camp as if he were describing a play, not a human tragedy. He was no longer the sensitive boy I had known in Izbica.

"The whole camp is divided into four sections: the garrison where the Nazis reside, and three others called Lagers. Lager I, where we are right now, contains the prisoners' sleeping barracks, the kitchen, and some workshops. Lager II, a couple hundred feet farther on, is where the prisoners sort the clothing of the dead. And Lager III, on the north side, is where the gas chambers are and where they burn the bodies."[2]

Even though we had heard of Sobibor, the reality of it hadn't sunk in until now. I tried to grasp the enormity of it, but I couldn't. I was quiet. Jozek gave me tips on who to look out for, what to do and what not to do, but I was hardly listening. Would I like to meet his girlfriend? The women's barracks were nearby, I heard him say.

We went indoors and clambered up to the second tier. Sitting there with some other girls was a very beautiful seventeen-year-old. She was introduced to me, we talked for a moment, and then we all went outside together.

We heard music and followed the sound to the rear of the tailor shop. There, in that accursed place, was a small orchestra and a couple dancing a tango! They danced beautifully, each movement unbelievably synchronized. Jozek said they were Dutch ballet stars from The Hague.

We moved on. Jews were standing in groups, sometimes in couples. I turned to my friend. "Jozek, what's going on here? How can they laugh, dance, make small talk, and think of women? Look around you . . . barbed wire here and there on every side. We will never get out of here. How can we?"

"Toivi," he answered, "don't be amazed. Only a few hours ago you were still free. You will get used to it if they give you enough time. We all know what awaits us. You see that fire over there? This very minute your whole family is turning to ashes, just like my family half a year ago. And I didn't cry, and now you're not crying. You have no more tears, you want to say? No, it's because we've become robots; our survival instincts have taken over. If we thought like normal people, we would all go mad."

I was thinking about what he told me, but still it bothered me the way he had said, *"turning to ashes, just like my family half a year ago."* No emotions, no sorrow, uttered so matter-of-factly.

We were interrupted by a whistle, signaling that it was time for bed. I lay sleepless on my bunk, afraid to think or let myself feel anything about my family and their apparent deaths.

The First Morning

Four o'clock reveille! I jumped up and hurried with the others to wash behind the barrack. A thin metal pipe ran the full length of the back wall of the barrack, a few feet from the ground; water dripped through little drilled holes. The crematorium fire was still burning, the flames reaching into the sky.

I stood in line for breakfast in the cold morning air. Only coffee was offered, because the small portion of bread given at supper was supposed to last the entire next day. Soon there was another shout: "Prepare for roll call." Prearranged work detachments started to form columns. The Kapos moved about nervously and quickly took a head count. Though the Germans were still far away, the Kapos yelled, "Attention! Caps off!"

We removed our caps and stood frozen at attention. When the Germans finally arrived, each Kapo handed a written tally to the head Kapo, who in turn reported the number of prisoners to the SS. The Germans checked each group against the written tally. Then the prisoners were ordered to march to work. The people working in Lager I went to their workshops. The rest were ordered to sing German, Polish, and Russian songs as they marched to designated work sites in other parts of the camp.

But our Izbica group, still without a work detail, waited. I moved closer to a friend of mine from Izbica, Zygmund Tuchman. He was very strong and healthy, and I decided to stick with him. And when a tall, mean-looking SS man named Gustav Wagner called Zygmund, I took a chance and followed.

Wagner led us to a pile of cut pine branches near the main gate. We were to weave pine branches into the barbed-wire fence so no one could see into the compound. A moment later Zygmund was called away to unload a truck with barrels of beer. He managed to do it so quickly that the German, noticing his strength, nominated him to be a Kapo.

At lunchtime we returned to Lager I. Each of us was given our own eating pot. Standing in line, we held out our pots for kasha and small pieces of horsemeat. We had an hour for lunch. Tired from the hard work, I lay down for a nap. After one o'clock roll call, it was time to go back to work.

With Zygmund gone, I had to finish the work on the fence alone. Five feet away I saw freedom, but Ukrainians armed with rifles stood along the fence, and in the watchtowers were guards with rifles. The job was easy, but I felt too conspicuous.

The workday ended at five o'clock. Our Kapo led us back to Lager I. I picked up my aluminum pot from under the pillow of my bunk and joined the others in line for supper. When my turn came, the cook at the dispensary poured out about sixteen ounces of black liq-

uid that tasted like lightly sweetened warm water. I received dark
bread with a warning that it should last me until the next evening.
People sat around the yard, eating quietly. Then we rinsed our pots
in cold water and awaited the last roll call. Before long, I heard sharp
whistles. The Kapos' whips lashed out until we were all assembled in
neat militarylike formations.

The reporting ritual was repeated. The Kapos stepped out and
reported to the SS man in charge, but this time some orders were
barked and a few prisoners stepped aside, took down their pants, and
one after another were beaten with long whips in front of everyone.
The prisoners were yelling, but the sounds I heard were loud numbers.

Jozek later explained that every day, after the last roll call, some prisoners were required to report for the punishment they had incurred
earlier at work. In pain, the prisoners screamed out numbers, until
they reached the number of lashes they had been sentenced to—normally at least twenty-five lashes. If they failed to count loudly, they
would be beaten to death. After this performance, we were told to
disperse. But we were not to rest—not yet. The SS men ordered the
Kapos to teach us various German songs to be sung during our
marches to work. Numbly, we complied.

Later that evening Jozek came to my barrack again. We talked a
bit. He told me that in March, just before I arrived, Himmler visited
the camp. In his honor, the camp commandant performed a sample
execution of seventy beautiful naked Jewish girls, specially selected
and brought from the nearby town of Włodawa.

We went out into the yard. Just then, a pretty girl stepped onto one
of the eating tables and sang a song familiar to all of us, "Mein Yid-
dishe Mamme." She sang in a clear, strong voice; the word "Mamme"
stretched in a note of longing, sadness, and grief. She sang in Dutch,
but I knew the words in Yiddish. I knew that it was an expression of
great love for her mother, and loneliness. I couldn't afford to break
down, so I moved on.

Behind the tailor's shop, a few prisoners were playing classical music
(violin and bass) as if it were the most natural thing to do. We moved
into another barrack. In a corner, Jews were drinking alcohol. Jozek
explained that the vodka was obtained secretly from a Ukrainian
guard, in exchange for gold prisoners had found when sorting the
victims' clothing.

From time to time, huge tongues of fire shot up to the heavens.

Handling the Raw Material

In the middle of the night I was awakened by a sharp whistle. My bunk neighbor explained that a transport had arrived, a Dutch one. This train usually came in around 3:00 A.M.

While the transports of Jews from Eastern Europe usually arrived at Sobibor in overfilled cargo wagons or trucks, the Dutch transports sometimes came in standard passenger trains. The Jewish administration in Westerbork, Holland, their departure point, provided them with doctors and nurses for the sick, maids for the handicapped and babies. Food and medicine were in plentiful supply in attached freight wagons.

Kapo Bunio tore into our barrack, and turning on the light, he shouted, "Porters and barbers . . . get ready!"

Groups of prisoners jumped from their bunks, dressed quickly, and went out to the square. Evidently a large transport was expected. Another Kapo dragged additional men from the bunks, myself included. A few of us were designated "porters" and a few others were called "friseurs," barbers.

The camp was well lit. Being led to the workplace, I could see some movement far off on the station platform [1].³ New arrivals were getting off the train. A narrow-gauge dumpcart passed by. Into it would be thrown, I was told, in addition to the large pieces of baggage, the sick, the old, the crippled, and all those unable to walk on their own. The rest would follow the SS men to a long barrack [31].

The eight-member group I was with was led to this barrack and told to wait for the arriving Jews. It was a large windowless barrack; its entrance and exit gates were wide open. Two prisoners were placed by the entrance gate, four in the center, and two by the exit. We were to tell the Jews passing through the barrack to leave their purses and small hand baggage there.

The first group of condemned drew near. First were the women. They were nicely dressed. I stood for a moment, dumbfounded. It was early in the morning, and many small children slept in their arms. They had no idea they were going to their deaths.⁴

The sudden crack of the whip reminded me not to be a passive observer. The veteran prisoners repeated a sentence in Dutch over and over again, informing the passing people that they were to leave their belongings here; I mimicked them. At the exit gate stood an SS man, and woe to us if someone passed by still holding something after crossing the length of the barrack.

Once in a while I would see bewilderment and suspicion on their faces. They had left their heavy baggage on the platform without worry, because all the luggage had tags, but here they were told to throw their very personal belongings into a huge heap. When someone refused to leave a purse or a handbag, the SS man would whip the victim until he or she complied.

The column of about five hundred people passed through. We could hear more wagons arriving on the camp's side track. Now this place had to be emptied.

The barrack had several doors that led to attached smaller barracks [32]. Several prisoners entered through these doors, and together we quickly loaded the heaps of hand luggage into blankets and carried them to the adjoining rooms. Inside were tables where women stood sorting the booty. We threw down load after load. Soon the barrack was empty and the sand floor had been raked clean.

Then the SS men led us to the gate of an enclosed courtyard and ordered us to wait. From inside the yard came a single German voice. I thought I heard the end of a speech. After a while the gate opened and we entered [33]. The yard was now empty and quiet. Only heaps of neatly piled dresses, suits, and underwear remained.

We loaded the clothes onto blankets and carried them back through the gate. I understood that they were left by Jews who had just been ordered to undress. Moving along with others, I found myself in a large warehouse [42, 43]. We threw the clothes onto large, short tables.

Now, with the next group approaching from the train platform, we were ordered back to the first barrack, where the purses or small packages were to be left. Again the same procedure. Later we walked to the undressing yard and waited for the gate to open.

This time we were earlier, and again we heard from the other side a voice in German. "The 'Preacher' is talking," whispered Szmul. I paid heed. It was a speech conducted in a surprisingly relaxed and polite manner, so unlike the Nazis' normal behavior. The speaker apologized to the listeners for the inconvenience. For sanitary reasons they must undress, put their clothing neatly away, and take a shower before relaxing in the comfortable living quarters that were awaiting them. He recommended that they take the prepared postcards and write a few words to their loved ones in Holland to assure them of their safe arrival in Poland and good health.

The soothing speech of the well-mannered SS man was effective. There was applause. I heard a commotion as the people rushed toward the free postcards, having no idea that those very postcards were a lure meant to reinforce the facade of "resettlement" for the next transport. If only the fence dividing us had been transparent, they would have seen the still-warm mountain of clothing from their predecessors waiting to be sorted and packed.

Suddenly I heard the sound of internal combustion engines. Immediately afterward, I heard a terribly high-pitched, yet smothered, collective cry—at first strong, surpassing the roar of the motors, then, after a few minutes, gradually weakening. My blood froze. I'm sure that the people in the undressing yard heard the scream, but they could not have known what it meant. The noise, muffled by the sound of the engines and the thick walls of the gas chambers, could be taken for a distant thunder, an approaching storm.

An SS man with a machine gun and a whip was watching over us, and we stood waiting as if frozen in time. Now the "Preacher" finished his speech, and applause could once again be heard.[5]

The people, like their predecessors, entered what the Germans sadistically called the Himmelstrasse (Road to Heaven). This was the path, flanked by a barbed-wire fence, that led to the hair-cutting barrack [45] and finally to the gas chambers [51].

Our job in this section done, SS Oberscharführer Karl Frenzel randomly chose four prisoners, myself included, and led us to the hair-cutting barrack, less than twenty feet from the gas chambers. Inside were simple wooden chairs. Josef Wolf, a short, dark, middle-aged SS man, stood in the center of the room. I was given large shears and told to wait. The women began to come. I didn't know what to do.

"Just snip quickly in bunches," a comrade told me. "It doesn't need to be close to the head."

I was terribly shy. I had never seen a nude woman before. Like all fifteen-year-olds I wanted to, but I felt embarrassed for the naked and humiliated women. I tried not to look directly at them, and they looked down and tried to cover themselves.

Not all the women reacted the same way. One woman resisted, refusing to move. When the Nazi hit her with the whip, she attacked him with her fists and nails, but the German bullet was faster and killed her instantly. Now most were resigned and passive. A teenager wept at the loss of her lovely locks, asking not to have it cut too short.

They were going to die in only a few minutes, and there was nothing we could do. After the women left, we packed the hair into potato sacks, which were then brought to a nearby storeroom.

After about three hours' work and over two thousand deaths, the SS men ordered us back to the barracks. We were being counted. Everything was tallied—both the number of the murdered and those still living. As we moved on, the searchlights enveloping us were shut off one by one. It was a beautiful starry night.

Nearing our barracks in Lager I, we heard rhythmic thuds coming from the direction of the gas chambers, like stones being thrown into a metal box. Later I learned what it was. Prisoners in the crematoria section were throwing the bodies onto the narrow-gauge dumpcarts that carried the corpses to the cremation site.[6]

When we arrived at our compound, we were counted again before being allowed to go back to our barracks and to sleep. In the morning, another group would finish the job of sorting and packing the booty for shipment.

A Slave

I became one of the hundred or so slaves who sorted clothes nine hours a day, six and a half days a week. I would pick up items from mountains of clothing and throw shirts to the left, undergarments to the right, sweaters here, pants there, and so on. But first I cut off the Star of David. The new owners wouldn't need it. All clothing was searched, and any valuables were put in a wooden box nearby. All pictures, documents, and Star of David patches were thrown onto blankets and taken to be burned. The sorting process was completed by tying the selected items in groups of ten and carrying them to specific storerooms designated for women's and men's clothing.

I had been sorting clothing for about a month when I became aware of the space where empty suitcases were stored. In the labyrinth of suitcases and boxes, I had seen a place where I could sit down, relax, and not be seen. I made a deal with the prisoner, nicknamed Berliner, who was in charge there: I had food I had stolen while sorting the luggage, but no place to eat it or to rest; he had the place, but no opportunity to acquire food. We made an exchange.

It was a sunny July day. The engine that pulled the narrow-gauge dumpcarts had broken down. Zygmund Tuchman, now a Kapo, was ordered to get three prisoners to push some carts, laden with cans of food, to the gate of Lager III, the gas-chamber compound. Prisoners from the other lagers were never allowed to see the inside of Lager III. Zygmund got his group to the gate, but instead of instantly turning back as ordered, they were a little too slow, and the gate leading to Lager III opened in their presence. The group was not allowed to return to Lager I. My friend Zygmund was gone.

This part of Sobibor was our nightmare. Transfer there was equal to unbearable exhaustion and misery, working in the process of cremating. My own encounter with Lager III came not long afterward. SS Oberscharführer Rudolf Beckmann, chief of the Administration Office, ordered two other prisoners and myself to go with him. He led us to a barren field between Lager II and Lager III. On a truck platform were two young girls about twenty years of age, one of whom was completely nude and probably wounded.

"You," he said, pointing at the other prisoners, "carry the naked one. And you," he pointed at me, "go with the other one. Bring them to Lager III."

The girls were frightened but silent. I sensed their unspoken question: What was Lager III?[7] Beckmann followed briskly a few paces behind.

As we walked, the girl whispered frantically in Polish, "I've got money. Bribe the German. Help me . . . do something!" She didn't know that the Germans would soon take her money as well as her life. "Aren't you a Jew, how could you do this, doesn't your conscience bother you? Help us." I didn't dare answer her. Beckmann was right behind me, and it would be death for me as well.

"Am I going to die?" she asked. Should I answer yes? What good was the truth? I kept quiet. We came to the gate of the gas chamber compound. My heart pounded. I was terrified too. Would he order me in as well?

"Go back!" ordered Beckmann. I turned and ran like the wind. Minutes later I heard shots. The girls had been executed. I returned to my interrupted work, shaken. Their pleading faces tormented me and left me no peace. They were so young, good looking, in the spring of their lives. And they were only two, out of hundreds of thousands like them.

As time passed and I became more familiar with the system, I noticed that the camp had two separate routines. For the prisoners, the daily routine consisted of work in different detachments at steady places of work, sorting clothes, shoes, valuables, and so on. The second routine began the moment a transport of Jews arrived. Then specially designated groups would emerge from the workforce to process the new arrivals. There were the Bahnhofkommando, who received the Jews at the train platform; the group manning the transit barrack where handbags were left; those who carried clothing to the sorting tables; those who raked the ground after the Jews passed through the "Himmelstrasse" corridor to the gas chambers; and the "friseurs" who cut the women's hair. After the new arrivals were slaughtered, things returned to "normal," and we prisoners returned to our previous assignments.

The Dutch Twins

Agonizing days passed. On May 7, 1943, another Dutch transport arrived and was processed overnight. We returned tired to our barracks in Lager I. It was four in the morning. The camp was quiet. Thousands of Jews had disappeared as if they had never existed.

In a corner, under a lamppost, I noticed about thirty new youngsters. Why are they standing around, I wondered. Everyone else was hurrying off to their bunks.

No sooner was I in my barrack than curiosity got the better of me. As I stepped back out, faint light from two directions dispelled the darkness. The sun was pushing up in the east, and the flaming pyres were lighting up the sky in the north.

Kapo Bunio was standing at the edge of the group. He spotted me, but said nothing, though he could have punished me for being outside my barrack. Visibly tired, the newcomers were quietly conversing with one another. All were finely dressed.

A tall man in a dark suit and tie beckoned me. Kapo Bunio was busy talking to Yosel and didn't notice as I joined the group. The man said something to me, but I didn't understand. The only Dutch words I knew were those the SS men taught me to say in the transit barrack—"Lay down your handbags"—and the words heard over and over again from the entrance to the death alley—"Gold, money, and watches to the cashier." He switched languages, I think to French, but still I didn't understand.

Suddenly I was aware of two identical girls, about fifteen years of age, tightly holding hands as if afraid of losing each other. They looked at me with deep blue eyes.

"Do you speak German?" one asked.

"Yes."

"We would like to know what this place is called. Is it Sobibor, like the station we saw?"

"Yes."

"Could you show me later which barrack my father and brother were taken to?"

Obviously this was a group freshly selected from the early-morning transport, replacement for those who were killed or had committed suicide in the last few weeks. Apparently the two sisters had been temporarily saved at the caprice of the SS supervisor.

What should I tell them? They had no idea where they were. A few who understood German closed in to listen, and I began to be dangerously conspicuous. I had to make it fast.

"What's your name?"

"Inge."

"My name is Toivi, I'm from Poland . . . I'll see you at breakfast. I can't talk now. Good-bye." And I slipped back to the barracks.

As I climbed up to my bunk, I thought of how they reminded me of golden-haired Rywkele Flajszman, a poor girl who helped mother in exchange for meals when I was a child. Rywkele was taken to Bełżec with her parents in early 1942. My conscience had always bothered me for verbally mistreating her, showing off to her that I was the boss's son. And now it was too late to explain that I really liked her.

I couldn't get the twins out of my mind. Although I was allowed to sleep until eleven o'clock because I had worked during the night when the transport arrived, I decided to stay awake for the morning roll call so that I might see them again.

The bugle sounded and I jumped down from my bunk. I asked the Waldkommando (forest brigade) foreman Podchlebnik, whom I had known from Izbica and was friendly to me, where the newcomers were. But he wasn't even aware of their arrival. I scanned the coffee line, but no sign of them.

Kapo Pożycki noticed me. Before I was able to explain that I had worked on the night shift and had permission to sleep late, he whipped me on the head and shoulders, screaming that I should join the roll call. By now the SS men were coming into the yard, and prisoners had to be either in the columns or out of sight. There was no time to return. So after the usual ceremony of the roll call, I marched to work with the others.

Luckily, Berliner, the luggage sorter, didn't mind that I found a big trunk and took a nap in it until lunchtime.

Inge found me in the food line. "Tofi!" I turned around and there were the twins. "We didn't go to breakfast," said one. "They kindly allowed us to sleep late after the long journey."

God! They don't know the truth! The word "kindly," coming from them, sounded convincingly innocent.

"Tofi, take us to our father and brother. Please, look for them."

I couldn't tell which one I had talked to the day before. Their voices, too, sounded the same. I noticed that they had no eating pots and so they might miss their meal. I asked them to stay in line and left to find them containers. I went to the son of the kitchen chief, Cukerman, who was an acquaintance of mine, and he helped me find pots for the girls. We were just in time.

I led them to the tables. "Eat," I said. "I'll explain everything later."

Every so often they'd stop eating and talk quietly in Dutch, glancing toward me as if to say, "What's wrong with him? Can't he answer simple questions?"

Many times I would talk about Sobibor with fellow prisoners, and we'd even joke about our only way out, with the smoke, traveling with the wind. But this was different. I wished they would find out by themselves or have someone else tell them. Why did they have to ask me?

They were so innocent and naive. The flames were high in the sky, the stench was everywhere. Why did they ask? Why?

"Inge, we must go back to work, I'll tell you for sure in the evening. I'll be waiting between the barracks, right after supper." By that time they would know . . . I hoped.

I thought of them all afternoon. I looked for them in the barrack where the women sorted, but they weren't there. As soon as the day's work was finished and we returned to our compound, I rushed to our meeting place between the barracks.

They were waiting. Surely they knew now. They were in a work group. The others must have told them.

We greeted each other. Sobibor was expanding, and we sat down on the wood panels being prepared for the new barracks.

"Where are you working, Inge?"

"In the chicken coops."

They were working alone. Then they still don't know!

"Inge, ask me and I will try to answer. What do you want to know?"

"Tofi, I want to know two things. Where can I see my father and brother, and how can I mail a letter to Holland?"

There was no way out. They would find out anyway. There was no escape. Not knowing how to start, I corrected my name.

"Inge, my name is Toivi, not Tofi. Tell me, when you left Holland, where did you think you were going?"

"They told us we were going to be resettled until the end of the war."

"And you believed it?"

"Why not? Even the Dutch guards and the Jewish officials told us so. We received cards from transports leaving before us."

"Well, have you noticed anything curious about this place?"

They pondered. Just then, with renewed strength, flames shot sky high from the crematorium behind the camouflaged fence of Lager III, and I continued, "For example, that fire? The smell?"

I blurted out, "Listen, you will never see your father or brother again, nor will you ever leave here alive. This is Sobibor. A death factory." They were silent. They looked around, still not able to comprehend.

"Listen," I repeated, "it's true. I'm not crazy. Please believe me. The smell is from dead bodies piling up for days in the hot sun, waiting to be burned. And the fire you see is burning them. This is a place that gasses and burns Jews."

In the weak light I couldn't see the expressions on their faces, but their eyes were fixed on me, and again they clasped hands. Then they began talking rapidly in Dutch, but soon realized that I didn't understand a word and switched back to German.

"Toivi, it can't be! They are alive. My father and brother are young. They must be working somewhere!"

I felt they believed me yet refused to accept the truth. "Inge, they are gone. You will understand when you are here longer. You will see it."

The sisters stood up quietly, looking at the fire. I was waiting for a tear, but their eyes were dry. I never saw anyone cry in Sobibor. Before I went to Sobibor it was hard for me to even imagine the death of one of my parents. I would have suffered terribly, and I'm certain I would have cried. In Sobibor I lost my close family in just one hour, and I closed my thoughts to it. Now it was the same with the girls. Maybe this was nature's way of ensuring survival. I felt like putting my arms around them. But we simply stood there . . . three lost kids.

Without asking, I told them what happened to transports, sparing nothing. The words came out in a wild stream. All the while their eyes were fixed on the fire. When I finished, knowing we felt the same spiritual bond of loneliness and suppressed feelings, I left them alone.

We met often and talked a lot about our pasts. Their parents were upper-class intellectuals. Their father had been a high official in the German justice department. With the rise of Nazism, the family moved to Holland, to the city of Scheveningen, where their parents soon divorced. Their father and only brother arrived with them at Sobibor.

Although we sometimes daydreamed together about the possibility of surviving the war, these conversations sounded artificial, like fairy tales, and at some point they abruptly stopped.

Later I was able to distinguish a difference in the twins. Inge was more curious and open. Once, when she was sitting close to me, the evening wind blew her blond hair toward me, and I caught it with my lips. But she noticed this gesture, and I felt ashamed and awkward. Though I was immensely curious about girls, and knew that Sobibor was the end of my life experience, I never tried anything with her again.

I thought constantly of escape. The Germans were doing some demolition work in the nearby town of Włodawa. A small group of Jewish prisoners, with Ukrainian guards and SS Oberscharführer Dubois in charge, went there by train each day to work. Before the morning roll call, I would hang around the group of prisoners designated to work in Włodawa. Maybe someone would get sick. Maybe they would take one more person. I waited for a chance. Within only a few days one prisoner was so brutally beaten by Wagner that he wasn't able to work. I asked to take his place, and the Kapo agreed.

It was still dawn when we left the camp for the village train station. Soon a regularly scheduled train arrived. The Germans took one car, putting guards at each door, and we made it to the town. We walked from the train station to the center of town, a distance of about a mile. On the way, a group of Poles was walking toward us on the narrow sidewalk. One man didn't get out of the way fast enough for our German guard. He beat the Pole until he was unconscious.

This day our work consisted of dismantling the ovens of a Jewish-owned bakery. Sobibor needed fire-resistant bricks. Although Włodawa was already officially Judenrein, about 150 Jewish girls worked there under local supervision, sorting the spoils of the abandoned Jewish households. We could see them nearby and thought we might be able to help them. Risking torture and death—the likely result of unexpected searches often conducted by the SS guards—we smuggled money and other valuables to Włodawa. We hoped that the female slaves would find them and use them to save themselves by buying false papers or food. Eventually, though, most of these girls were brought to Sobibor and gassed.

As we marched to and from work we were forced to sing. Poles stopped on the streets in confusion and looked at us. When had they last seen Jews, let alone young and healthy-looking Jews, singing happy songs? They didn't know what to make of it. When they found out we were from Sobibor, the whole street emptied in fear.

In a few weeks the brick transfer was finished. There had been no chance to escape. Not only did the Germans watch us closely, but the prisoners watched each other. We knew that if anyone escaped, everyone would be held responsible. And a mass escape in the middle of a town full of Nazi collaborators would be doomed to failure.

Road Builder

I observed that prisoners who always worked in one place became dangerously conspicuous, their faces familiar to the SS man in charge. Any deviation from the routine could be easily noticed.

A new extension of the camp was being built, called Lager IV, or North. Bunkerlike storerooms were being constructed. Rumors were that this would be a sorting center for Soviet ammunition. From conversations with prisoners working there, I found out that watchtowers on the newly enlarged perimeter were not yet completed and some stretches of forest were not yet fenced in. The Ukrainian guards there were cruel, but the area seemed not to be guarded heavily. Maybe this was the way to escape!

I saw my chance. Prisoners from Lager I were building a road in the North camp, and I volunteered to go there. In charge was SS Scharführer Arthur Dachsel. At fifty-five, Dachsel was the oldest Nazi in Sobibor. He was also one of the least vicious; he seemed to protect "his" prisoners from beatings by other guards, if only to keep us in good working condition. I cut down the small trees, cut the trunks into fifteen-foot segments, and laid them aside to use as a foundation for the new wooden road. I kept myself clean and walked straight. Dachsel took notice.

When there were no more saplings in the immediate area, he put me in charge of a group of tree cutters deeper inside the forest. It was an easy job. I'd line up the men and march them off like an army platoon: "one, two, left . . . one, two left . . ." We were guarded only by Ukrainians, and I would have the men sing racy Ukrainian songs to keep the guards in a good mood and thereby prevent beatings. My strategy worked.

One day, as I was marching my group to work, SS Karl Frenzel suddenly appeared.

"Halt!" he shouted.

"Abteilung . . . Halt!"—I stopped my group.

"Bend over!" He lashed at me once.

"Now why did I beat you, Kleiner [little one]?"

I had no idea what I had done wrong. I was in panic and didn't answer. Frenzel beat me again, this time five lashes. Again he asked if I knew how I had earned this punishment. Desperate, I looked to Kapo Bunio, who was standing beside me.

The Kapo looked at Oberscharführer Frenzel, as if asking for permission. Frenzel nodded his approval.

"You were out of step," the Kapo said coldly.

Instantly I snapped to attention and gave an order to the group: "Abteilung Marschieren! [Unit march forward!]" This time I marched in step with the rest. Frenzel was in a good mood. He smiled and left.

I denuded one area of young trees and moved very close to the fences surrounding Lager III. At first I thought it was just another fence in the forest. But once I heard a commotion on the other side, behind the fence and the trees, and the piercing screams of people in terror, I knew I was behind the gas chambers.

A few days later, while marking trees to be cut, the guard ordered us to sing. While the Polish Jews knew Ukrainian or Polish songs that the guards could understand, the Dutch Jews did not. The Ukrainians noticed the "uncooperative" Hollanders and became angry. They began to torture and beat the Dutch prisoners. Most of them were wounded and bleeding. SS Dachsel, from whom I could probably ask protection, was on the other side of the compound, and I was powerless. Dachsel had a relatively subdued temper. He never yelled, and although he carried a whip like the others, I had never seen him use it.

The same day, after roll call, I went to the barrack where the Dutchmen had their bunks. I had become friends with many of them and felt sorry for them. For them the shock of Sobibor was devastating. While the Polish Jews had years of degradation and suffering behind them, the Dutch went from relative security to this hell virtually overnight. And they broke down quickly. I heard their weak groans coming from the barrack. The next day, the morning rays found many of them hanging from their bunks.

I became aware that although some of the forest area was not fenced, we were watched by many guards, and it was impossible to escape. It was best to fade out from Lager IV. The next day I took a chance and asked SS Dachsel to release me from the tree-cutting force. He agreed and put me in charge of another group building the road. We dug long, narrow channels for larger logs, which would form the main support for the new wooden road. It was to run for about three hundred yards, through Lager IV.

Where the road was to make a left turn, I made an engineering mistake. Not understanding the instructions given by SS Dachsel, I built the turn flat instead of with a higher angle at the curve. The angry but still even-tempered German relieved me of my "instructor" job, and I was again a regular worker. Shortly thereafter the road was finished, and I returned to Lager II.

I decided to try the Waldkommando next. The work performed there also took place outside the barbed wires of the camp. This particular group supplied wood for the crematorium by cutting down trees and digging out the stumps. Although the area was heavily guarded, we were out of view of the guards in the towers. Maybe, just maybe, there was a chance to escape. I had been looking for an opportunity to merge into the Waldkommando to check the possibilities there.

One morning I asked Foreman Podchlebnik to permit me to join his group. I was accepted. The group was composed of twenty Polish Jews and twenty Dutch Jews. Each morning we went to the forest about three miles outside the camp.

It turned out that we were in fact heavily guarded, one guard for every two prisoners. True, we had "weapons"—axes and saws to cut down trees—but the Ukrainians used a special strategy in guarding us. They stood at a greater distance from the prisoners than usual, their weapons ready at all times. The work there was tortuous, supervised by the cruel SS Hubert Gomerski and SS Werner Dubois. With the foreman's consent, I again exchanged my place with a prisoner from another working group.

On June 18, 1943, a transport from Lwów arrived. As my friend in the Bahnhofkommando told me later, when the cattle-car doors were opened, dead bodies of naked men, women, and children slid out onto the platform. Some were so swollen and decomposed that when they were loaded onto the narrow-gauge dumpcarts body parts fell off. Out of 1500 arrivals, only a small fraction were alive, and they were half-mad from hunger and exhaustion. Normally the journey took three days at the most, but this transport had been on the rails for over a week.

At the end of the same month, suddenly, during lunch, we were ordered to go to our barracks and the doors were closed behind us. Onto the Sobibor rails puffed a strongly guarded train. This time they didn't call the Bahnhofkommando, barbers, and porters. This transport was apparently special. The Germans were taking extraordinary precautions.

Even so, as the new arrivals were being led to the gas chambers, they began to realize their fate. They threw themselves on the Germans and scattered in different directions. They were shot and killed as they ran. They did what we had talked about many times: throw themselves on the Germans. A quick death by a bullet was preferable to the long, agonizingly painful end in the gas chambers.

From notes found hidden in the clothes of the dead, we pieced together that they were death-camp prisoners from Bełżec. The camp had stopped its deadly activity at the end of 1942, but cleanup work and the burning of bodies had continued. These prisoners had been promised work in a similar camp. So as not to arouse their suspicions, they were put in roomy cattle cars, and given food and drink. One note said:

> We have worked one year in Bełżec. We don't know where they are transporting us. They say to Germany. In the wagons are dining tables. We have received bread for three days, canned food, and vodka. If this is a lie, you should know that death awaits you, too. Don't trust the Germans. Take revenge for us.[8]

A few days later, in the middle of the night, Oberscharführer Wagner asked for volunteers. Because I was always on the alert for potential escape routes, I volunteered, despite Wagner's reputation as a volatile killer, especially when the job was to be done at night. A group of twenty Jews assembled in pairs. SS Wagner led us to the main gate. From there, under heavy Ukrainian guard, we marched outside the camp. The night was beautiful. In the moonlight, I could see the village train station and neighboring cottages. It was so peaceful. If not for the silhouette of the tall SS man and the outstretched rifles of the guards, it might as well have been an evening stroll. Wagner led us along the railroad for about five minutes, finally stopping next to a pile of neatly stacked reserve railroad rails. Beyond the alert chain of guards, the forest tempted me with its dark wall of trees. But it was impossible to get away.

Now we were ordered to pick up a rail. The gates opened again and we were back in another hellish world. We marched straight in the direction of Lager III and left the rails near the gate. This was simply the way the burned-out grates of the pyres were replaced. I was wondering why, with all their might, the SS stole the rails at night. But I assume that the clever SS Wagner had found this eliminated the hassle of going through regular channels.

Escapes and Reprisals

There was no way out of Sobibor except, as the saying went, "through the chimney." But I remember one daring escape attempt that *was* successful.

It was a dark, rainy night. We hadn't had such a storm in a long time. One usually sleeps soundly in such weather, but that night some of us were awake. In the morning there was the usual daily routine: wash-up, breakfast, and preparation for roll call. Suddenly, like an electric shock, news spread from mouth to mouth, "The wires are cut . . . They ran away . . . We don't know how many . . . The roll call will show."

Nervous Kapos ran to notify the Germans. I snuck behind the men's barracks. I saw the cut wires hanging loose. I knew retribution awaited us, but I didn't hold it against those who had escaped. Instead, I was jealous.

The SS arrived immediately, and although it wasn't the usual time, they held roll call then and there. Soon it was discovered that two prisoners were missing—Josel Pelc from Tyszowice and a mason from Chełm whose name I don't remember. Wagner was on vacation, and Frenzel set the sentence. As punishment, two Jews from every work group would be executed.

"Attention! About face." It had begun. Usually we envied those who were already dead, yet at the same time some wild, primitive instinct for life succeeded in keeping all of us straight and strong, so as not to catch Frenzel's eye. We knew that the Nazis always picked the weak and the sick.

SS Frenzel moved slowly to the front of the first formation and selected men at will. Those chosen moved to one side; the group to be sacrificed grew quickly. I noticed my friend Hersz from Grabowiec standing among them. He smiled to himself, shaking his head with self-pity, as if to say, "Finally my time has come." Frenzel came close to my group. I was overcome with fear. I was small and very skinny. Only a few days earlier I had been lashed and beaten with a stick for moving slowly, and was left barely alive.

Because each formation was standing in two rows, he chose one man from the front row first, then walked behind the back of the second line and ordered another victim to step out. I was standing in fear. His steps came closer. I could hear the heavy breathing of this fat and angry man. "God, help me," I begged silently, "don't make him choose me."

Down the line from me was a distant relative from Izbica, Yczy Mojsze Waks. His leg was bandaged, and this was decisive. The German touched him with the whip and told him to get out. His seventeen-year-old son was left to watch helplessly. Once the selection was completed, the condemned were led toward Lager III. We heard shots, and later the dumpcarts returned with their clothes to be sorted.

After this escape, security was strengthened. There were already three rows of barbed wire surrounding the camp as well as the watchtowers with machine guns. Now military engineers were brought in to mine a fifteen-meter-wide section of land around the perimeter of the camp. Painters were ordered to make signs reading "Danger! Mines!" which were then posted around the camp. In addition, a deep ditch was dug between the two outer fences of Lager I and was filled with water. The mines and the moat were not only to make escape more difficult, but also to hinder the advance of partisans who were becoming active in the area. Finally, chains and padlocks were put on the doors of the barracks to lock the prisoners in at night.

In the latter part of June 1943, in the middle of the night, two loud explosions were heard. Soon all the prisoners were called out from their bunks for an unusually speedy roll call. Sometimes special roll calls were held when a mine was set off by a deer or rabbit and the SS suspected an escape. But this one was different.

The counting went on for over half an hour. Then the guards surrounded us in a horseshoe formation, increasingly tightening the half-circle. Our orderly ranks dissolved as we were pushed tightly against the walls of the barracks. Now we were enclosed on all sides. Some of us began to pray. Our time had finally come—the inescapable day of our own liquidation.

Meanwhile, the sound of machine guns rattled from the north side of the camp. And high above, silently witnessing, the full moon lit up this surreal scene. Time passed and suddenly, after two hours, the Germans, without any explanation, told us to go back to sleep.

The next day Ukrainian guards disclosed that enemy partisans had ap-proached the northern fences. The Germans, alerted in time, had repelled them.[9]

It was July 20. I walked with other prisoners toward a burning pit, carrying on our backs blankets stuffed with documents to be destroyed.

"Look!" said my friend Karolek. With a shocked expression, he pointed to the railroad track that ran on higher ground outside the camp, parallel to the camouflaged fence.

A group of people was being forced to run quickly, their hands held high above their heads. At first I thought they were a group of Jews caught in the forest by neighboring farmers and brought to the camp for reward, five kilograms of sugar for each Jew caught and returned. But looking closely, I recognized familiar figures. They were our people from the Waldkommando! Something unusual must have happened.

A few minutes later, an alarm sounded. It was roll call for all of Lager I. The Nazis ignored their usual counting routine and instead put us in one column, four abreast, then led us under heavy guard in the direction of the crematoria.

We didn't know what had happened. Nevertheless, we were certain these were our last minutes. Every step brought us nearer to the gas chambers. We whispered quietly among ourselves. Is this our last moment? Should we throw ourselves on the Germans? One thing we knew for sure: we would not be led peacefully to our deaths.

Finally, we were ordered to stop and form a semicircle in the center of the meadow between Lager II and Lager III. Now I noticed a group of people sitting on the grass with their hands behind their heads.

SS Untersturmführer Johann Niemann made a speech: "Some prisoners in the Waldkommando tried to escape. Only the Dutch Jews showed their integrity by not trying to run away. As a reward for this, they will be allowed back to work and they will not be punished. In a moment, the recaptured Polish Jews of the Waldkommando will be executed, and this will be the destiny of anyone who even dreams of running away."

A few yards from the condemned stood two Ukrainian assistants who carried out the executions. Two at a time, the prisoners were motioned forward. Apathetically they moved to the appointed place. All spent their last seconds of life looking straight ahead at the pointed rifles.

Of all those sacrificed, only one protested—Podchlebnik, the foreman of the Waldkommando. A second before he was executed, he spat toward the Germans and yelled, "Remember, there will come a time when we will be avenged!"

Another man from Izbica, whose name I can't remember now, tried to beat his destiny. In the split second before the shots rang out, he fell to the ground, but was noticed; he was ordered to get up, and was shot again and killed. Then SS Niemann went over to those who were still alive after the firing had stopped and ended their lives with a pistol.

The next day another execution took place when seventeen-year-old Leon Blatt from Izbica (no relation), one of the Waldkommando escapees, was caught hiding in the forest. As punishment, he was to be whipped and beaten to death. To make it worse, the sentence was to be carried out by a Jew nicknamed Radio, a friend of Leon's. The execution was done in the courtyard of Lager II, for all to see.

For a long time the whip flew as he lay on the ground. Screaming in pain, Leon begged and pleaded to be dispatched by a bullet. And since Radio didn't know where to hit to shorten Leon's pain, the display of suffering lasted even longer. At last, taking the whispered advice of nearby prisoners, Radio struck Leon on the head with the handle of the whip, repeatedly and with great force, until the boy lost consciousness and died. Only by hastening his inescapable destiny could his terrible suffering be ended.

Being forced to watch his beating was one of my worst experiences in Sobibor. I thought to myself, how is it that one death can be so much more unbearable than the knowledge of thousands gassed in agonizing pain? And the Nazis knew that—they knew that by making us watch such horror they could more easily keep us in line.

After the war, I learned the details of the escape attempt. The Waldkommando worked in the forest outside the camp, chopping logs to stoke the crematorium fires. The work was difficult, and under the hot sun the prisoners were suffering from thirst. Two men, Szlomo Podchlebnik (cousin of the executed foreman) and Josef Kopf, along with a Ukrainian guard, would leave each day at noon to get water at the well in the nearby village of Złobek. On the way, the prisoners approached their guard, offering gold in exchange for vodka, as was often done. But this time, as the Ukrainian examined the money, they disarmed him, knifed him to death, and escaped.[10]

Meanwhile, those remaining in the forest waited for the water. When the group didn't return in the allocated time, the impatient Germans decided to look for them. Halfway to the village they found the dead body of the Ukrainian. An immediate roll call was ordered. Everyone knew something serious had happened. When the body of the guard was brought in, the Jews were sure of their fate. They were immediately surrounded by the fierce and angry guards. At that moment one voice sealed it.

"Hurrah!!" yelled young Leon, as he threw his ax at the Nazis. It electrified the resigned and fearful victims, and moved them into action. Except for the Dutch Jews, all followed Leon's example, throwing their axes and saws at the Nazis and running. Leon actually managed to get out of the camp, but unfortunately became disoriented in the forest, ran in circles, and was finally captured by the border police. His slow and painful death was to be an example to the rest of us.

Betrayal

I awakened. There was a hand on my shoulder, shaking me. It was Fiszel Białowicz, my bunk neighbor. "People are escaping!" he whispered nervously.

"What do you mean?" I mumbled, half-asleep.

"Toivi, listen . . ." In the Kapos' section of the barrack, I heard a door creaking as if blown by a draft. There was whispering in the barrack, and some footsteps. I decided to check with a friend in the Bahnhofkommando. Maybe he knew what was going on.

I crawled down and made my way quietly toward the Bahnhofkommando section of the bunks. As I neared, I heard whispering again, but I couldn't make out a single sentence. The night was dark, and I could see only faint outlines. I reached my friend who occupied the first bunk to the right by feeling my way in the darkness.

Moniek, what's going on?"

Unexpectedly, I received a blow on my forehead with a hard object, a warning not to intrude. "Don't worry, it's not your business, go back to sleep," a voice said.

Something strange was taking place. But, relaxed by the knowledge that the Bahnhofkommando didn't seem concerned, I returned to my bunk to sleep. It was near dawn, and another miserable day lay ahead; I had to be alert to survive.

The next day it still wasn't clear to me what had happened. But slowly I gleaned from bits and pieces of information that a group of Kapos had devised an escape plan with the help of a bribed Ukrainian guard. However, at the last moment, when they were ready to leave through the window and cut the wires under the cover of darkness, someone alerted the Bahnhofkommando. A quarrel followed, and this naturally paralyzed the action.

To many of the prisoners, the Kapos' attempted escape was already a public secret. If they had gone through with it then and succeeded in escaping, it would have brought immediate reprisals to many of us, and would have helped only a small group of hated Kapos.

In the morning, as they did every day, the Kapos' whistle announced roll call. Everyone formed working groups and, after routine checking, we marched off to work. It was about ten o'clock. I was talking to a friend and pretending to sort clothing when I observed an unusual scene. Most of the Kapos were walking in a very tight group, surrounded by guards, with Governor (head Kapo) Mojsze Sturm at the front. Slowly they passed us, moving in the direction of the gas chambers. Obviously they were being led to their deaths.

I was sorry for them, especially for Mojsze. He was a young fellow, about twenty years old, of wiry build, blond with blue eyes. Though he hit me occasionally, I didn't hold it against him. I think my fellow inmates also did not hate him. Often, in the presence of Germans, he would use his whip and make us work faster, but the moment he was sure the Nazis were gone, he would tell us to take it easy and slow down.

The group slowly disappeared from view. Immediately it was rumored that someone had betrayed the escape attempt to the Germans, but no one knew whom. An hour later, the puzzle was solved when a new Governor appeared in Lager II. It was Berliner the luggage sorter, who was, until now, a little-known figure in the camp. I could hardly recognize him now. He looked ridiculous: over fifty years old, short and awkward, already in a new Governor's cap, new gabardine riding pants, long leather boots, and a whip—an unmistakable sign of authority. He would have absolute power of life and death over us, and we understood it. I was afraid of him now, and saddened. The traitor was rewarded and the Nazi message was clear: "Look how generously we reward those who are loyal!"

After the execution of the Kapos involved in the escape attempt, their clothes were delivered for sorting. At lunchtime roll call, Berliner was officially presented as Governor. The big questions now were: What kind of man will he be? How will he use his power?

As it turned out, his personality completely changed. He became power-mad. He began by ordering us to address him as "Herr Governor" while standing at attention. His predecessor had been so approachable we would call him by his first name.

Until now, Jews working as sorters in Lager II were occasionally able to smuggle foodstuffs to Lager I. Now this became increasingly difficult. Berliner watched us like a hawk. He frequently conducted searches and beat his fellow Jews without pity. And each day his behavior worsened.

Fireman

After a short intermission, new transports began to arrive again. I was determined to maneuver myself into a job where I would have little contact with the Germans. Not far from the sorting sheds was a big pit where teenagers Szmul Wajcen from Chodorów and Meir Ziss from Zółkiewka worked burning documents, photo albums, letters, and so on. It was an ideal place to work. The ditch was deep and always surrounded by thick smoke. The Germans did not come close, and there was no supervision.

In the beginning, when carrying blankets from the sorting area full of items to be burned, I would throw in some food for Szmul. After a while we became friends, and when the papers piled high, I pitched in to help. The SS didn't object, because I was assisting in cleaning up the place. Szmul didn't object either, especially when Meir was busy elsewhere. Eventually Meir moved on, I continued to help, and in time everyone accepted this as my steady work. The Kapos and SS called me Fireman.

Later a special oven was built in an enclosed building to prevent burning papers from being dispersed by the wind. The pit was leveled, and we were now hidden in a building out of view. Szmul later was transferred, and I was put in charge of the burning and given another helper, Blind Karolek, so nicknamed because he had only one good eye. Finally, I had a relatively isolated place where the work gave me access to money and food.

My first duty each morning was to clean out the ashes and remove any debris. Because some of the things put in the fire were noncombustible—the metal parts of luggage, metal toys, and so on—some ashes could not fall through the grates to the container below. With a long, hooked metal rod, I cleaned the grates, but before dispersing all of this on the sandy ground I sifted it through my fingers, looking for gold. Often prisoners delivering trash from the sorting area to be burned secretly threw valuables into the collecting blankets instead of giving them to the Nazis. The paper money disappeared without a trace, but gold could still be found in the ashes; only its luster was gone.

This part was dangerous. I worked carefully. If a German noticed any valuables in the ashes, Karolek and I would undoubtedly be killed. I quickly hid the coins I found.

To start a fire, I laid out some wood, identification papers, and torn books, and lit the pile. The oven, ablaze again, was stuffed to capacity. The flames hummed and crackled through the tall chimney. All books were supposed to be burned, but I always tried to save some to look at if I could get away with it. I had always loved books, and I would risk my life to smuggle out a book to read in some barrack corner.

A huge transport of Dutch Jews was being cremated. The enclosure near the incinerator was filled to the ceiling with refuse. Blankets full of documents were still being brought in for burning. After loading the oven, I shut the steel door and leaned against the wall to catch my breath. I reached for the book I had put aside—a German encyclopedia. I turned the pages and stopped at an interesting picture: a chastity belt. I had learned something about sex by secretly reading books on the subject, but this was something new to me. Soon I was completely absorbed. Karolek, my coworker, focused on the canned food hidden under the trash, also was neglecting to keep an eye out for unexpected visits.

But resting was forbidden at Sobibor. I suddenly became aware of the shadow of a German peering in through the grimy window. Startled, I dropped the book into the fire. SS Wagner rushed in and immediately inquired, "Fireman, were you sleeping?"

My mind worked fast. If he had asked me whether I was reading, I undoubtedly would have admitted it, knowing he could have seen me. But his question betrayed that he didn't really see me clearly and wasn't sure what had taken me from my labor. I stood at attention and answered, terrified, "No, I wasn't sleeping."

He asked me again and again, trying to break me down. But I knew that sleeping or even resting on the job drew the penalty of death. And so I answered consistently, "No, no, I wasn't sleeping."

Unsatisfied, but apparently unsure of my guilt, Wagner beat me with the cleaning rod. I tried to shield my head with my hands and ran for cover behind the oven. He chased me as a cat does a mouse, beating me along the way. Finally Wagner pushed me out the door and, pointing to a barrel, announced that Karolek and I would each receive the minimum penalty of twenty-five lashes. Immediately, without a word, I took down my pants and stretched over the barrel.

SS Beckmann was passing by, and both men—one standing on my left, the other on my right—began to whip me. I had witnessed many beatings, and was aware that I must be conscious and loudly count at least twenty-five lashes—otherwise I could be beaten endlessly.

Each lash felt like a hot iron rod was being applied to my body. But, biting my lips, I counted. With the scream "Twenty-five!" I stood up without an order. As if there were a gentlemen's agreement, they allowed me to leave.

Now it was Karolek's turn. First he was panicky, then petrified with fear. When called, he lay still on the sand. Then Wagner brought his nail-studded military boot down on his face and kept it there as he whipped him. The grinding boot stripped the skin from Karolek's face, and his bones were showing.

This made me panic and I slipped away to a nearby sorting barrack. But soon I heard "Feuermeister! Feuermeister!" and I knew Wagner was looking for me. Failure to answer when spoken to by a Nazi was also punishable by death. So was helping a prisoner to escape punishment. When other prisoners begged me to give myself up, fearing for their own lives, I returned to Wagner, my heart pounding.

When Wagner demanded an explanation, I answered, "I went to the pharmaceutical storeroom to rub my butt with talcum powder," hoping that somehow he would find this entertaining.

And he did laugh for a minute. Then he began beating me with the metal rod again. He finally stopped and stood in front of me. He announced that he was giving us two days to burn all the trash and that we should report to him after the evening roll call when we finished. Then he left, letting me live. It didn't matter this time. The order was as good as a death sentence.

We were a sight: Karolek, bloody, a piece of flesh ripped from his face, and me with a crippled hand. We looked at each other in despair. How could we incinerate in two days what usually took us a whole week, and in our condition? Only a miracle could save us. Although I was weak, I started to work. I fed the oven like a steam engineer. Karolek, however, was at the end of his endurance.

Governor Berliner appeared out of nowhere. His cruelty and his compliance with the Nazis were already known, and, even though we had helped each other before, I didn't expect pity from him.

"Toivi, I see you will not make it," snapped Berliner. Apparently he already knew of SS Wagner's order. I didn't know what this statement meant, sadistic relish or sincere concern, and I didn't answer.

"Do you hear me? You are doomed, you bastards!"

I thought I detected a tone of sorrow. "Yes, I know," I answered resignedly.

To my surprise, Berliner took off his jacket and grabbed a shovel. "Come on. Let's go. Open the oven." Working with unexpected strength for a man his age, shovel after shovel, the trash disappeared. I couldn't believe it. That wasn't all: In the afternoon, he appeared with another man and worked again.

The next day I felt worse. My hand was swollen, my body ached all over, but I persevered and returned to my work. Karolek, sick in the barrack, was resigned to dying. Berliner soon appeared with the same man and went straight to work, stopping only when a German was visible.

Mysteriously, the delivery of fresh trash also slowed down considerably. Had Berliner ordered the flow of trash to be curtailed? I wondered. The results were soon visible. Luckily, no new transports were coming in. At the end of the day the building was clean; even my books went to the fire.

Back in the barrack, Karolek was impatiently waiting for me, for he, too, would pay the price. His face was swollen but clean, and his friend had applied a bandage. His one eye peered at me with quiet acquiescence.

"Karolek, it's okay. We made it," I reassured him. And I told him how Berliner had continued to help until it was done.

I was grateful to Berliner, but I couldn't understand why he did it. He turned against many of his friends, yet he helped me. I remember him telling me once that he had arrived at Sobibor with a close relative my age. Maybe he helped me because I reminded him of his relative, now lost forever.

It was time for roll call. The whistle sounded again, and the row of prisoners stood at attention. After the last roll call of the day, there was the customary penal report to the Germans. I told the Kapo about my duty to report to Wagner. My heart was pounding uncontrollably. When my turn came, I stood nonchalantly in front of this rabid murderer and calmly reported, "Herr Oberscharführer, the job in the incinerator is completed."

Berliner acknowledged that it was so, and I was dismissed. It was over. My life was saved, temporarily.

Death of the Traitor

When I returned to Izbica from the Stryj ghetto in April, I learned, to my dismay, that the pages from my diary I had given to my teacher,

Mr. Śliwa, before my journey vanished when he was taken to Auschwitz. I summarized the missing events and started a new journal. Most entries were only short notes. Being afraid of a sudden roundup, I kept them in my pants pocket together with the telegram from the Stryj Jewish Hospital informing my parents about my death. Because the roundup on April 28 was sudden, I did not have time to give the pages to gentile friends for safekeeping. They wound up with me in Sobibor.

Even in Sobibor I never thought of my papers as useless, and I kept on writing. Because my work at this time was disposing of trash, the safest place to keep my diary was hidden in the heaps of papers and documents I burned daily. But now that everything had been burned and the premises were clean, I again kept the diary in my pocket—that is, until the next transport filled up the bins once more.

Every once in a while, the well that supplied the Germans' drinking water developed a funny smell. In such cases, SS Wagner called prisoners to empty the well. If one was so unlucky as to be in his line of sight, nothing was left to do but to run toward him. It didn't matter if he called only three or five prisoners; everyone in sight would run, stopping in terror a few feet in front of him, afraid that he would suspect them of being lazy.

One evening I had the misfortune to be in the yard at such a time, and I was taken to the deep well. Two ladders tied together at the ends were lowered into the well, a few buckets thrown in, and the prisoners were ordered to jump down. Other prisoners, on the ladder, passed the buckets full of water from one to the other, and above us stood the worst murderer and sadist of all, SS Gustav Wagner.

If the bucket didn't come out in a flash, continually and rhythmically, and if it did not descend in the same manner, there would be trouble. Wagner simply threw the metal buckets down the well, not caring whether they hit someone on the head. And it was unforgivable if the bucket sank. The guilty one no longer had a reason to come back up. If he did, he was beaten to a pulp or pushed back down and drowned. I worked for about three hours, and luckily was only bruised, bleeding, and exhausted.

The pain was excruciating, but added to my sorrow was the discovery that the pages of my diary were soaked, ruined beyond repair. And with them my "promise," my guarantee—the letter from the hospital in Stryj reporting my death to my parents. My father's words were always in my subconscious: "You will survive the war. When somebody is mistakenly declared dead while he is still alive, it means the opposite. You will live a long and healthy life."

In the summer of 1943, transports from Holland arrived regularly. The victims' belongings were routinely loaded onto waiting trains for shipment outside the camp. When engaged in this loading procedure, the Germans, Ukrainians, and Kapos formed a human alley from the storeroom to the train, through which the prisoners were forced to run, carrying packages of clothing on their backs.

It was exhausting. Many of us collapsed, but Berliner was elated. Always breathing down our necks, he screamed at us sadistically and beat us as we ran with our heavy loads: "Maybe you are tired, maybe you want to sleep? Maybe you need help?" Even the Germans adopted his way of mocking us. Our hatred of Berliner was intense.

A couple of weeks later, a heat wave struck the area, and high humidity only made it worse. Although there were only small, irregular clouds in the blue sky over Sobibor, dark clouds in the east and the murmur of distant thunder announced an approaching storm. I was sweltering, working in the heat of the incinerator, and felt an irresistible urge to sneak off to a spot I had noticed once before while loading hay onto a cart. I thought I could get a few moments of rest there.

I figured I could slip away from the incinerator without danger, since my old partner, Szmul Wajcen, now worked with me again. He was very sharp, and I could trust him to explain my temporary absence with a good excuse. We all understood that here rest wasn't only rest; it was essential for survival.

Passing the sorting area, I slipped through the gate to the disrobing yard, and went beyond it to the food warehouse. I was a bit scared, for it was directly opposite SS Beckmann's office. Carefully looking to see that no one was close by, I slipped quickly inside the building. Immediately to the left of the entrance were narrow steps. Racing up a few steps at a time, I found myself in the attic. It was quiet, and there was the sweet smell of hay. A strong ray of light cut sharply into the darkness through a small louvered window. I stood there for a long time, gasping at the beauty of the countryside, the loveliness outside Sobibor.

Suddenly I heard steps. I slipped into the darkness and shivered, waiting. There was no place to hide and, anyway, it was too late. My eyes were fixed on the entrance. It was Berliner. I held my breath. A flashlight beam wandered around the attic and finally fell on me.

Again we stood face to face. I hadn't spoken to him, or even thanked him, since he helped me in the incinerator. Though he had hit me once with the whip since then, as I ran with others loading packages onto the train, this was a random attack and in the presence of Germans. Would this new transgression be too much for him?

He stood before me with his flashlight shining in my face. As if recovering from shock, he shut off the flashlight and whispered, "Toivi, what's happened to you? Are you crazy, do you want to die?"

Intuitively, I felt that the tie I had with him formerly was still influencing him. "Berliner, listen . . . I'm tired. The heat from the incinerator is unbearable, and I must take a rest, otherwise I'll crack."

"Toivi, I'm too old to be fooled. I know why you come here. For the same reason I come here." He spoke in a quiet voice, and I knew the danger had passed. He had guessed. It was not the food, not the quietness and stillness of the place, not to rest, so much as it was the little attic window, the unlimited sky above it, the golden Polish wheat fields and little cottages with smoking chimneys far beyond, the whistle of swallows in the beams, and longing for scenes of the past. We both stood quietly, looking out the window—not the feared and hated head Kapo and the lonely, frightened slave worker, but simply an older man and a fifteen-year-old boy, consumed with the same feelings.

We went down together. He escorted me to my place of work, and without a word he went away.

During the lunch break, I was dozing on my bunk when a voice awakened me. I immediately snapped out of my sleepiness. From the height of my top bunk, I looked down on the gorillalike figure of Kapo Pożycki directing someone to position a bench in the middle of the barrack.

"Go get Berliner!" he yelled, motioning to a young boy. "He's probably in the women's barracks!"

The messenger ran off and soon returned, alone. "Berliner says he can't come. He's eating."

Pożycki knew what would make him come. "Go again," he said

stubbornly, "and tell him that somebody needs his butt whipped."

It worked. Berliner arrived, smiling and bouncing his whip off his high boots. "Well, now," he said, looking around, "who lies down?"

Pożycki closed in, grabbed him by the collar, and yelled, "You, butcher, you lie down!"

"You're joking!" said the Governor weakly, forcing a laugh.

Pożycki kicked him toward the bench. "Lie down, I said!"

Shocked, Berliner lay down over the bench. This demigod of life and death was now sobbing like a baby, pleading for mercy. He would have happily conceded to any of our wishes, anything to prevent him from being flayed by that leather-covered wire coil, the same whip he used to cripple other prisoners.

One man sat on Berliner's neck, forcing him to lie on his stomach, while another held his legs crossed under the bench so he couldn't move. "Count fifty!"

Each of the three Kapos (Pożycki, Bunio, and a Dutch Kapo) gave him fifty lashes. The onlookers were surprised and shocked by the scene, but then a wild excitement overcame them and they joined the lynching.

I watched from my bunk. Berliner was shrieking for pity. "Did you have pity on us?" they answered. Using his own words with the same ironic intonation, they mimicked, "Are you tired? Would you like to sleep? Can I help you in any way?"

At last, when it looked like he was lifeless, they eased their hold. But he was strong. He hadn't worked hard in Sobibor, and he'd had good food. Unexpectedly, he got up and tried to walk to his room. He was returned to the bench and again beaten without pity. This time, to finish him off, he was hit in the liver with the hard handle of the whip, but he held on to life. Suddenly SS Wagner appeared in the yard. Before he could be seen, Berliner was whisked to the Kapos' room.

At evening roll call, Pożycki, in Berliner's place, reported to the German commander that Berliner was ill. Then he ordered Symcha Białowicz, who worked in the medicine warehouse, to prepare a strong poison, which was mixed with tasteful kasha. The next day, during the morning roll call, Berliner's body lay in front of the column, wrapped in a gray blanket. This time Pożycki reported that "the Governor died from an acute illness." Some said later that SS Frenzel, taking the report, winked at Kapo Pożycki and ordered the body to be burned immediately.

It seemed that everything happened with Frenzel's approval. He never forgave Berliner, because Berliner made a basic mistake when he betrayed the Kapos' escape attempt. Instead of reporting the case to Frenzel, who was directly responsible for Lager I, Berliner went over Frenzel's head by talking to SS Wagner. Afraid to be in conflict with his higher-ranking comrade, Frenzel himself did not punish Berliner.

Also, the Kapos fed Frenzel fictitious stories of Berliner's arrogance, such as how he prided himself on being more important than SS Frenzel. Whatever the circumstances, it appeared that Frenzel had given his permission for Berliner's murder.

The few Kapos who had survived Berliner's betrayal took their revenge. All prisoners were relieved at the hated head Kapo's demise.

Transports from the East

For some time again there had been a lull in transports. Food was scarce, and we were hungry, because we previously supplemented our diet with the food we found in the luggage of new arrivals. Suddenly the Nazis ordered us to prepare for a transport that would arrive the next day. Somewhere on the distant rails of Poland, a doomed train was rolling toward Sobibor.

Karolek turned toward me and said, "Tomorrow there will be plenty of food."

I thought: Are we still humans?

Again Sobibor received victims day and night. Now the long trains came mostly from the ghettos of Eastern Poland and the Soviet Union. In September, close to fourteen thousand came from Wilno, Lida, and the Mińsk area alone. These Jews brought no luggage, just some small packages of food—usually bread and onions.

For the next four days, similar transports arrived. The workload was overwhelming; we didn't have a moment to think. The warehouses were again filled to capacity, and the sky over Sobibor darkened from the low-hanging smoke.

One morning, on September 23, 1943, one of these transports stopped at the Sobibor platform. I was curious, I wanted a closer look, so I picked up the hoe with which I mixed the burning material for better combustion and moved toward Lager I. If stopped, I would just say that, with the Kapo's permission, I was going to exchange it in the blacksmith's shop because of the charred end.

Instead of moving closer to the west side of the camp, which was the regular route to Lager I, I walked slowly along the eastern fences, in a direct line with the visible platform. I had never been on the platform when other transports arrived and was curious about the proceedings. Halfway, I stopped and pretended to remove a pebble from my shoe.

All the Nazis were on the platform. I wasn't able to hear any normal conversations, but Frenzel's and Gomerski's loud and wild commands easily reached me. The other Nazis were surrounding the Jews with outstretched rifles and machine guns. "Carpenters and builders, step out!" yelled Frenzel.

They needed new prison labor. God only knew when it would end. As expected in such situations, the prisoners grabbed the opportunity. It was always better to be needed. They began to push forward chaotically, just as they did when I arrived in Sobibor, and this did not please the Germans' sense of order. Swinging his whip, Gomerski beat the people. Finally, a group of young Jews, mostly those in some kind of uniform, were taken out. The rest began to move northward in the usual way—toward the gas chambers.

Suddenly SS Frenzel came down from the platform and walked in my direction. It was too late to disappear, and I pretended to be at work with my hoe.

"What are you doing here?"

I'm going on the Kapo's order to the blacksmith to exchange the hoe."

"I have seen you standing."

"Only to remove a pebble from my sandal."

SS Frenzel stared in my eyes, contemplating for a moment, then he grabbed a two-by-four. I threw away the hoe and covered my head with my hands, but the blow fell on my right side under my ribs. Immediately I felt short of breath, and, knowing that the next blow would probably kill me, I started to run toward the gate of Lager I. I don't remember now, but I probably ran past the startled guard toward my barrack; once inside, I fell down on the lower bunk.

Kurt, the orderly, was in the barrack. I wasn't able to speak, so with my eyes I begged him for help. Kurt's only answer was, "He is coming. God help you."

Frenzel was standing over me, the two-by-four still in his hand.

The end is coming, I thought, and I was prepared. To be in the wrong place in Sobibor means death, and to run from an SS without permission was unheard of. As if from another world, I heard a voice saying, "How do you feel?"

"It hurts," I heard myself saying.

"Rest little one. Then back to work." And with this he left.

Kurt stood for a moment in shock and disbelief, then left, returning in a moment with a cup of cold water. Although my side hurt, my bones were intact, and soon I felt strong enough to leave the barrack. It was a dangerous place to be during working hours. I entered Szlomo Szmajzner's blacksmith shop, and while preparing a new hoe, I told him about the selection on the platform.

In no time the selected group arrived and was left in the middle of the yard. Kurt, notepad in hand, took names and allocated bunks in a huge, newly built barrack.

I eyed the newcomers with suspicion. Who were they? Some of them had uniforms. Their coats were loose and unbelted, and on their caps were imprints left by Soviet five-pointed stars.

Soon they left the barracks and moved about in groups in the yard. I was still curious, so, despite the danger of my unauthorized presence, I stayed in the blacksmith shop waiting for some news. Only Kurt had had any contact with them. Hearing Szlomo call, he turned and entered the workshop.

"Kurt, who are they?" asked Szlomo.

Being from Czechoslovakia, Kurt understood Russian perfectly, but the information he had was scant. The "Russians" were Jewish Soviet POWs who had been sent to the Minsk ghetto and later, with other Jews, to Sobibor.

By now it was close to the lunch break; in half an hour we would be counted, and I could be missed. I had to return to my work at the incinerator. In no time I was back with a new hoe.

The Nazis made a critical blunder that later proved fatal for them. Sobibor Jews to date were untrained in the art of warfare, but in the group of newly selected men were Soviet soldiers, including some high-ranking officers. Despite their time in the ghetto, their spirit seemed unbroken. Many had heard of the German defeat at Stalingrad, had heard the German Army was retreating from Soviet territory, and knew that the enemy was not invincible.

That same evening, the new prisoners watched in shock as the flames shot up in the sky. They knew the truth.

Kali Mali

The next day Kapo Pożycki ordered about a hundred of us to move into the new barrack with the "Russians." I was among those selected, and from experience I sought out the best place—in a corner on a top bunk, far from the front doors, where prisoners could be immediately exposed to intruding Germans or Kapos. There I came in contact with my first Russian Jew, a man nicknamed Kali Mali. He was short and dark, had a long face with burning black eyes, and spoke only Russian. He was at least ten years older than I was. He reminded me of my Uncle Jankel, the storyteller.

Although we couldn't write in Russian, most Poles could easily communicate in other Slavic languages. Noticing the "Russian" group sleeping on sparsely outfitted bunks, I approached Kali Mali and asked if he would like a blanket, or better still, if he would like to move next to me. He hesitated at first, but after talking a while, he said "Harascho" [good]. I made the arrangements. I promised the prisoner next to me some vodka if he would move to another bunk. He agreed, and the Russian took his place.

Kali Mali was a poet and a dreamer. His real name was Alexander Schubayev; he was a railroad engineer from Donbas (Ukraine). We talked until late in the night. I told him the Sobibor story, and although he was already aware of the overall purpose and function of the camp, the details shattered him. Exhausted, I fell asleep.

I heard a voice saying, "Toivi . . ." No matter how tired I felt, I was always immediately alert, a necessary condition for survival.

"What is it, Kali?"

"You told me that many people come here with their tools of trade."

"Yes?"

"What do they do with them?"

"Some we use here. The rest they send out."

"Toivi, can you bring me a balalaika? For sure musicians have come here, too."

"I haven't seen a balalaika, Kali, but I can bring you a guitar from the Dutch transports."

"Bring me one."

Over the next couple of days I had orders to fill: a guitar and vodka. Although the sorting groups sometimes found vodka in the victims' belongings, none ever reached my incinerator.

When transports arrived, we stole food from the victims' provisions. Nevertheless, some of the prisoners risked their lives by bartering with the Ukrainian guards, exchanging gold jewelry (taken when sorting the victims' clothing) for sausage and vodka. Such risky behavior may seem baffling, yet this deadly game served a psychological purpose for some people, as I found out myself when I tried it.

After the next transport passed through the alley to the gas chambers, I grabbed a rake and attached myself to a small group of prisoners who were cleaning the debris from the passage. I had always been hurried through this section at night, on our way to the haircutting barrack further on. I had never seen the Road to Heaven, as the Nazis called it, in the daylight.

It was shocking. Every step in the sand told a story of defiance, cries for help, footprints never to be seen again. Hundreds of steps evened out in every pull of the rake, the large steps of adults and the small steps of children; the one-legged steps of invalids held up by friends; the long, dragging mark of somebody being pulled, a cripple perhaps, whose prosthetic devices were left in the undressing yard, or someone who had fainted.

And mixed with the other debris left behind were some very finely torn red and green particles that slipped through the teeth of the rake. I bent down to pick up the pieces. It was money. The red seemed to be Soviet paper currency and the green American dollars.

So they had no illusions. Some realized that this was the end and their last act was one of defiance. Naked and powerless, on the way to their deaths, they methodically destroyed what little they had left so that the Germans could not profit. I understood how they thought and felt. They were heroes in their own way.

There were also signs of hope. From under my rake, I pulled out a few pieces of paper. One read: "People, my name is Perlmutter from Wilno. Give my brother the message that Natasza was here." Such notes were similar to those thrown from the wagons of transports crisscrossing Poland on the way to the death camps, in the vain hope of informing loved ones of their destiny.

So as not to arouse suspicion, I collected debris by the fence, then moved close to where a Ukrainian guard was standing. I had never dealt with the guards before and decided to take a chance with a stranger, hoping he would not shoot me immediately, or worse, deliver me to the Germans. As if understanding, the guard came closer.

"Would you bring me a bottle of vodka and kielbasa?" I asked.

He answered simply, "Under the bush here . . . when a transport arrives," his lips barely moving.

"All right," I said, and moved on.

On the way back to the incinerator, I realized we had not agreed on the price, but it was too dangerous to return to the alley when the work had already been finished.

As I arrived at the incinerator, I could see everything was running smoothly. A dark cloud of smoke was coming out of the incinerator chimney. Szmul had been moved to another job, and because Karolek was keeping the fire fed, evidence that our work was proceeding, no Nazi came around to check.

An hour before work ended, I went to see Josef Duniec. He was a Polish Jew who had emigrated to France and been brought in a French transport to Sobibor, where he became an Underground member.[11] He was not a Kapo, but for a time he was in charge of a work group in Lager II. He was a decent person, and in the past we had worked together sorting clothing. I found him in the men's clothing warehouse and called him aside.

"Josef, is it possible to get a guitar for Lager I?"

"Toivi, are you crazy? A guitar?"

"We have musicians among us. They play instruments in the evenings. What's wrong with a guitar, Josef?"

"But only with the Nazis' permission!"

"Josef, the Germans wouldn't remember if they allowed a guitar or not. Anyway, I promised it to one of the Russians. Just tell me where the instruments are stored."

"All right, I'll take you there, but I will have nothing more to do with it." I thanked him and followed. Right behind the canned food storeroom was a separate section. Hanging from the ceiling, like an inverted forest, were violins and guitars. On the floor were boxes full of harmonicas, stacks of accordions, and many other instruments. I picked a guitar in fairly good condition, similar to one I had seen in my grandmother's home, and asked the girl working there to put it aside for me.

I had a plan. When the next transport arrived I would attach myself to the group transferring shoes from the undressing yard to the shoe storeroom between Lagers I and II. With that first step done, I would look for my next opportunity.

It arrived two days later with a transport of about a thousand people. In the incinerator building, I pushed aside collected trash and reached for a hidden paper box. Inside I kept some gold watches, coins, and jewelry. Now I picked out a new gold watch, put it in my pocket, and waited until the rakers were called to the alley. In the alley, I moved close to the bush were I was to collect the booty from the Ukrainian guard. There was a different guard now, but he winked knowingly, as if he had been informed about me.

"It's all there," he said softly, and moved away.

As if I were picking up trash, I reached with my hand and felt a bottle and a kielbasa. With the guard's back to me to obstruct the view, I put the bottle and kielbasa inside my trousers and made sure the belt kept everything secure. In return, I placed the gold watch under the bush.

I was excited and felt strange. The guard, who was my enemy and of whom I was supposed to be afraid, was human. I could see in his eyes that he was even more frightened than I was. While I was trying to postpone my death here, he was free. But now he was on my level— for a short time, we were both afraid of the same enemy. I now felt I had power over my oppressor, and it made me feel good. I was not just a "Nassen sack" (wet sack), as they called us; he had to reckon with me.

After a while the work in the alley was finished. With my shirt pulled out over my pants and my belt tightened, there was no sign of my cargo. I went to the sorters and picked up a blanket with food-stuffs for delivery to the storeroom.

At this time the Germans were usually on the transport-unload-ing platform and the Kapos supervised in their absence. With no Germans in sight, their oversight was less rigorous, as long as every-one kept moving. So when I had completed the delivery of the food,

I entered the music section of the nearby storeroom and threw the guitar into the empty blanket.

With no time to be wasted, I mingled with the shoe gatherers and collected shoes that were lying around. I threw them into the blanket with the guitar. When the blanket was full, I hoisted it onto my back and left for the shoe storage with the others. There I threw the shoes onto a heap for sorting and made sure the guitar was left in the blanket.

Behind the barracks were heaps of pots and pans. Initially I thought of hiding the instrument there until I had a chance to retrieve it. But then I thought: Why should I do this piecemeal, first smuggling in the vodka and kielbasa and then later the guitar? For each discovery I could be punished by death. Why take the risk more than once? So I loaded a blanket full of pots and pans and proceeded to carry out the last and most dangerous part of my smuggling operation. I walked as casually as I could past the guard at the gate of Lager I.

"What have you got there?"

"I'm bringing pots to the kitchen." He glanced at the pots and pans protruding from the top of the blanket and let me pass.

When I got to the kitchen Cukerman asked, "What's this?"

"Extra pots for the Soviet newcomers."

"OK, dump them at the back of the kitchen until suppertime."

I had succeeded so far. Now it should be easy to hide my stuff in the barrack. We had a sand floor, and it would be easy to dig a hole and bury the vodka and kielbasa. I hid the guitar under the blanket on my bunk. It was safe for today. I ran back to the incinerator.

After the evening roll call, I delivered the vodka and kielbasa to my former bunkmate, Mojsze. This account was settled. As for Kali Mali, I had seen him in the women's barrack, busily talking with a tall woman, and I didn't want to disturb him. I waited for him in my bunk. At nine o'clock that evening he arrived.

I have your guitar," I said, and pulled out the instrument.

"Unbelievable!"

I had forgotten the pick, but he used his nails, and a few notes flew in the air. It was uncomfortable sitting in the bunk, and we slipped down to the floor. Someone brought a chair, and Kali touched the strings again.

I still remember the songs he sang—"Dark Eyes," and songs of soldiers longing to return to their loved ones—and even now I treasure my records of those familiar tunes. After so many years, I can still see his sorrowful face and hear his melodic voice, just as it was then.

Sadness is all around me,
The road ahead is cheerless,
The past seems to be a dream
That torments my sore heart.
There were only lies and deception.
Gone are the dreams and peace.
But the pain of unhealed wounds
Will stay forever with me.
Coachman, don't ride the horses so hard.
I have nowhere to rush . . .

Scourge and Sanctity

As if there were not enough brutality, SS Wagner created the notorious Straffkommando (penal brigade). For any wrongdoing, a prisoner was sentenced to three days in this commando. In actuality, this was a death sentence—a slow death with terrible suffering. A Jew in the Straffkommando was marked with red patches on the chest and back. He worked an eighteen-hour day. Only a few minutes intermission was given for water and bread, to be taken standing. The few hours of sleep were often interrupted with roll calls.

The work was terrible and senseless. Prisoners were forced to run, beyond their endurance, carrying heavy rocks from one place to another. All the while they were savagely beaten. Even the worst Kapos felt sorry for the unfortunates. Though new prisoners filled the Straffkommando, the total never increased. No one sentenced to the seventy-two hours ever survived the ordeal.

In spite of our subhuman working and living conditions in a place seemingly accursed and abandoned by God, I watched couples fall in love, care deeply about one another, grow jealous, and experience all the "normal" feelings of men and women.

Still others sought fulfillment through their faith. They searched in the victims' belongings for prayer books, held daily services, and observed Jewish law as strictly as possible. On every holy day small groups of pious Jews gathered. One cantor from Turobin hid behind piles of clothing and valises to pray daily with the others, ignoring the potential danger of getting caught. At risk of their lives, a few prisoners had found and saved rice for the traditional meal preceding the Yom Kippur fast. On the eve of Yom Kippur, they came to my incinerator and begged me to boil it for them.

Sealed off from the rest of the world, we were thirsty for true information. The Soviet Jews infused us with hope and a vision of Hitler's defeat. Although we were sure we would not live to see it, it was good to know that the Nazis' end would soon come and that someone would avenge us.

There was proof: SS Oberscharführer Graetschus, now commandant of the Ukrainian guards, returned from leave in Germany with wounds inflicted during an air attack that occurred on his way to Sobibor. His hand was bandaged.

My fellow prisoners already knew from the last Izbica transport about the Warsaw ghetto uprising in which Jews stood up against German tanks and the enemy retreated. Now we heard news of the German defeat on the Eastern Front 350 miles away; we grew confident of an Allied victory.

It was now the end of September 1943. The Sobibor Nazis sensed their desperate situation and felt nervous, just as we prisoners gained courage. One day when ordered to sing, instead of the usual German army songs, the Russian Jews started with a Soviet air force song, and most of the rest of us joined in. The Ukranian guards were infuriated. "Halt!" they cried. Then they commanded in quick succession: "Lie down!" "Get up!" "Lie down!" "Crawl!" "Get up!" "Run!" This penal exercise went on until we were unable to breathe. We had hit them in a sensitive spot.

The stream of oncoming transports began to subside. Yet the fires howled day and night, continuing to burn the old corpses. Then, one day after lunch, when we were ready to march to our work stations, we were ordered not to move. Outside the barbed wire, every ten yards or so, Ukrainian guards stood with rifles at the ready. From every watchtower a machine gun covered us. We were kept standing hour after hour. This was strange.

At about 3:00 P.M., we heard gunfire coming from Lager III: at regular intervals two shots rang out. At first we paid little attention, but when the shooting went on for twenty minutes without stopping, we realized what was happening. They were liquidating the prisoners in the crematorium site! The day had finally arrived. We would be next! We stood quietly, terrorized by the SS guards and the barrels of machine guns.

Finally the shooting stopped. While still under guard, we were ordered to go back to our work. That same evening the proof of our fear was confirmed: the clothing of those executed was delivered to us for sorting.

The rumors, probably started by the Nazis to pacify us, were that the Jews attempted an escape by digging an underground tunnel. For this they were executed. Soon afterward, they selected from among us thirty prisoners to replenish the 150 Jews in Lager III who had been killed.

The Underground Organization

We knew our fate. We knew that we were in an extermination camp and death was our destiny. We knew that even a sudden end to the war might spare the inmates of the "normal" concentration camps, but never us. Only desperate actions could shorten our suffering and maybe afford us a chance of escape. And the will to resist had grown and ripened. We had no dreams of liberation; we hoped merely to destroy the camp and to die from bullets rather than from gas. We would not make it easy for the Germans.

Amid despair, the core of a conspiracy came into being. The leader was Leon Feldhendler, a thirty-three-year-old flour mill worker, a rabbi's son, and former head of the Judenrat of Zólkiewka, a small city in eastern Poland.

Although I was not yet in the tightly knit circle of the conspirators, I knew everything that was going on. Szmul's older brother was in the group; he kept his brother informed, and Szmul in turn informed me.

With the arrival of the eastern transports, Leon immediately seized upon the opportunity to recruit trained military officers into the Underground. His attention fell upon a tall man, thirty-five years old, who still wore his Red Army lieutenant's uniform. This was Alexander (Sasha) Aronowich Pechersky from Rostov-on-Don.[12] After a period of observation, the Underground contacted Sasha.

On September 29, a transport of Jews from Białystok arrived but wasn't able to enter Sobibor because the loading platform was taken up by a freight train full of bricks, probably to be used for the expansion of the camp. Prisoners were quickly lined up to toss bricks hand to hand from the train to a site about two hundred yards away. As always, humiliating and indiscriminate whippings accompanied the work. A brick slipped and fell on my friend Mendl's leg and broke it. As if he were a useless horse, SS Wagner shot him.

The same evening I observed Leon and Sasha talking casually outside the women's barrack.

On October 7, Sasha, under the pretext of a date with pretty eighteen-year-old Luka in the women's barrack, received from Leon detailed information about the camp—security, daily routine, topography, and Nazi personnel. Sasha presented his ideas for the operation. Possibilities were discussed and plans outlined. From this time on, various escape projects were analyzed in rapid succession.

One proposal was to dig a tunnel under the barbed wire and minefields, originating under the stove in the cabinet shop and extending to the outside for a distance of about thirty-eight yards. After some calculation this plan was rejected. The odds against it were overwhelming, not the least of which was the impossibility of 550 people crawling out through a narrow tunnel unnoticed in the still of the night. Other plans were also deemed unacceptable.

On October 9, Szmul told me that Leon Feldhendler would like to talk to me after work. We had only spoken occasionally; despite Leon's friendship with my father in Izbica, where he had lived for a while, we were not close.

When I met Leon that evening, he took me aside, and after some small talk, he got down to business and asked me if I could keep a secret. I promised. Then he explained the current situation and asked about the layout of the trash-burning compound. He told me that tomorrow at work I should stack some trash against the windows to obstruct visibility and allow Kali Mali to enter whenever he came.

The Plan

On the evening of October 10, the core of the organization had a meeting in the carpenter's shop. Despite some objections, it was necessary to include Kapos Pożycki and Bunio in the conspiracy, especially as Pożycki was suspicious already. Also, the plan could be carried out much more easily with their help. With their authority, the safe movement of the operational groups to targets in different sections of the camp was more likely to succeed.

A record player played old Russian folk songs while the conspirators quietly talked, their voices inaudible over the music. A consolidated command was formed, and though Leon was the initiator and head of the conspiring group, at this point Sasha assumed full responsibility for technical planning and military matters. The crucial element was strictly enforced secrecy, not only to keep the Germans from discovering the plan, but to keep fellow prisoners from discovering as well. The planning took into consideration the Germans' brashness and power-hungry mistreatment of the seemingly subdued Jews, their consistent and systematic daily routine, their unfaltering punctuality, and their greed. Simply stated, the plan involved the secret killing of as many Nazis and Ukrainians as possible within a period of one hour maximum.

A heavy responsibility was placed on the few who, because of their work, had authorized entry to places vital to the Underground. The *putzers* (young Jews selected by the Nazis to serve as valets) and girls who sorted the captured Soviet ammunition in Lager IV were in charge of stealing ammunition, if possible. Combat groups of three persons each were established, including a detachment for an attack on the armory. They would be armed with knives and axes, specially prepared by the carpentry and blacksmith shops to fit inconspicuously under their belts and be covered by their jackets. The Germans would be enticed with promises of quality leather coats and boots. The tailor and cobbler shops would lure the Nazis for fittings in a series of appointments that were synchronized to enable executions every few minutes.

The gate leading from Lager II, where most of the prisoners worked, would be closed to passage except for members of the Underground. Setting the camp on fire while escaping, although discussed by some privately, was not seriously considered for obvious reasons.

At the time of the breakout, the prisoners had to be in Lager I preparing for roll call. To keep our elimination of the SS secret until the last minute, nothing unusual could take place.

Phase One would start between 3:30 and 4:00 P.M. It would be a period of preparation, with no exceptional danger expected. This phase would last about half an hour. The knives and axes would be distributed and the assassination squads posted in ambush by Kapos Pożycki and Bunio.

Phase Two provided for the actual elimination of the SS. It would last sixty critical minutes, from 4:00 P.M. until 5:00 P.M. During that time all accessible Germans would be secretly eliminated. Everything depended on discreet and prompt execution. SS men supervising certain work groups were free to leave at this time. Thus, if a Nazi should fail to see his already murdered comrade at his post, he would not be unduly alarmed. The preliminary elimination of the Nazis required silent weapons only. So as not to betray the operation, pistols acquired from the assassinated enemy were not to be used at this stage. Above all, it was imperative that no visible changes in the daily rhythm be noticed. Leon even urged the Kapos to make use of their whips as usual. It was decided that a fellow Jew could be killed if he threatened the security of the revolt. If everything went well, the prisoners, led by the Kapos, would return to Lager I just as they had done daily at 5:00.

The outcome of Phase Three—the open revolt—depended on the number of Nazis killed, weapons at the prisoners' disposal, and the effect of surprise on the guards in the camp and in the towers.

Now back in Lager I, the rest should be quickly informed and prepared to fight. At this time, the camp's electric generator would be put out of service by the electrician, Walter Schwarz, a German Jew.

Even a minute's delay past 5:45 P.M. could destroy the chances for success of the revolt. While the disappearance of a SS from his post would not worry his colleagues earlier, now the Nazis would begin to gather in the prisoners' yard for the head count. The surviving Germans could then easily detect the inexplicable disappearance of their henchmen.

Kapo Pożycki would blow the whistle for roll call a bit earlier than usual. The prisoners would form a column, but instead of waiting for the Germans, they would be led by the Kapos in regular formation toward the main gate. The idea was that, without the key Nazis around, the guards would think the Germans had ordered us to march for some work assignment, and this would allow the prisoners to come as close as possible to the main gate without arousing suspicion.

When passing the armory, a special group would detach and assault it by surprise. Next, a couple dozen feet farther on, the strongly secured main gate would be taken by storm and the guards overpowered. Then, while fighting, they would yell to the Ukrainians not to shoot, that Stalin was winning the war, urging them to escape with us while they were able.

If some problem developed and the plans needed to be changed, everything would have to be played by ear. If the conspiracy was prematurely exposed, the fight would begin accordingly. To avoid the mined area, Pechersky suggested that the main route of escape be through the fences close to the Germans' housing, assuming, and rightly so, that this particular area would have only signal mines. In any case, sticks and stones were to be thrown to detonate the mines. In the carpenter's shop, some ladders were prepared to reach over the fences.

Because of the memory of earlier failed escape attempts, especially Berliner's betrayal, the number of conspirators involved was kept to an absolute minimum. Out of a total of about 550 Jews alive at the time, fewer than 10 percent had any knowledge of the escape plan. Also, to the organizers' dismay, there was no possibility of contacting Lager III, where about thirty Jews were now working. They would have to be left behind. The escape date was set for October 13.

On October 11, another small transport from the east arrived and soon a volley of shots and screams was heard coming from Lager III. We were all ordered to stay in our workplaces and not look out. But soon it became clear that the newest victims, already undressed and realizing what would happen to them, had resisted and were running naked to the fences. Many were killed on the run; the rest were captured and executed.

That same day SS Frenzel returned from vacation in Germany and soon inspected the barracks. A few Jews were lying on the bunks sick. Such "malingering" infuriated him, and he chased them with his whip into the yard and escorted them to the gas chambers. For some reason he spared the only woman, Selma Wijnberg, and ordered her to return to work.

One of the condemned was a young Dutch man whose mother, a

Viennese, was a favorite among the SS men in the camp because her beautiful yodeling was appreciated by SS Wagner, himself an Austrian. When she saw her son being led away, she threw herself on him, screaming and calling the Nazis murderers and scum. Refusing to leave him, she supported her weak boy to Lager III, where they perished together.

SS Haupsturmführer Reichleitner and SS Gomerski had been out of the camp for a few days. Now, with SS Frenzel back, it was SS Wagner's turn for vacation, and the next day, October 12, Wagner was seen leaving with stuffed suitcases. Wagner's departure gave us a tremendous morale boost. While cruel, he was also very intelligent. Always on the go, he could suddenly show up in the most unexpected places. Always suspicious and snooping, he was difficult to fool. Besides, his colossal stature and strength would make it very difficult for us to overcome him with our primitive weapons. We needed him out of the way.

October 13 arrived. This would be our day of revenge. After workday started, I sneaked into the men's clothing warehouse and outfitted myself with winter underwear and a warm coat; then I waited excitedly for things to happen. Close to noon, I heard some whistles and loud noises coming from the Nazi garrison area. I was terrified. We are betrayed, everything is lost, I thought.

I soon found out that, unexpectedly, German SS soldiers from the nearby labor camp Osowa had arrived at Sobibor. At first it was feared that the conspiracy had been betrayed, but when laughter and drunken singing were heard, it was understood that this was a friendly visit from Nazi cohorts. Nevertheless, the action was called off. The guests could reinforce the enemy manpower, and the German appointments in the shops would be questionable. Arrangements were hastily made by the heads of the shops to reschedule the appointments with the main SS staff members for the next day. Luckily, this was accomplished without a hitch.

At an emergency meeting that evening, the conspirators seemed depressed and apprehensive. They saw the incident as a bad omen, and the following day was Succoth, a religious holiday. However, Leon, the son of a rabbi, agreed there should be no delay. The revolt would take place the following day, on the same timetable. Knives, hatchets, small axes, and warm clothing were distributed.

Revolt

On October 14, 1943, the sun rose slowly over the horizon. It would be a warm day. SS Oberscharführer Bauer drove out to Chełm for supplies. The remaining Nazis in the camp went about their business as usual. Only a small group of Jews knew that this was to be a fateful day.

After the midday roll call, Kapo Pożycki, as planned, used his authority to take several conspirators—Sasha Pechersky, Siemion Rosenfeld, Boris Cybulski, Kali Mali, and Arkady Wajspapier—out of their normal work detachment and transfer them to Lager I. They assembled in the cabinetmaker's shop and set up headquarters.

At about 2:00 P.M., SS Unterscharführer Walter Ryba entered Lager I with a machine gun and took out four Jews, including Kapo Pożycki. Had there been a betrayal? A short time later Kapo Bunio arrived and reported that Pożycki and the others were taken to work in Lager IV, temporarily piling wood. The Nazi had been armed with a machine gun only because he had been the sole guard of these Jews.

At precisely 4:00 P.M. the stage was set. Now everything depended on the nerve of the attackers, their faith in themselves, and a lot of luck. Since Commandant SS Reichleitner was absent, Untersturmführer Niemann was the acting commandant. He would be the first to be killed. Shubayev and Yehuda Lerner were waiting in the tailor shop in Lager I with their axes hidden.

A few minutes earlier than appointed, Niemann rode up on his beautiful white horse. Dreszer, the twelve-year-old putzer, ran up to hold the harness. Niemann entered the tailor shop. Mundek the tailor was ready, holding the new uniform. The German, without suspicion, unhooked his belt with its pistol in the holster and casually threw it on the table.

As tailors have done for ages, Mundek patted and turned Niemann at his will. Finally he told him to stand still while he marked the alterations with crayon. Then a terrible blow fell from behind. The Nazi dropped like a fallen tree, his head split.

Lerner stood for a second with the bloody ax in his hand, then struck again. Unexpectedly, the cap maker standing by broke down and began to stab the dead body hysterically with his scissors, calling out the names of his wife and children killed in Sobibor. When no one could quiet him, he was gagged and put in a closet. Niemann's body was taken to another room, and the bloody floor was cleaned with rags. The horse whinnied as if it sensed something wrong, and Dreszer took him to the stables. Shubayev rushed to Sasha's quarters to deliver the first pistol. There was now no turning back.

In turn, SS Oberscharführer Siegfried Graetschus, the German then in charge of the Ukrainian guards, arrived at the cobbler shop to pick up his order. He was asked by Yitzhak Lichtman, the cobbler, to sit down and was helped to remove his boots so as to try on the new ones. While Yitzhak held the Nazi's leg in a firm grip, pulling off the boots, Wajspapier and Rosenfeld slipped out of the back room and split the skull of the Nazi with an ax. The cobblers barely had time to hide the body when his deputy, the Ukrainian Klatt, entered, calling the boss to the telephone. He was attacked by the same pair of conspirators and soon joined Graetschus on the floor, dead. Now, with their two prominent commanders dead, the Nazi staff was practically leaderless.

I prepared the incinerator building in Lager II in accordance with Leon's instructions days before. I shoved heaps of unburned documents against the window to obstruct the view.

Impatiently awaiting the arrival of the assassin group, I was looking through the open door. Suddenly I saw Kapo Bunio come in from Lager I with Cybulski, a thirty-five-year-old truck driver from Donbas, and another man I didn't know. I was surprised when the group went past the incinerator and continued toward the warehouses. Soon Sender, a tall Jew from Łódź, came to me and explained the last-minute change and the reason for it. The incinerator was too close to the fence and the guard towers. Even if the assassinations of the SS were successful there, the guard in the towers could become suspicious of the Germans' prolonged disappearance. Instead Sender ordered me to take up a position at the gate leading from Lager II to Lager I to prevent unauthorized persons from leaving their workplaces. If anyone were to ask me why, I was to say it was a German order. This was a very sensitive area close to the warehouse where the killing of some Nazis was planned, and there were many people who could discover the plot and panic.

I dug out from under the trash a beautiful, large, folded knife that I had hidden. It had a pearl-like handle and the Hebrew inscription

Kosher l'Pesach (kosher for Passover), obviously a ritual item. There were many of them in the luggage of the Dutch transports. I opened the blade and pushed the knife under my belt. Next I dug up from my hiding place, under the documents waiting to be burned, the valuables I'd hidden in preparation for escape—a fortune in diamonds, gold, and paper money.

While leaving for the assignment, I noticed in the yard a fourteen-year-old boy, Fibs, standing at attention before SS Unterscharführer Wolf, reporting to him that a brand-new leather coat, exactly his size, had been set aside for him in the men's warehouse. The short, dark-haired Unterscharführer took the bait and went without hesitation in the direction of the warehouse, disappearing inside the huge wooden barrack.

In one of the many partitions of the warehouse, a few "special" prisoners were stocking tied packages against the wall, each containing ten articles of clothing. The bait—the coat—lay to one side.

SS Wolf entered. "Attention!" barked Kapo Bunio. The slaves froze. "Help the Herr Unterscharführer with the coat!" ordered the Kapo.

An inmate fetched the coat and held it for the German. The Nazi put his arm into the sleeve, and in a split second the scenario changed. With a strike of the ax by Cybulski, the enemy fell. They finished him off with knives, and the lifeless body was hidden under piles of the victims' clothing. The blood on the floor was covered with sand. With this done, the executions in Lager II began. The trap awaited the next Nazi.

I took up my position at the gate opposite the warehouse. Soon a prisoner approached to pass the gate. When I stopped him, he started to argue with me. I saw Sender standing nearby and called to him for help. Sender took over, and I went to fetch other Nazis.

At this time the dumpcarts with the food rations were on their way to Lager III. I flagged down SS Scharführer Vallaster, the driver, and told him that SS Wolf needed him urgently. He was led to the same warehouse and killed there.

The motionless carts were standing on the rails near the warehouse, and I stuffed my pockets with canned food. My friend Karolek was amazed and said, "Toivi, you are pretty sure you will survive." I nodded my head in confirmation.

The communications were kept alive by inconspicuous young

couriers. They reported to the staff of the organization on the progress in Lagers I and II. Perfect examples of German punctuality and order, most of the Nazis came at their appointed times for their rendezvous with death. Others were lured to the traps. So far everything was going according to plan.

SS Beckmann was summoned to the warehouse. I observed him approaching. At the doorway of the huge barracks, he stopped, hesitated as if by intuition, then turned around, and, without a word, headed to the administration building, where he had his office.

After Sasha was notified about this hitch, a second emergency group—consisting of Leon Feldheldler, Chaim Engel, and Kapo Pożycki's younger brother—was ready to attack Beckmann. Beckmann's office was small, and he was alone. Still, it was necessary to take him by surprise. Pożycki's brother knocked on the door, asking permission to enter for some clarification. Permission granted, they entered. Expecting only one person, SS Beckmann seemed upset. In seconds the intruders went into action. Caught by surprise, it was too late for him to react. Pożycki immobilized him in a headlock, then Chaim plunged the knife into his chest several times. The blade slipped on the German's rib, cutting Chaim's left hand. The Nazi tried to regain control, and, although severely wounded, he managed to let out a loud scream for help before succumbing. Pożycki took his revolver. They left him slumped behind his desk. In the next office SS Scharführer Steubel was then killed.

Close to 5:00 P.M. Cybulski returned to Lager I and reported to Sasha the successful elimination of four SS men in Lager II: Wolf, Beckmann, Vallaster, and Steubel. Shubayev also reported the severing of the telephone line.

Back in the garrison area, SS Unterscharführer Ryba had entered the car garage by chance. The prisoners working there seized their opportunity: he was killed immediately. This worried the organization's leaders, because the garage was open, located in the administration area, and could be prematurely discovered.

Meanwhile, in Lager I, Szlomo Szmajzner picked up his stovepipes and headed for the guards' barracks. The Ukrainian guards were on duty with the working prisoners, and Szlomo hoped that the other Ukrainians, free of duty, were probably amusing themselves with the Polish prostitutes who came from nearby towns. They hung out in the barracks just outside the camp. Everybody knew that Szlomo was the tinsmith and often fixed roofs, stoves, and related problems, so he did not arouse any suspicion. He was scared but decisive. "Today is the day," he was heard to repeat to himself.

He put the pipes away and climbed onto the roof to check the chimney so as to establish his presence there as legitimate. Back in the barrack, he made sure that no Nazis were inside and then searched the squad leader's room. Szlomo saw a couple of machine guns hanging on the wall, but they were too big to conceal in the pipes. In the other room he noticed rifles and ammunition belts with only a few cartridges. Satisfied, he nervously tried to put the rifles into the stovepipe. Because of the unlocked rifle bolts, they didn't fit easily. For someone familiar with rifles, locking the bolts would have taken just seconds, but Szlomo was holding a rifle for the first time in his life. Not giving up, he managed to fit two rifles into the pipe and rolled it in a blanket, together with one more rifle. Carrying the blanket with the rifles over his shoulder, he casually, without incident, passed the Ukrainian guard at the gate of Lager I.

From the main tower came the sound of a bugle announcing the end of the day's work. Kapos now assembled their work groups in various parts of the camp and returned to Lager I in customary military fashion. Their marching songs in Yiddish, German, Polish, Dutch, Ukrainian, and Russian echoed far beyond the barbed wires of the Sobibor forest.

It seemed like any other day. In the courtyard, unsuspecting prisoners were standing in line for their coffee and bread. Their life or death would be determined in a matter of minutes! The operation, prepared and executed in secrecy, had gone like clockwork so far. Except for a few, the overwhelming mass of inmates had no idea what had already been accomplished.

Unsuspectingly, SS Unterscharführer Friedrich Gaulstich entered the area. Keeping his cool, Szlomo Leitman immediately asked him to come to the newly built barrack where he was working because of some problem with the bunks. The Nazi took the bait, but the untrustworthy Kapo Schmidt followed them. Pożycki, having returned with his group from Lager IV, intervened. He casually approached Schmidt from behind and whispered into his ear, "Stay away, don't mix in." When this was reinforced with the point of a knife, Schmidt understood. From then on Schmidt was under observation. The moment SS Gaulstich entered the barrack, his fate was sealed; an assault group took care of him. On average, from 4:00 P.M. on, one German was killed every six minutes.

The door to the blacksmith's shop was wide open. I was waiting for Szlomo Szmajzner inside; a few Russian Jews were standing in a corner talking quietly. Then Szlomo entered with the load in his arms. He was sweating and breathing heavily. He opened the blanket, and out fell three rifles. Before the Russians grabbed them, he was able to secure one for himself. A young girl, Zelda Metz, slipped in and dropped on the bench some ammunition she had stolen while working in Lager IV. Sasha was there too, manipulating a German revolver. Soon Walter Schwarz dropped in and reported the sabotage of the electrical transformer.

At the same time, a frantic search for SS Frenzel was still going on. On Pechersky's order, Siemion Rosenfeld was still waiting for him in the carpentry shop with an ax, but Frenzel had disappeared. Critical minutes were passing, and he was still out of reach. He was one of the main executioners at Sobibor and very dangerous.

At 6:00 P.M., as was customary, the German staff would gather for the evening roll-call. At that crucial time, the surviving Nazis would notice the conspicuous absence of their cohorts and sound the alarm. Most of the Jews remained unaware of what was occurring around them. They were standing in line for more coffee, or were busy eating or washing their pots. It was now 5:30 P.M. On Sasha's orders, Pożycki blew his whistle for roll-call preparation. It was fifteen minutes early, but the Kapo's authority was never disputed. People began to assemble.

Now the news spread like wildfire. While standing in formation, I noticed religious Jews returning to the barracks to get the prayer shawls they had hidden. They assembled near the kitchen, saying Kaddish, swaying back and forth. Seeing no hope for salvation, they said the prayer for the dead—for themselves. Believing that all was in the hands of Divine Providence, they resisted their oppressors by openly sanctifying God's commandments.

An elderly tailor twisted his fingers in desperation and walked back and forth, lamenting to himself, "What do we need this for? We could live for a few weeks more. Now this will be the end." A few young men were sitting on some building material near the barracks.

I recognized a buddy of mine with a blanket on his shoulders. He had been ill for two days, so it was possible that they were a group of sick and weak Jews. It was obvious that they had decided to stay: they appeared resigned to their fate. Others were saying good-bye to their friends and were looking for suitable weapons. Then more and more inmates nervously congregated in the yard.

Sasha, trying to form a column to march the people to the main gate leading outside, according to the original plans, heard gunfire and understood that something had gone wrong. (SS Bauer had returned from Chełm. Discovering that SS Beckmann was dead, he started shooting at the two prisoners unloading his truck.) He decided to act immediately. He jumped up on a table, looked down, and made a short speech in Russian, his native language. His voice was clear and loud so that everybody could hear, but he spoke composedly and slowly. He informed the people that the majority of the Germans had been killed, that there was no return. A terrible war was ravaging the world, and each individual is part of that struggle. He reminded them of the power of his motherland, the Soviet Union, and promised that, dead or alive, we would be avenged, and so would the tragedy of all humanity. He repeated twice that if by some miracle one might survive, he should be a witness to this crime forever. He ended with a call: "Comrades forward! Death for the Fascists!!!"

The guns in the towers remained silent. The guards probably thought that the nervous activity was normal. Before a roll call, the slightest shortcomings were heavily punished. And they were too far away to hear what was being said.

The mass of prisoners, coming from most of the nations of Europe and speaking diverse languages, now understood. From the assembled Jews, all of a sudden, a single, strange, and impatient voice was heard. *"FORWARD! HURRAH! HURRAH!"* It was quickly picked up, and, in a flash, the entire camp answered the call to defiance. Most of the Jews spontaneously divided themselves into two groups. A smaller group stormed the fences in Lager I, frantically cutting the barbed wires with axes and shovels, without concern for the ditch full of water and the mines. Some threw planks of wood to detonate the mines. The second, larger group, armed with an assortment of weapons, pushed its way forward toward the exit of Lager I to reach the main gate.

At that moment, a guard commander, the Volksdeutscher Schreiber, was riding his bicycle through the same exit. Not understanding what had happened, he yelled "Why are you pushing like cattle? Get in line!" When he understood, it was too late. He was immediately surrounded, thrown from his bike, and knifed. His pistol was confiscated. Not far away, I saw another guard in visible shock, continuously turning himself around as if set in motion, his outstretched hand still holding his rifle.

Another group of fifty prisoners, mostly Russian Jews under the escort of SS Scharführer Wendland and Ukrainian guards, were returning late from their construction work in Lager IV when shooting was heard. Seeing prisoners on the run, they instantly became aware of the revolt. They threw themselves on their guards, initially overpowering them, but then were showered with bullets from the tower. Most fell, but a few prisoners, with their work tools—shovels, saws, and axes—and their killed escorts' rifles in hand, ran to the gate and joined in the attack on the armory, which was then in progress.

In the armory, there were only a few complete rifles available to the Jews. Most were disassembled for cleaning. SS Dubois, in charge of the armory, was hit with an ax. While trying to run away, he was shot in the chest. The prisoners grabbed whatever weapons they could and hurriedly left to join the fight.

Not worrying about the gunfire, I was running forward. To my right I saw SS Wendland standing flat against the wall of the canteen. Slowly retreating to hide behind the corner, he sprayed the running prisoners with fire.

I also saw SS Frenzel reappear on the scene with his machine gun. He, together with SS Bauer, mobilized the stunned Ukrainian guards. They effectively blocked the passage to the main gate, where many of the prisoners were being killed. I could hear the bullets whistle by me. I saw a friend fall in front of me, then others.

The frontline Jews fell back for a few minutes. I stopped, my long knife of no use to me now, and backed off about fifty feet, then headed to the right of the Germans' quarters as a new wave of determined fighters, in a suicidal thrust, pushed forward again toward the main gate. A small group, including Sasha, Szlomo, Sender, myself, and another man with an ax, ended up between the fences in the peripheral guards' corridor. In the confusion, we had run into the entrance of this corridor, and in this way we did not have to pass the two barbed-wire fences and ditch; they were already behind us. Ahead of me lay only one more barbed-wire fence and fifteen meters of mine-field. I stopped. Someone was trying to cut an opening in the fence with a shovel. Sasha, armed with a pistol, stood waiting, as did Sender and myself, both with knives in hand. Only Szlomo Szmajzner, calmly shooting his rifle, was able to silence the guard in the tower. I still remember marveling at his composure. Within minutes, more Jews arrived.

Not waiting in line to go through the opening under the hail of fire, they climbed the fence. Though we had planned to detonate the mines with bricks and wood, most of us did not do it; we couldn't wait. We preferred sudden death to a moment more in that hell. People were scrambling for freedom. When I was only halfway through the fence it crumbled and fell on top of me. I thought this was the end for me. Instead, this probably saved my life, for lying under the wires, trampled by the stampeding crowd, I saw mines exploding and bodies torn. And I realized, had I been able to get through earlier, I would have been killed with them.

Corpses were everywhere. The noise of rifles, exploding mines, grenades, and the chatter of machine guns assaulted my ears. The Nazis kept their distance while shooting at us, and we had only primitive knives and hatchets. The wave of escapees finally passed over me. Now I was alone, lying amid bodies. I tried to extricate myself, but it was difficult. The wire barbs were deeply imbedded in the thickness of my leather coat, taken at the last minute from the warehouse. This managed to trap me under the fence. I thought to myself: "Is this the end? I don't want to die!" Suddenly I had a flash of insight, and then it was relatively easy: I simply slid out from under my coat and left it tangled there. I ran through the exploded minefield holes, jumped over a single wire marking the end of the minefields, and I was outside the camp. Now to make it to the woods ahead of me.

It was so close . . . I was behind the last of the fugitives. I went down a few times, each time thinking I was hit. Each time I got up and ran farther . . . one hundred yards . . . fifty yards . . . twenty more yards . . . and at last the forest. Behind us, blood and ashes. In the grayness of the approaching evening, the tower's machine guns shot down their last victims. The thirty Jews from Lager III, still unaware, were left behind.[13]

❖

Freedom – The Illusion

Freedom – The Illusion

I was running as fast as I could. I understood that these hours were crucial in the escape; the Germans would not enter the forest at night, and the farther I got, the better my chances. I didn't stop when I reached the woods. Tripping over branches and roots, I ran and ran. I was ready for anything. I would fight with my teeth and nails if someone tried to stop me.

How long I ran I don't know. The silhouettes ahead gradually slowed down. Finally, sweating and panting, we stopped in a clearing. The forest, like an old friend, embraced us, took us in, and shielded us from enemy fire. We had made it!

Of course, we were not out of danger, but the feeling of freedom, even momentary freedom, was exhilarating. Still, I could hardly believe it. Had I actually escaped that accursed place, or was I only dreaming?

Suddenly I realized that, miraculously, my right hand still held the big knife I had taken from the last Dutch transport. I looked around. We were being joined by more and more escapees. The moon provided the only light as the exhausted survivors gathered in the forest. The head count revealed that close to forty Jews were in our group. An inventory of weapons listed four pistols and one rifle, but very little ammunition, some axes, and a dozen knives. Sasha was with us. Standing straight and tall in his Red Army uniform, he was unmistakably our leader.

"Listen," he instructed, "from now on, move in single file. That way we won't leave a beaten-down path like this. And for God's sake, be silent and don't smoke! If you see a flare, or if we're fired at, just hit the ground."

After a short pause to rest, our group continued directly southward. The forest ended, and we entered a flatland of fields and meadows. On a stretch of pastureland we encountered a deep irrigation ditch about ten feet wide. We moved alongside it, looking for a shallow place to pass. The night was foggy, and we could see only about a hundred feet. Suddenly, a whisper came from the front: "Shhhh! Germans! Freeze! Lie down!"

I dropped to the ground. Now I could see them—some silhouettes appeared, moving toward us from the other side of the ditch. They were getting closer, we could not escape. It was too late. A cold sweat came over me. Were they Germans? They would not take us alive! They did not notice us and were moving nearer. Obviously their intention was to cross from the opposite direction. Someone up ahead stood up, "They're ours . . . ours!" he cried.

Another group of Sobibor escapees! We all stood up and moved alongside the ditch on opposite sides until we found a narrow spot allowing us to finally meet. We were looking for friends and exchanging observations. I saw Szmul Wajcen, Karolek, and Kali Mali . . . but I kept to myself. Like most, I was still in a state of shock. The one I was really close to was Jozek Bresler, the doctor's son, and I hadn't seen him. The Dutch twins were also missing. I didn't even know if they had tried to escape. As a participant in the revolt, I was bound not to tell anyone of the escape plans—and I didn't tell them. Did they make it? I wondered. They must have been with another group. I had seen a few Dutch girls on the run, so there was hope.

Sasha was very happy to encounter Kali Mali, who was leading about twenty escapees. There were some warm greetings and embraces, and then we moved on. Now we numbered close to sixty Jews with four rifles and eight pistols. We were even more vulnerable as a larger group, but, on the other hand, we gained three rifles and a few revolvers.

October 15. At dawn we reached another forest and rested in the thick undergrowth. The birds awakened and the forest came alive with chirping. It was autumn and cold there in the marshes. My boots were wet and I was freezing, but I was filled with the overwhelming glory of freedom.

Around midday, a faint buzz was heard. It got louder and louder. Between the treetops I could see a plane circling low over the forest.

We were hidden by the foliage, and though I knew it was probably impossible for the pilot to see me, I pressed against a tree and held my breath. Soon it passed. We maintained vigilance under tree cover during the daytime and moved only at night.

When darkness came we were on the move again. Sasha was at the head of the trail while Arkady Wajspapier held the rear. It was our second night; the air was crisp and the sky was clear. We passed through the forest and climbed a slight hill. Kali Mali moved up and down the line to make sure everything was all right. Noticing me, he stopped. I could see the handle of a German Luger pistol sticking out of his belt.

"This is Wolf's," he stated casually, as though it were a loan from a friend. "The magazine is stuck, though, and I can't reload it."

"Let me see it," I said. I had handled one gun before—the one I bought in Izbica and had never used. And I watched in Izbica once as two drunken German gendarmes loaded and reloaded a Luger pistol. Maybe I could do it, I thought. But no such luck. "Sorry, Kali," I said, handing it back to him. And I thought, how strange, I actually held the pistol of a Sobibor Nazi, a Nazi killed by a Jew.

We moved on. Near a summit, I looked back and froze at the sight of a long thread of people stretching like a gigantic snake. I knew it was impossible not to be discovered eventually, now when they were searching for us. Then and there I decided to detach myself from the others at my first opportunity.

October 16. As dawn approached, the group ahead sped up. In front of me was a French Jew, about twenty years old. He was weak, breathing heavily, and could not keep up. The distance increased between us and those at the front of the line. We were moving in between rocks, and there was no way to bypass him. People behind me became impatient, wanting him out of the way. Nervously, I pushed him and he fell aside. We sped up again.

I started to think about the French boy, obviously at the end of his endurance. I felt bad that I had pushed him and left him there. Moving out of the line, I sat on a stone, waiting to see him. The last people passed, and there was no sign of him. A few minutes later, he approached, moving slowly and unsteadily toward me. He sat down next to me on the stone.

"I can't make it . . . I'm weak. This is the end," he said in Yiddish.

"Come on, come on. Don't stay here. It's too close to Sobibor," I implored.

"I can't. I want to die . . . It's no use." I stood for a moment, sadly, then left without a word. Now I had to run quickly to make up for lost time. From far away I felt the tremor of a passing train. We stopped and, still not knowing where we were, decided to set up camp.

For the first time I observed closely the faces in our group. There were seven women among us. Mostly we were young, in our twenties; the oldest was close to sixty years old—Kapo Pożycki's father, who had worked as a cobbler in camp.

October 17. After spending the whole night marching through the meadows, we came to an open area sprinkled with occasional large trees. Again the low-flying reconnaissance plane circled frequently overhead.

Two other escapees crossed our path. They informed us about the heavy concentration of Germans on the crossings of the Bug River.[1]

The armed men moved aside, talking quietly; the rest of us sat waiting nearby. Szlomo, barely taller than his rifle, was not included in the discussion. Just then Sasha announced, "We've got to find out where we are. A few of us are going on a reconnaissance mission, and we need money to buy food." Dreszer was given a cap in which to collect money from those of us who had the foresight to hide gold and paper money in preparation for the escape. Soon a Soviet Jew approached Szlomo, asking for his rifle, but Szlomo steadfastly refused to give it up.

Alarmed that Sasha had chosen all the armed men, the rest surrounded them and protested. Finally a compromise was reached: Szlomo would keep his rifle and stay with us; Sasha solemnly promised to return as quickly as possible.

My heart was heavy. I felt, as the others did, that this talk about reconnaissance was only an excuse to leave, that we would be abandoned by our leaders. Fearfully we watched as Sasha, Kali Mali, Cybulski, Wajspapier, Ickowicz, Mazurkiewicz, and two others departed.

Time passed. We heard dogs barking far away. One hour passed, then two. We sat on the grass like ghosts, some alone, others in groups, our eyes wide open, searching the open space for a sign of our returning scouts. Another hour went by. We were wet from the dawn mist. Sasha was still not back. The glow of the rising sun seemed to emerge like a distant fire. We had lost hope. Despite his promise, he had defected. They had taken our money and guns and left. Or had something happened to them?[2]

We were now without leadership or firearms, except for one rifle. Our group was getting unruly. It would be dangerous to remain where we were any longer. Sadly, we moved back to the edge of the forest.

We Break Up

We were people of different origins and ages, and we spoke different languages, but we all had come from the depths of hell, determined and prepared to fight to our last breath. We were prepared to never again fall into German hands alive! With the weapons we initially possessed, a good fighting unit could have formed. In any case, Sasha chose differently, but I don't think any one of us today would point a finger of judgment at him.

Now a real tragedy unfolded among the remaining people. Separate groups of two and three began to form according to age, origin, and friendship. Quarrels started. Those who were older and less resourceful lamented and begged not to be abandoned by the quickly departing groups, who, nevertheless, refused to be burdened by those who were weaker.

I realized how difficult survival would be for so many people. At the end of 1943 there were no more open Jewish areas to which the hunted could return. The shtetls and villages once vibrant with Jewish life were empty; many of the houses had been demolished by vandals looking for hidden treasures. True, we had just escaped certain death in the gas chambers, but we were still far from safe—the specter of death had receded only slightly. There was now the problem of where to go and what to do. Under Nazi law, Jewish presence in any public place meant certain death.

The forest offered no real security either. Various partisan groups and roving gangs of bandits roamed the country, robbing in order to exist. There were Polish anti-Nazis, Communist and anti-Communist groups; there were Ukrainian pro-Nazi groups, who fought the

Poles and Soviet partisans. Despite their differences, they had something in common: generally all, except the Soviets and some Polish
leftist partisans, robbed and killed any Jews they might encounter.
Without weapons, only enterprising individuals had a dim chance of
evading the enemy and surviving.

All along I had my mind set on going my own way, but not alone.
Wandering among the groups, I approached Szmul Wajcen. "Szmul,
you want to go with me? My hometown, Izbica, is only thirty miles
away. I know every spot there and have Polish friends."

Szmul answered without hesitation, "Okay, Toivi." With him was
his friend, Fredek Kostman, a tall, handsome teenager.

Karolek, standing nearby, asked to be included. "I'm going with
you, too, boys," he stated. Then, out of the blue, he said, "Toivi, do
you still have food left?"

I said with a big grin, "I've got a can of fish paste!"

Just before escaping I had taken a few cans from the dumpcarts
and put them into my pocket. Karolek had teased me then: "You think
you're going on a picnic? You will not live to eat it!" He was mistaken.
With the help of my knife I opened the container and divided it
evenly. We had our "picnic." It was delicious.

Little Dreszer approached Szmul. They had been very close in the
camp. "Szmul, you'll take me with you . . ." It was half a question,
half a statement. Szmul hesitantly agreed. At the end, instead of two
of us, we suddenly had seven.

We knew each other more or less. There was a strongly built man,
Mendl, who headed the bakery in Sobibor, about twenty-five years
old; Fredek Kostman from Kraków, twenty-one; Walter Schwarz, the
electrician from Germany, thirty-five; thirteen-year-old Dreszer from
Zólkiewka; Szmul Wajcen from Chodorów, seventeen; "Blinde" Karolek, nineteen; and myself, fifteen.

We secretly detached ourselves from the rest, crossed some fields
and reached a forest. We figured that we would sit there for the rest
of the day. Suddenly Mendl, who had acted strangely from the beginning, began to tremble and cried out that we would be caught. They
would torture us, he said. Then Schwarz announced he was leaving
the group. He was the oldest, well-built, and somehow gave the illusion of protection. We couldn't lose him. From then on, we followed
his every movement.

After a few hours, tired, we lay down in the bushes for a nap. Half-asleep, I felt a sharp tug on my arm. It was Dreszer. "Toivi, Schwarz and Karolek are leaving!" Opening my eyes, I saw the two men moving silently away. Szmul and Kostman were awake, too, and in a few minutes the whole group caught up to them. An argument followed.

Schwarz wanted to take only Karolek with him, leaving Fredek, Szmul, Mendl, Dreszer, and myself to form a second group. The problem was what was to be done with Dreszer, who was only a child, and Mendl, who was now on the verge of a nervous breakdown, shaking, stuttering, and whimpering like a baby.

I talked it over with Szmul and Fredek, and we came up with what we thought was a fair division of the group. If Schwarz would take Mendl, we would take Dreszer. Unfortunately, Schwarz only wanted Karolek. We couldn't agree. We catnapped, trying to keep a constant vigil on Schwarz, for fear he would try to slip away and desert us.

October 18. Mendl awakened us. Schwarz was leaving again. We ran after him and stopped him. "What do you think you're doing?"

His eyes flashed with anger. He would gladly have strangled all of us if he could. Strong as he was, he knew we outnumbered him and carried knives. Finally, seeing no way out, he agreed to our earlier proposal.

He would go with Karolek and also Mendl, so as to balance the strengths of each group. Now his group had an experienced older man, a strong young man, and one risk, Mendl. In my group remained Fredek, Szmul, and our risk, Dreszer. We separated.

About five minutes later, Mendl suddenly appeared through an opening in the trees. "What happened? Where's Schwarz and Karolek?" we asked him.

"They chased me away," he sobbed.

We knew that Schwarz couldn't have gone far. Running, we caught up to him. We gave him an ultimatum: either he takes care of Mendl or we all stay together—nobody leaves! Happy or not, he took Mendl, and we departed in opposite directions.

Less than half an hour later we heard loud screams in the distance. It sounded like Mendl. Though we didn't know what had actually happened, we suspected it was something horrible. (In fact, after the war, survivors told me they saw Mendl lying in the forest with a broken leg.) We didn't investigate, and none of us spoke. We knew that if we tried to rescue him, tried to move with a disturbed man, our fate would be sealed. Slowly and sadly we moved on.

We plodded along to the far end of the forest. By now it was daybreak. In the distance, smoke curled upward from the chimneys of peasant huts. But hungry as we were, we were more terrified of asking for food. One never knew what kind of people lived there.

Little Dreszer decided that he was the bravest. He went directly to a peasant hut. We watched from a distance and waited. Hours passed, and he did not came back. Perhaps he felt unwanted, perhaps he felt his chances were better alone. Maybe a good person decided to shelter him, or maybe he was captured for delivery to the Germans. There was nothing we could do, and to tell the truth, in a way we were glad that the group was now smaller.

The Road "Home"

After trudging along for an hour or so, we came upon a lone cabin about two hundred yards from the edge of the forest. It was not so much hunger we felt now as the desire to know where we were.

We sneaked carefully up to the door and knocked. No answer. We stepped inside. The warmth of the place engulfed us. I looked around. I saw a table, two chairs, and a bed. On the bed was a feather quilt with a tomcat snuggled in it. What I would have given to lie down on this bed and think of nothing, without the ever-present feeling of danger. Oh, to be this tomcat! That would be true bliss, I thought.

I looked at my companions. They, too, were mesmerized by the peaceful atmosphere. It was a humble cottage, typical of the very poor areas in eastern Poland. Though family and livestock shared the same roof here, to us the earthen-floored home was the palace of our dreams.

A woman came in from the barn side of the hut. She was still obviously young, yet worn, her face wrinkled and ravaged by difficult years. Silently she approached the bed and awakened a little boy we hadn't even noticed, as he was hidden under the quilt.

"Good morning," we said as she turned and calmly faced us.

"Good morning, gentlemen."

"We would like to buy some food. Could you sell us some?"

"As you can see," she answered, "I am poor. I am alone on this farm without a man, but I'll give you what I can."

She brought bread and fresh milk. We drank it all and asked for more. She filled bottles for us with what remained in the pail, leaving just a little for herself. We quickly ate our bread. As we were ready to leave, Fredek took out a gold ring and offered it to the good woman, but she wouldn't hear of it.

"What for? For the food? You were hungry and I gave you what I could, but not for money." We tried to persuade her, but she stead-fastly refused, saying, "Jesus said, 'Give food to the hungry and water to the thirsty.'"

As we were about to go, the woman looked at us and said, "I suppose you boys are from Sobibor, where they burn people. Yesterday they searched the neighboring village. You'd better get away from here."

We were stunned. Here we'd been afraid to tell her we were from Sobibor—we thought she would fear not only us but also the Germans hunting us. "Sobibor" was a word spoken only in whispers; it evoked terror in most people. And yet she said it so calmly, so mat-ter-of-factly—"Sobibor, where they burn people." We stood there for a moment. Then, afraid to put into words what I feared might be true, I asked, "How far are we from the camp?"

"Sobibor," she said, thinking slowly out loud, "must be about a mile from here. On a clear day, you can see the top of the big tower."

My legs felt weak. We had been running for nights and were only one mile away! We must have been going around in circles!

Being native to this part of Poland, and my two companions strangers to the region, I took the initiative. "Which way is Lublin?" I asked. She pointed and wished us luck. We thanked her again and left. Actually, we needed to head in the opposite direction, but we wanted to keep our true destination a secret in case she were interro-gated by the forces chasing us. Returning to the woods, we hid in a thicket and waited for dusk. Night was our friend.

October 19. Our plan was to reach Izbica and get help from gen-tile friends of my family. Though the forest was protection, it had disoriented us and slowed us down. We were afraid of getting lost again and ending up right back at the camp, so we trudged down the open highway. We realized the risk we were taking, but decided that the oncoming darkness would conceal us. For a long time we encountered no one. Then, past midnight, as we came to a sharp curve in the road, a man appeared. We kept moving straight ahead. After all, he was alone, and there were three of us. As we passed, we pretended not to notice the stranger, and he didn't appear to notice of us. We never learned his identity. Perhaps he was another escapee from Sobibor, or a partisan. Just the same, it was a lesson to be more careful on the open highway.

Soon the forest that bordered the road gave way to open fields. We moved quickly, almost running. We could hear a car coming and hid in ditches alongside the road until the car, lights dimmed because of the war, passed by. Our next stop was a hole on the road filled with rainwater. What luck! We lay on the ground and lapped it up. How refreshing it was! At daybreak we hid in the forest and slept.

The early darkness of October fell again. We passed isolated cottages and were nearing a crossroads when a group of people suddenly appeared. They were obviously drunk, pushing each other, singing and talking nonsensically. We simply went on.

"Halt!" came a shout.

We fell to the ground, crawled away into bushes, and kept still. Time passed, and no one chased us. When we got up carefully, they had disappeared. We figured they were probably drunken Poles who, as a joke, ordered us authoritatively to stop. When we instead fell army style, they probably thought we had weapons and would shoot.

October 20. We were now near the town of Piaski. At dawn we approached a peasant hut and again asked if we could buy food. The farmer eyed us with suspicion. Fearing we were well armed, he politely gave us rye bread and salted pork. We handed him money and shoved off to the nearby woods to sleep for the remainder of the day.

After a while we heard a loud voice coming from the road nearby: "Hey! You Jews, come out. If you come out voluntarily, nothing will happen to you!" We were hidden in the bushes near the forest edge and could see the road. There stood a single civilian with a rifle, yelling the order to come out. He did not dare to enter the forest alone. After a while, not getting any results, he left.

At nightfall we resumed our journey, bypassing the district seat of

Krasnystaw. As a new dawn was breaking, we trudged dead-tired down the hills to the main road. Finally, we reached the sign proclaiming "Izbica—12 kilometers"—my town, my home. From here I knew the road like the back of my own hand.

October 21. Nearing Izbica, in the village of Wólka, we came upon Zawada's farm and a big, beautiful haystack to hide in! We jumped a fence and headed for it. We pushed ourselves up the slippery wall of hay to the top, using a wooden pole for support, and dug deep into it. Three feet down, we hit what appeared to be sealed wooden crates. We figured the farmer probably used the hay to hide and camouflage his valuable possessions from the bandits that roamed the area. We made ourselves comfortable. And just in time, for rain began to fall. It was quiet for a few hours, then suddenly a dog barked ferociously, jumping up against the haystack. We heard the door from the house open and footsteps.

"Is someone there?" called the farmer Zawada.

We didn't answer. The barking became frenzied. I could hear old Zawada and his son discussing what to do. A ladder was laid against the haystack, and I could hear the weight of somebody climbing. We looked up. Staring at us was the peasant with his pitchfork.

"What are you doing here?"

"We're Jews, Mr. Zawada. I'm Leon Blatt's son."

There was a pause, then, "Come down."

We slid down the straw. Standing there was Zawada's son with an ax in his hand. The farmer was now looking inside the haystack, probably to see if his treasure was still intact. Then he came down.

He motioned to the cottage, "Come inside."

We didn't know what to expect. But he was kind. He fed us, but he refused to hide us, even until darkness came. He was too afraid.

By now the day was in full swing. Cowhands were already out with the cows. We could be seen. We had to hide quickly. We ran through the fields and entered the Orlów forest.

I was somewhat familiar with this area from my childhood. We hid in a clump of bushes and waited for night to come. Izbica was close now; we had almost reached our goal. It was agreed that I would go into town and talk to Mrs. Bazylkowa with the proposition that she hide us for a generous fee. She had been a close friend of the family, and earlier she had helped to hide my brother. Besides, she had many of our possessions. When we first split up the family, we gave her all of our precious belongings, knowing that soon we could be forced to leave.

The three of us shared an implicit understanding: trusting anyone—even each other—could cost us our lives. As I was the one who knew the Izbica area, the others needed to ensure my return. I was to leave all my money and jewels with my comrades as a guarantee that I wouldn't desert them. I handed everything over to them.

Bending the blade of my pocketknife halfway to simulate a gun and raising the collar of the coat Fredek had given me to hide my face, I set out in the gray dusk.

This was October 1943, long after Izbica had been made Judenrein. I prayed I would be perceived as a Pole. Surely no one would imagine a youth walking openly through town could possibly be a Jew.

I passed a familiar building on the outskirts and continued to the town. Then I stopped, amazed. I, a native who knew every corner, could hardly recognize my own town! Where Jewish homes had stood there were only open spaces, so thoroughly had they been dismantled and plundered by gentile neighbors seeking hidden treasures. Finally I reached Mrs. Bazylkowa's house.

"Who's there?"

"Toivi."

"My God, go away! I'm afraid."

I begged her to open the door for just a moment. The key grated in the lock and the door opened a crack. Her frightened face peered out.

"What do you want?"

Knowing her deep respect for my father, I lied that he was with me and offered her a large sum of money.

"I don't want to hear about it," she cried. "I can't help you . . . I'm afraid. Please go away." She was closing the door.

"Give us some food at least," I begged. "Please, we're hungry."

There was a long pause. "Wait," she said.

In a few moments she returned holding a small piece of buttered bread. I started to put it in my pocket so I could bring it to my comrades.

"Eat it here," she commanded me, "or give it back to me."

I complied. She was afraid someone might find me with the bread and I'd betray where I got it. She knew only too well the Nazi law that any gentile caught harboring or helping Jews in any manner was subject to the death penalty.

"Please hide us," I pleaded. "We don't have anywhere to go, and it's almost winter."

"No, Toivi, I can't! You know yourself my husband was taken to Auschwitz.³ My daughter drowned as a child. All I have is one son and I want him to live. I refuse to listen." By the terror etched in her face, I could clearly see we represented a deadly plague, the Black Death of the twentieth century.

The door closed in my face. Discouraged, I began the trek back to my comrades. It was now very dark. Close by, a shot rang out. Frightened, I started to run. Half an hour later, as I approached the place where my companions were to wait for me, I whistled softly as we had agreed. No one answered. I began to backtrack, still whistling, frightened that I had lost them.

This time a voice called me softly from the bushes near the road. "Toivi, Toivi." They had probably let me pass by earlier to make sure I wasn't being followed by strangers. I explained the situation. With this disappointment we became very depressed. Hope had eluded us again.

Our situation became critical. The forest was as dangerous as the town. To seek a friendly partisan group was too risky; our fate would most likely be murder by a hostile group. We would need exceptional luck to encounter friendly partisans who would take us in.

Sitting on the edge of the forest, we could see the flickering of light in the window of a farmer's hut about two hundred yards across the road. We decided to take a risk and ask for food. We left the woods and approached the isolated farm. A dog sensed us and began barking ferociously. Frightened but desperate, we entered. The hut was lit by an oil lamp. We could see no one, yet our eyes were hypnotized by a hot pot of soup on the table. Nevertheless, we did not dare touch it. We went out, stopped at the barn, then the stable. Finally we called out, "Anybody home?" Silence was our reply.

We returned to the cottage and this time went ravenously at the soup, without even sitting down. Fredek nervously insisted that we leave at once since no one was around. It could be dangerous, maybe a trap. The dog was still barking and jumping about furiously in the yard. From afar we caught a glimpse of a flashlight.

"Gospodarzu! [Farmer!]" I called out, and there emerged from the bushes a boy about twelve years old. Immediately recognizing us as Jews, he called to his family, who were hiding in the fields, that it was safe to come out. It seems that upon hearing the dog bark and seeing us emerge from the woods, the family ran away, fearing we were a hoodlum gang.

Then came a surprise. The peasant's name was Bojarski, and his daughter was once a classmate of mine. We recognized each other and things warmed up considerably. Farmer Bojarski asked us to supper. We had our first good hot meal. We were delighted with our good fortune. We sat in the clean, warm peasant house and ate until we were full. I asked him to give us shelter and offered good pay. Just in case, we gave the farmer's wife a gold ring and his daughter a pair of gold earrings. He said we should return to the forest while he considered the deal. We went back to sleep in the woods.

Something was bothering me. Faint pictures from years past moved in my mind.

I was then in the second grade, probably seven years old. One Friday evening after supper, the Sabbath candles twinkling, I was sitting on my father's lap, moving my hand against his beard, when somebody knocked on the door, opening it at the same time. In came a tall man dressed in a long sheepskin coat, the kind the country coachman wore. He appeared drunk.

From the talk, I understood that this coachman was hired to deliver the wooden containers filled with bottles of vodka for my father's store. The warehouse was in the city of Zamość, and once a week my father used this service to replace the sold stock. Many times, as I can remember, my father complained about the losses he suffered because of the coach-man's dishonesty. When the shipment was unpacked, he always found a few broken bottles inside. Curiously, the packing material, although wet, did not smell of alcohol.

It was expected that some vodka would vanish during the voyage, but this time it seemed that the coachman not only drank on the way but also took some home. To my father it was an intolerable loss, especially because the liquor board set the prices, and it was impossible to pass the losses on to the customer.

My father complained to the coachman. Curses and angry words, then threats and racist slurs followed. Then the coachman kicked a chair and left. I was shaken. I had never witnessed such an explosive scene.

Maybe ten minutes later a scream echoed from outside. "Es brent!!! Es brent!!! *[Fire!!! Fire!!!]" We ran outside. About three doors down, smoke poured out. People were ripping shingles from the roof and pouring buckets of water.*

The next day rumors circulated in town that a peasant had tried to burn down Blatt's home. Somebody outside overheard the angry conversation and later noticed the departing coachman entering our neighbor's porch, lighting matches. His screams scared the man and alarmed people in time to put out the fire.

The coachman's intentions were obvious. The few houses on our side were attached to each other. If the fire had not been controlled immediately, the whole block would have turned to ashes. The coachman's name was Bojarski.

I was tormented. Should I tell them about this farmer? He now seemed well-off, so friendly and sympathetic. And his daughter seemed genuinely happy to see me. So many years had gone by. Maybe here lay the chance to survive. It was getting cold in the forest, winter was approaching. Where else was there to go?

The Wooden Cage

October 22. Very early in the morning I awakened Szmul and Fredek. After listening to my story, we decided to return to the cottage after all. After a breakfast of eggs, bacon, bread, and milk, the farmer told us to wait until evening in the haystack nearby. He loyally brought us lunch—cabbage with bits of pork and potatoes. When night came, he asked us inside to wash and have supper.

After some talk, we displayed some of our treasure on the table: diamonds, gold, and jewelry, as well as German, American, Russian, French, and Dutch paper money, and gold coins. This, including what we still withheld, amounted to a fortune unknown in this area.

The peasant's eyes were shining. His wife picked up a beautiful gold chain, which we let her keep as a gift. But the farmer was still afraid and couldn't make up his mind. Once more he wasn't ready with the decision. He didn't ask us to return to the woods for the night, but told us to wait again under the haystack for his answer.

At midnight he came. "I've decided to give you shelter," he said. "I know the Russians will be here soon. Tomorrow I'm going to prepare a better hiding place for you." Happily, we bade each other good-night and went back to sleep beneath the hay.

October 23. We were brought breakfast, later some soup for lunch. Finally, after the darkness fell and the dog was unleashed, we were invited inside. After supper, we gave him a considerable sum of money, gold, and diamond jewelry.

Then he led us outside to the corner of the barn opposite the stack of hay where we had been hiding all day. He twisted a small bent nail and moved a wooden panel aside, revealing a tightly packed wall of straw. Near the ground there was a hole barely visible in the dark, about two feet in diameter.

"Squeeze in," he said. I went first, then Szmul and Fredek. Once inside, complete darkness engulfed us.

"Bojarski, sir," I implored, "please give us a kerosene lamp until we get settled."

He left, then returned in a minute with a safety lantern, the type Polish peasants hung from the back of their carriages when traveling on the road at night. The panel clicked back into place.

We were greatly relieved. It was like a stone off our chest. At least we were safe. At least it was a place to stay where nobody would tell us, "Go away, I'm afraid." Yes, there were good people in this world, too.

Examining the construction of this tomb, we concluded that we were apparently under a large table, maybe eight feet long, about four feet wide, and four feet high. The sides were packed with thick paper from old cement sacks, dry leaves, and straw to insulate us from the harsh Polish winter.

Soon our furnishings arrived, two old blankets smelling of horse sweat and a two-gallon metal pot. When we found old and torn newspapers inside, we understood the use of this household item. The farmer promised to feed us three times a day, and let us out each night after dark for fresh air and exercise.

So nine days after the escape, we luckily evaded the dragnet and finally settled into a safe shelter. God was watching over us, and we were thankful.

The first few days everything ran smoothly, even though our world was suddenly reduced to eighty cubic feet. But after a few weeks, the farmer reneged on his promise to feed us three times daily, and we made do with what was provided.

Our life in the shelter went somewhat like this: we knew of daybreak by the crowing of the roosters; we talked on various possible and impossible subjects to pass the time; when we heard Bojarski's son returning from school we knew it was midday; after that, we waited for nightfall and now our only meal.

First we would hear careful steps around the hiding place. The farmer was making sure everything was okay before opening the panel secured by the bent nail. Each night we took turns at the opening. The one on watch waited to receive the pot of food; at his side was the other pot to be exchanged.

After our meal, the peasant returned, opened the panel, and called us outside. One by one we crawled out. The first breath of fresh air overcame us, then we followed the farmer. Bojarski, with his alert dog at his side, walked with us around the barn. He did not speak a word; when the dog barked, maybe because of a passing rabbit, we froze in terror. After about fifteen minutes he told us to return. After a week the farmer refused to take us out. It was too dangerous he said. We agreed.

The nights were mostly cold and dark, and a peaceful quietness engulfed us. Each day Fredek would add another straw to the matchbox; our calendar. A month had gone by. At first we had quite a bit of trouble sleeping, since each of us went to sleep whenever we felt like it, and day and night had a way of getting mixed up. Then, when one wanted to talk another would want to sleep. However, we put an end to this and instituted rigorous discipline. From cockcrow until supper we were forbidden to sleep. In a short time we felt much better.

I remember being curious as to how I looked, for we had no mirror. However, one glance at my two buddies convinced me that we all looked the same: half-naked, bearded, unkempt, and wild.

One day, when our kerosene was exhausted, Bojarski refused to buy more. He was afraid it would start a fire, he said. Now we seemed to be living in a tomb; everything was done by touch. We ate and slept in total darkness.

Once, when I was receiving the bowl in the dark, I was scalded by the boiling soup. My hand and stomach were badly burned, and I suffered from boils and blisters for some time.

Although it was already the end of fall, the leaves and straw acted as good insulation, and it was rather warm inside. Fredek, the only one of us who smoked, couldn't fight his addiction. He tore bits of coarse paper from the old bags that had formerly contained cement, crumbled some dead oak leaves from our bedding, and lit it. There was more stink than anything else, but he couldn't resist.

The feeling of safety put us in a friendly and relaxed mood. Fredek and Szmul talked about their lives before the war, their homes, and their towns. I listened in disbelief. It was like a dream. Although I had once passed the big city of Lwów and had seen the very big buildings, I was never inside one, except, perhaps, when I was in jail in the city of Stryj.

They told me of train stations with many trains on many platforms at one time; to reach them one had to go through long tunnels, on top of which other trains were passing, without fear of collapse. They talked about cars, Simcas and Citroens, names I had never heard before. I always thought that there were only two brands of cars—Opel, which the town doctor, Mr. Lind, had owned, and Schultz's Fiat.

I was intrigued when they mentioned toilets that were actually inside their own apartments—with flushing water! In Izbica I had seen only public toilets, one in the middle of a field close to school, one behind the synagogue, one close to the mikvah (ritual cleansing pool), and others scattered about town. They were always overflowing and impossible to enter. Once in a while they were drained; a horse and carriage pulling the dripping waste container was a normal sight. Many people preferred secluded places out in the fields. As a child, my favorite spot was a ditch on a hill with a beautiful view of the town—that is, if I climbed the hill and made it in time. During the night people used chamber pots. One year, just before the war, a local fabric merchant named Pomp built himself a new house and actually put in a toilet and running water. It was a hit. Half the towns-people, as well as those from outlying areas, stood in line to see this wonder, but I never had a chance.

Their stories sounded incredible, and I voiced my disbelief. They soon discovered the ignorant "peasant" among them and were happy to spend time teasing me. They were city boys, and they stuck together. Not being able to impress them with my hometown Izbica, I switched to my story of buying a gun, my escape to Hungary, and the jails.

This was too much for Szmul, and when I stopped talking he said, "You finished, Toivi?"

"Yes."

"Then flush."

It took me a while to understand the connection. What did this have to do with my past? But soon I understood. So, my talking was only shit! Their rejection hurt me terribly. There we were—after Sobibor, after hell, sharing the same fate—and they didn't believe me.

I wasn't able to fall asleep, it bothered me so. The only rational explanation was that they had been taken directly from the ghetto to Sobibor in early 1942. They had no contact with the hostile world that had developed in the meantime. Come to think of it, I, too, had react-ed with disbelief when I returned to Izbica in 1943 from the ghetto of Stryj and heard terrible stories about Poles murdering and betraying the few Jews who managed to escape to the forest or to neighboring villages, and about the various organizations' zeal in eliminating Jews.

I realized that daily life for a prisoner in Sobibor was actually in some ways more secure than that of Jews who were hiding on false papers, or in the forest, or in bunkers, freezing and searching for food, counting their every surviving day as a miracle. In Sobibor we knew what to expect. Sobibor was the end. Sobibor was a matter of waiting for death, being resigned to it. Outside, there was a fierce struggle for life.

Weeks went by and life in the shelter became routine. So what if our necks and backs ached from crouching in our cramped quarters and we saw no daylight? We knew that sooner or later all this would end, and in the meantime we were safe. We still would have preferred to join some partisan group, but Bojarski adamantly refused to allow us to contact anyone. He stubbornly maintained that he didn't know anyone he could trust. He was suspicious of those armed men roaming the countryside, and perhaps, too, he feared that by joining them we might be induced to make him return the fortune at gunpoint.

And so we lived in our hole. The boundary between us and the rest of the world was a small plank of wood, yet it imprisoned us more surely than jailers and prison bars. With us was the knowledge of the gas chambers.

One night Bojarski asked Fredek to lend him his boots to wear to church. Fredek gladly consented. This was the beginning. After that we had to "lend" him other items, one by one, until one day we were left with only our underpants, one pair of overalls, and one sweater to share among the three of us. But we weren't sorry. We didn't complain. We wished only to survive.

Life in the Shelter

Then misfortune struck. During the night the dog began to bark fiercely. We heard voices from the outside coming closer. Someone entered the barn. There came the sound of someone digging into straw, overturning objects. Who could it be, we asked ourselves. Then we heard a strange voice in Polish.

"Where the hell do you have the Jews?"

"Sir, have pity, there are no Jews here, no strangers here."

"So how come you are so well-off and nicely dressed lately? Who is paying for it? People can see. You can't fool them. C'mon now, hand over the Jews. We will honestly divide their gold with you. We'll fix 'em good!"

Bojarski began to cry. "I swear by God I'm not hiding anyone. There are no Jews here!" He knew that if they discovered us, not only would we be killed, but he would be forced to hand over his fortune to the bandits.

The intruders, however, didn't seem to believe him, for they went on snooping around the barn for some time. They poked at the straw with sticks a bit more, without reaching us, however, for we were too deeply hidden. We crouched, praying quietly, holding our breath with each thrust of the stick and rustle of straw. Finally they left. Temporarily, the danger was gone. That night Bojarski entered our hideout and sputtered, "You see now! Just a bit more and they would have killed all of you. What do we do now?"

He was right, of course, but we consoled him, telling him that now that the bandits were convinced he didn't shelter Jews, they'd leave him alone.

Bojarski left. What should we do? The possibility of having to leave this shelter, the uncertainty, was devastating. We heard a chain jingling and the dog being turned loose. Soon all the farm noises quieted down. It was night, and we lay down to sleep.

"Toivi, Szmul, listen, the farmer wants money. That's all there is to it. Let's give him more."

"Okay," said Szmul after a slight hesitation. "We'll each give an equal amount."

"Szmul," said Fredek, "I don't have much, only the few dollars my friend gave me at the last minute."

"I don't care," came the curt reply from Szmul.

Of the three of us, Szmul had the most valuables. Many of mine had been lost in the coat I had to leave under the fence while escaping. Fredek had little because he did not know about the revolt until the last minute. But Szmul insisted on equal amounts. Fredek dug out some money and threw it on the blanket. I matched his five hundred U.S. dollars, and Szmul added the same. From then on Szmul lost a friend. Fredek never again allied himself with Szmul against me.

The next day Szmul was in a bad mood. For nearly an hour he didn't say a word, but busily checked his pockets and dug with his hand in the straw.

Fredek was curious. "Szmul, what is it?"

The answer was unexpected. "You boys stole my money," he said angrily. I hadn't done it, and I was sure Fredek hadn't either. Probably it fell out the day before when he opened his little cotton bag to give his share to Bojarski. We helped him search. In a corner close to the chamber pot, I felt some metal. It was a ring and some coins. I reached for Fredek's hand and let him feel it. Then I waited for his reaction.

"Szmul, do you really think we have stolen it?" Fredek asked matter-of-factly. I understood that in Szmul's answer lay Fredek's next move.

"Yes, there are only three of us here."

Fredek covered the gold and said nothing. It was our secret. From this time on something hung over us. Though destiny and circumstance had thrown us together, we had different backgrounds and personalities. Szmul, with light brown hair, green eyes, and a slender build, was a handsome but selfish seventeen-year-old. Fredek, about twenty, a tall and slim fellow with intelligent blue eyes, a big-city boy from Kraków, was slow and peaceful. And I, the youngest, was just a village boy. Szmul often pointed out my ignorance and lack of sophistication.

Even so, when we were running together in the forest it was I who knew exactly what to do. Even before Sasha left us, as I watched the long line of fugitives trailing through the forest I made up my mind to detach myself. I was in full charge and did not follow any of the big fellows, but chose my own companions and decided where to go.

One would think that our situation should tie us together. But it was not to be. I felt that if freedom came the next day we would probably part and never speak to each other again. We were constantly together, touching each other day and night, for weeks and months. Although terror kept us together, our personalities kept us distant.

Now Bojarski didn't allow us to get out at all at night, calling it a security measure. He brought us food only once a day, in the evening—a bowl of soup, a chunk of bread, and three spoons. In general, things went from bad to worse. We asked Bojarski for a talk. He complained, "I thought this would be only a short time. I figured on a few weeks, maybe two months, but there's no end to it."

"Please, Bojarski, sir," we pleaded. "Give us back our clothes and let us get some exercise at night. We haven't stood up for months!"

"I can't," was his answer. "Suppose you're caught by unfriendly partisans and you betray me. You can be sure, if I'd known this would last so long," he repeated, "I'd never have let you in." We looked at each other, gave him some more gold, and asked that he at least give us better food. Now he happily agreed.

Mid-December. For several days we heard dull detonations. When delivering food at night, our landlord whispered gleefully, "The front's coming closer—it'll soon be all over. Boys, I'm with you now, no matter what. I'll keep you until the Russians get here. They've started their offensive. If everything goes well, they'll be here in two weeks. Say, you don't regret giving me that money, do you?"

We assured him we didn't. He was greatly pleased. Then, since he had neglected us, he voiced his uncertainty concerning my family house in Izbica, which I had promised him earlier. We assured him that we didn't hold this against him; we knew how much he and his family were sacrificing in helping us, and little things he had neglected to do didn't matter. He left full of good humor and hope, and we felt the better for it, too.

Soon he brought us more news that lightened our hearts. A partisan group ambushed and killed Jan Schultz, the major of Izbica, on his way to Krasnystaw. His end finally came. The other Volksdeutsche were fleeing Izbica. The Russians would be here soon. After this talk, our meals came regularly three times a day, and Fredek received cigarettes and matches. But we were still in darkness.

Days went by. The sound of heavy gunfire gradually ceased and the Volksdeutsche returned. We learned that the fighting had not been between the German occupation forces and the regular Soviet army, but a clash between the Nazis and one of the larger Soviet partisan groups. Bojarski became angry, and our treatment became worse.

In general, throughout the entire hiding period, food became our political barometer. When it was good and plentiful, we knew that the situation on the front was favorable; when meager, we knew the contrary was true.

A few days before Christmas, Bojarski squeezed into the hiding place, crying to us that he couldn't take it anymore. The Russians weren't coming, and he was afraid.

"God," he said, "what shame and disgrace would descend upon my family if people found out that I was sheltering Jews!"

In the dim light of his kerosene lamp I had seen the large cross he wore, inscribed with the letters INRI. "Do you believe in Jesus?" I asked him calmly.

"Yes, of course."

"Do you know what the letters on your cross mean?"

He looked at me angrily and said nothing.

"Jesus of Nazareth, King of the Jews. Jesus himself was a Jew. The picture on your wall shows them gathered around the table. All twelve of those apostles were Jews."

Such an insult was too much for him. He grew angry and abrasive. We knew he wanted more gold. Without another word, we gave it to him. We were relieved he extracted it in this manner rather than simply killing us and taking it all, as other peasants had been known to do in similar situations. Most other peasants would not risk their lives for any money in the world. True, he had very favorable conditions: he was isolated, living outside town, much apart from his neighbors. But still, if betrayed for harboring Jews, the Germans would have killed him and his entire family.

Christmas 1943

Each time Bojarski gave us the meager soup and a piece of bread, he carefully closed the entrance panel. We were constantly hungry, and I promised my friends that if by chance the board was ever unlatched, I would get out, go to Platto (my first shop boss in Izbica), and try to obtain more food. On December 24, my chance arose.

As Christmas Eve approached, we were happily anticipating the good food of the holiday dinner. Maybe we would even eat a piece of pie! He certainly would not forget us. One thousand nine hundred forty-three years ago Jesus was born on such a night. Wouldn't he respect His teachings?

Time went by, and no one came to feed us. Our appetites increased as we visualized a share of the holiday feast. Finally, above the whistling of an oncoming blizzard, we heard steps outside.

The panel opened; someone pushed in a pot with soup and didn't wait to receive the other pot. Szmul, who had picked up the food, said that it had been the farmer's young son. We bent over the pot. Usually he gave us about a gallon of barley soup. Now he gave us less than half a gallon of cabbage soup, less and worse food than usual, and without the usual bread! This was our holiday fare? I suspected he was feeling bad about feeding Jews, the "ones who killed Jesus," on such a holy Christian holiday. Suddenly, a thought struck me.

"Szmul," I called, "take a look. Maybe in his hurry he didn't close the panel." Szmul checked and found I was right. I was free to leave!

Earlier, when the political situation seemed to improve, Bojarski had returned some of our clothing to us. Putting it all together, I had an outfit of sorts. I eased out of our hideout, opened my switchblade, and held it as I would a pistol as I headed toward town. It was dusk.

A blizzard stormed, howling and whistling through the trees. Trudging through the deep snow of the fields, I passed the Maliniec farm, then descended from the hills to Platto's house near the train station.

I heard voices within. The room was lit, but curtains prevented me from seeing who was inside. I went around to the front of the house. The door was locked. I knocked lightly, and a dog barked angrily from the hallway. I panicked and ran. In the past, the German supervisor from the nearby train station was quartered in Platto's home, and he owned a dog![4] I fell into a ditch and sprained my ankle. I hadn't had a chance to run for three months, so now I could barely move. With great difficulty and in great pain, I went uphill, trying to return by the shortest route.

To make matters worse, it was very dark and the blizzard was sweeping down waves of snow. The wind was so strong that I was only able to move forward slowly by bending and cutting through it headfirst. In this fashion, I made it to the road in the canyon that would lead me straight to Bojarski's farm. Now it was a little easier. The canyon walls weakened the wind's force, and the snow didn't hit so hard in my eyes.

Hours were passing. I should have reached my destination, yet in front of me the road stretched on and on. I came to a small wooden bridge. I raised my head and saw that I was in the middle of a forest.

"Where am I?" I wondered. Then it dawned on me. This was the "Red Bridge" in Kulik Forest! With the roads blanketed in new snow and poor visibility, I had missed the path and had taken the wrong fork in the road a mile back.

I was losing strength. The terrible cold pierced my body. I was very, very tired and wanted desperately to sleep, but I remembered stories my uncle had told me about Jewish peddlers traveling through the villages, peddling their wares in the winter. Sometimes in a blizzard they would get lost, tired, and then freeze to death in their sleep. I knew instinctively that the biggest danger now would be to give in and lie down, that if I surrendered I'd be lost.

By some miracle and with a lot of willpower, I found the strength to go on. I finally returned to the proper road in the ravine. I knew I wouldn't be able to make it all the way to the shelter. Exhausted, I tried to find the haystack I had noticed on the way to Platto's. I knew it must be close by. Reaching the field, I moved by instinct. I could barely make out a gray shape through the blizzard. It was a haystack! With my last ounce of strength, mechanically, I dug in deeply. Surprisingly, inside I found an empty space and some rags. Who knows who had used this place previously?

In spite of my terrible exhaustion, I slept uneasily. I knew I must return at dawn, before anyone could notice my absence, so every once in a while I stuck my head out of the hay. Finally the blizzard had stopped; the fields were soft and white as down. I stepped out and ran on.

It took me longer than I had figured. I was late. Bojarski was moving through the yard. I hid behind the fence, wondering what he would do if he knew of my outing. When he went into the house, I ran into the barn and lifted the panel to the hiding place. My buddies pulled me in. The dog didn't bark; he knew me. The boys were disappointed—I hadn't brought anything to eat. My feet were swollen, I felt sick and hungry. On top of it all, expecting food, they had eaten my share of bread.

We daydreamed and fantasized how it would be when we would be liberated. We imagined ourselves kissing the first liberating soldier and carrying him through the whole town on our shoulders, yelling with joy.

And so time went by without change. Our youth and the desire to survive produced miracles, for in spite of our unnatural, cramped existence, we never became ill.

It was now February 1944. Months had passed since we last stood upright, went outside, or had seen daylight, except for my outing to Platto's in December. Again the time came when, tired of this endless waiting and inactivity, we asked Bojarski to return all of our clothing, let us have a shave in his house, sell us a revolver, and let us go. He promised us everything except the gun, but the next day he broke his promise. He had a new plan.

"Boys," he said, "I won't let you down. If we perish, we'll go down together. But I'm worried. The Germans are looking for partisans in our area; they're searching all the farms close to the woods. I'm afraid they'll search mine as well. So I'm going to put you in a more secure hideout, which I have been preparing for a while."

The Execution in the Shelter

In a few days he let us out. It was nighttime as we crawled out of our present shelter and were led behind the barn to a covered patio storage area that housed some farm equipment. I noticed a wheelbarrow; in it lay a large object, round and gray.

He held us each by the armpits and lowered us into the ground through a narrow hole dug in the earth. We asked for the kerosene lamp so that we could arrange ourselves in our new quarters. He gave it to us without a word and closed the opening by tightly pushing in straw.

I looked around. We were in a small dugout, about four and a half feet long, three feet wide, and three feet high. Along the "ceiling" was a strong pine pole and across it some smaller pine poles—all of it covered with straw and branches. On top of it must have been soil. The small, round entrance in the corner of the roof was now jam-packed with straw.

While wondering where the air vent must be, we heard light footsteps, then the sound of something heavy being rolled. In a moment, an object fell with a great thud over our heads. The main pole began to crack slowly in the center and formed a V.

Szmul immediately supported the ceiling with his shoulders so that it wouldn't collapse upon us. I tried to push the straw out of the opening in order to call the farmer. It was impossible. Then I began to pull out big clumps of straw, and found that something else was blocking the entry!

"What's wrong?" Szmul cried out.

"It's blocked!" I gasped. "It's blocked!"

The kerosene lamp began to flicker and waver, and finally went out. We mustn't panic, I told myself, we mustn't panic. I tried to light it again. The match lit for a few seconds and went out. "Why the hell doesn't it burn?" my thoughts screamed. The answer came instantly; we were lacking oxygen.

We were now short of breath. In the dark we couldn't see each other; we could only hear our raspy breathing. Panicky and struggling to breathe, perspiration began to pour down my forehead into my eyes.

"Move over, let me try," gasped Fredek.

We changed positions. He was the strongest . . . maybe he could do it. But he couldn't get into a balanced position for pushing. He was too tall. It was very dark and cramped. Without oxygen we were exhausted, close to fainting, and trembling with fear.

Finally, with superhuman effort, Fredek, gathering strength, managed to move the heavy object blocking the entry hole just slightly. It shifted a little toward the crack of the bent-down ceiling. A stream of fresh air quickly revived us all, and we squeezed out!

As we stood there, it flashed through my mind that there was a change in the surrounding scenery. The wheelbarrow was now partially over our new hiding place. The handles were high up and the body of the cart was slanted down to the ground. Next to it was a heavy millstone. We didn't try to figure out what it was all about. Fredek went immediately to inform Bojarski of the accident. In a minute he was back.

"Bojarski's getting dressed and will be right out." And, grinning, he added, "You know, when he saw me coming toward him, for a second he stared at me like I was a ghost. Then he clasped his head and wondered aloud, 'How did you get out?'"

We laughed. It still hadn't occurred to us that he had actually tried to bury us alive, that the wheelbarrow with the millstone had been expertly prepared to seal off the entrance and make escape impossible. Only the sudden force from the edge of the fallen millstone, breaking the main support of the roof and forming a slide, made shifting the weight possible. This saved us from death. There was no way we would have been able to move it had the roof been straight.

Bojarski was an interesting character. It wasn't until some years later, when I was more mature and had time to reflect on all these happenings, that I tried to understand him. I am convinced that he gave us shelter with the intention of saving our lives. The fact is that for five months he carried out this difficult task. It's possible that with his family living under the fear of discovery and the threat of death, he had gradually become used to the idea of getting rid of us. We were only Jews, "Christ killers," as he was told in the local church. Then, somehow or other, the breaking point came. Perhaps it was the temptation of getting the rest of our money and jewels. Perhaps he feared that we would take revenge for mishandling us. Perhaps this combination suddenly broke his spirit and propelled him toward murder, turning a man of goodwill into a criminal.

Then, however, we had no time for psychological analysis. Bojarski was coming toward us, carrying a kerosene lamp. We watched his huge barefoot figure grow larger in the murky night. "Well, boys," he said, "too bad, you'll have to return to the old hole. We'll think of something else later."

Not until we were settled in our old place under the table did we begin to have serious suspicions. It did seem strange that, fearing an inspection, he had not made a hiding place in the fields far from the farm, as he had himself suggested, but on the contrary had put us into that hole behind the barn, which could be more easily discovered. And yet, when one drowns, one will grasp even at straws to pull himself out, as the saying goes. We tried to reject these thoughts, tried to argue that it was merely an accident. After all, had he not kept us safe for several months? Thus we reasoned it out in our small prison.

Five and a half months had passed since that cold fall evening when we first knocked on Bojarski's door. It was now April 23, 1944. I had strong hunger pangs and couldn't sleep. I kept thinking, as I had in jail, of freshly baked bread. I could almost smell it. It was already nine o'clock and we'd had no supper. I gave up hope.

We got into position for sleep. Fredek and Szmul were in one corner while I was at the other end near the entrance. Today it was my turn to receive the food. I felt cold so I got between them, the way we used to during the cold winter months. "I don't like this, it's too crowded," said Fredek, and he moved to my place by the entrance.

We were lying quietly, resigned to our dreams, when we heard faint footsteps about the barn. We recognized Bojarski's tread. Perhaps he was not as mean as we thought; he was bringing us food. We heard him stop before the entrance.

Although it was my turn to pick up the food, Fredek was now close to the entrance. He stretched out on his belly and edged through the opening in the straw to the board, which would open any moment for our food. We heard the catch open and the board move.

Suddenly, a flash of light and the crack of a gunshot disturbed the stillness. I heard Fredek wriggling, screaming, "Son of a bitch . . . Germans . . ." The rest became a mutter, and then an unrecognizable gurgle.

The board was swung back in place. Silence. Only Fredek's hoarse gasping was heard. Szmul and I were sitting up against the wall. Fredek, in his convulsion, threw himself about, spraying us with his blood. After a moment of shock and confusion, we realized that he was dead, and knew it was our turn! Still, we felt it was impossible: it was a kind of dream, a nightmare. But Fredek's blood was only too real. Those few moments seemed to last hours. Again we heard steps and voices.

To reach us through the entrance they had to crawl flat on their stomachs. Perhaps they were afraid to take the risk now—we could be too dangerous for them. We heard the straw covering the shelter in the barn being pulled away. We knew these would be our last moments. Cornered and unarmed, we felt like rats in a trap.

The last bundles were being yanked out. Szmul crawled to the other corner where he burrowed into untouched straw. I followed him. We waited. Now the big table was being pulled out, leaving a bare square area surrounded by a mess of straw.

"They aren't here," said a surprised voice.

Then a thin layer of straw covering me, was removed. "I got him!" shouted a young fellow. His kerosene lamp shone in my eyes. His pistol was aimed at my head.

"Please," I begged him, "don't shoot. Please don't kill me!"

He was about two feet away. He was young, about seventeen years old, skinny and blond, a stranger to me. Filled with terror, I faced the muzzle of his old rusty gun. He looked straight into my eyes, his face full of scorn. I could expect no mercy. Quietly, coldly, sadistically, he said, "Where's the first one?"

"He's dead."

"And where's the second?"

"Next to me," I answered, terrified and desperate, staring straight into the barrel of the gun.

I heard a bang and felt the sharp, burning bite of a bullet under my jaw. My ears rang. Fully conscious, I instinctively took a deep breath, closed my eyes, and slid down.

Seconds went by. I felt no pain. I realized that I was thinking. I wasn't sure if I was alive or if this was life after death. Once, in early childhood, my uncle told me a strange tale. For three days after death, he said, you can hear and feel, and your hair and nails grow, but you cannot react. Perhaps that's what was happening to me now, I thought.

I tried to slightly open one eye. In the dim light I could see the man who had shot me. He was talking in a low voice with someone. So I'm alive! Then the thought struck me, should I ask him to shoot me again? If he left me with a bullet in my head I would only suffer and die later. Or he would bury me alive. I wrestled with the thoughts of surrender for a long excruciating time, but I kept quiet.

I felt a noose around my feet. I was being pulled outside; evidently I was in the way of their reaching Szmul. After dragging me for a while, I was thrown down in the mud. The night was cold. I was only in my underwear, and it was raining. I opened my eyes and watched in the dark the barely visible silhouettes of people in front of our hiding place.

My thoughts raced. Should I try to escape? I sat up in the mud. I heard steps and lay down again. Men approached, stopped, and one said, "Might be better to give him another bullet." I froze, recognizing Bojarski's voice. I was shocked. So it was Bojarski!

We were so accustomed to the rhythm of farm living that any change did not escape our attention. Now I understood why, earlier that evening, I heard his children say "good-night" as they left for an overnight stay with their uncle in Izbica. Probably Bojarski didn't want his children to witness his crimes. There was another clue that had escaped our attention earlier. Just before Fredek was killed I heard the whining of the dog, as if he were resisting being dragged into the house. The farmer always took him in when someone was expected, to avoid having the dog bark needlessly.

These thoughts lasted mere seconds, and ended abruptly as my survival instincts took over and I feigned death. I had seen before how people became stiff after death, but I did not know how much time must pass for that stage to set in. Hopeful that the murderers did not know either, I tried to look as stiff as possible. I was already so cold from lying there that my body trembled uncontrollably. In the dark it probably was not noticeable.

Just then, someone bent over me. At this point, however, with great willpower I stopped the trembling. He put his hand over my mouth. My eyes were slightly open; I had seen the shadow of the hand coming down and I held my breath. At the instant when I thought my lungs would burst, he removed his palm. He then touched my fingers in the dark, feeling for rings, and said to Bojarski, "Let's not waste a bullet; he's already stiff."

The moment he went away, the trembling I had been controlling overcame me and shook me in spasms. I wasn't thinking of running away now. There were people moving about the yard. Among them I recognized the form of Bojarski's plump wife.

Suddenly I heard Szmul scream. "Don't shoot! Don't shoot! I want to live! I will be your slave forever. Just let me live!" There was a shot, then another. Again Szmul screamed. There was another shot, and silence. Seconds went by . . . a last muffled shot, then complete silence.

They returned to me, pulled me inside the barn and left me face down on the ground. The blood from my wound flowed faster in this position, but I couldn't turn and give myself away.

In the meantime, the murderers rummaged excitedly through the jumble of hay and overturned the table. Hunting for our scattered treasure, they were happy, like children, as they found a watch or a gold ring. Finding no more, they picked up our remaining clothes, and as they were leaving one said to another, "Let's look through the Jew rags inside and call it a day. We can bury them tomorrow, they won't rot before then. Besides, we can search the straw more thoroughly in the daylight."

Run! I thought, or it will be too late. I thought of Fredek. I'm alive, maybe he is alive too. In the dark I stumbled over his body. I touched him and whispered, "Fredek . . . are you alive?" But there was no answer. I was now wearing only underwear; they had already taken my pants, which held some pages of my diary. Without another thought, I removed Fredek's bloody overalls and put them on.

Then I recalled that Szmul had his jewelry pouch in his pants pocket. I would try to retrieve it from his body. I knew from the conversation I overheard that they hadn't yet taken his clothes, perhaps because he was buried so deeply in the straw, way back near the wall. All I felt was that a miracle had spared my life, and I must do everything I could to fight for it still.

I crept into the straw tunnel left by Szmul and reached his body. This time I didn't ask if he was alive. It seemed impossible after four shots. In order to get to the pocket of his pants, I would have to turn him. At that moment I felt his breath, very faint.

"Szmul, are you alive?"

"It's you, Toivi? I thought you were the bandit!"

"Can you move?"

"Yes. I'm not badly hurt. Only one bullet hit me."

"Have you got the jewelry?"

"No. I threw the purse to the bottom, below the straw, so they couldn't find it. It must be close by."

He rummaged in the depths for a while and found the satchel. We crawled back to the loosened panel of the hiding place. Szmul got out and had to pull me after him; my legs were extremely weak.

The farmhouse was so close you could hear the conversations from within. Now! I thought, run from this place, and for God's sake, run fast because it could be too late!

Again on the Run

We ran for the woods. We had barely reached the edge of the sparse forest when suddenly I felt sharp pains in both ankles. I fell to the ground, not knowing what hit me. I couldn't go on. The pain was excruciating with each step. Could it be my sprained ankle hadn't healed since Christmas? Or was it the result of trying to run after being mostly prostrate for so many months?

"Szmul," I said, "I'm sorry but I can't go any further. In the condition I'm in, they'll catch us in no time. With so few trees to cover us until we reach the depth of the forest, we're plainly visible, and the first place they'd search would be here. Go alone. You can run fast and soon be deep in the forest. I'll look for another place to hide."

Szmul wouldn't leave me. "If we die, we die together," he answered.

We decided to go toward Izbica. Not far from Maliniec's farm there was a demolished brick factory. I remembered as a child I had played cops and robbers there, hiding in the broken-down brick ovens. I decided to go there. Bojarski would never dream we'd be crazy enough to give up the security of the forest and go directly into the town.

After half an hour we were in despair. I couldn't move at all any-more. I had crawled and slithered in every possible way, and even rolled like a barrel, taking extreme care not to let my bare feet touch the ground, for then the pain would shoot through my whole body. Szmul tried to carry me, but he, too, was weak and gave up. In an hour we had gone barely one-quarter of a mile.

Hearing voices, we turned around. There was a commotion on the farm road, and we saw the flickering light of kerosene lamps. They were heading for the forest. They were looking for us!

We went on. Though it was only one and a half miles to our des-tination, we had now spent at least five hours trying to reach it. Now, as dawn broke, we could see the outline of the brick factory ruins; our goal and our hope lay on the little hill ahead of us. We prayed no one would notice the two strange creatures, one crawling and rolling through the fields. Oblivious to the pain, I concentrated all my strength on our goal.

Thank God, we finally made it. The openings to the ovens where we intended to hide were outside. Now they were covered with debris, and it was dangerous to remove it in broad daylight. So we went inside the ruins of the building. We were afraid of being discovered, but there was no other place to hide for now.

It was all ruins: there was no roof, the walls alone remained. The sky had cleared up after the rain. Here and there, grass grew in clumps. Outside was a willow tree. I was overcome with sadness. The branches just beginning to bud were beautiful, but we needed full foliage to protect us. Where were we to go from here? The forest did not accom-modate refugees very well in springtime.

We heard a rustle, but it was only a frightened cat scurrying by. Again I was jealous, jealous of a cat's carefree life. Now, for the first time, I sat and reflected on what had just happened. I looked at Szmul, and only then did I notice that his hand was wounded. Noting my observation, he explained, "After they drew you out, they came for me. I guess they were afraid to dig into the straw to get to me, because they shot at me through the tunnel I left behind as I was crawling. I was screaming and begging for mercy, but they shot three times and missed. Suddenly I realized it was better to pretend to be dead, and I shut up. A man with a flashlight squeezed into the tun-nel and was facing me, I was so afraid, I put my hand to my mouth to keep from screaming. He shot me at close range. When the bullet hit, I was terrified. But this time I didn't scream. I didn't even move. The guy was sure I was dead, so he slid back out."

He showed me his right hand. His index finger was straight and he was unable to bend it. The bullet was visible, lodged right in the joint. I was conscious now of my own wound. With the pain in my ankles, I had forgotten it. A stream of blood, now dry and caked, stretched from my right jaw to the overalls, where it mixed with Fredek's blood. Gingerly, I felt my jaw. I imagined it to be a terrible wound, but all I could feel was a little hole. I theorized that the bullet had hit my jaw and then ricocheted out.[5]

It was around noon when a woman came to the ruins to relieve herself. As she was about to leave, she noticed us. She was ashamed and angry. I knew this woman well: she was my wet nurse, Ola. Again she didn't recognize me, but it was clear to her that we were Jews in hiding.

"Are you from Tarnógora?" I asked.

"Why do you ask?" she answered abrasively.

"I just recognized you . . . I'm Blatt's son."

She couldn't believe her eyes. It had been exactly a year since she had last seen me, when my father had paid her to go to the hospital in Stryj to find me. I had obviously changed a lot during that time.

"Please, will you bring us food? We'll pay you well, and please don't tell anyone we're here," I begged. She showed no emotion, no warmth, no feeling, and asked no questions. Coldly she promised to get food and left. I never saw her again.

Every minute seemed like an eternity. I prayed to God for pity, prayed that no one would come by and spot us.

Finally, when it was dark, we went outside. At the bottom of the wall were semicircular openings from the brick-burning ovens. Being careful not to make loud sounds, we cleaned the interior of one of the ovens. It was hard work and took all our energy for a long time. We threw out all but two bricks, to be used as pillows. Those outside we used to camouflage the entrance. Then we were ready for sleep.

I was so weak that just raising myself up on my elbows induced heavy breathing and a pounding heart. That night and the next day we just lay in the oven, quietly resting. About noon, we heard children running and jumping around the brick factory.

"Jews! . . . Where are you Jews?" they yelled. Luckily, we were already safely camouflaged. Was it possible that Ola talked too much and let our dangerous secret out? After a while the voices faded and we relaxed again.

Three days passed in hiding. We were hungry. My legs improved but were still very badly swollen. When it was dark I decided to go to the home of my former elementary-school teacher, Mr. Podgórski. I thought I was one of his favorite students, because many times he gave me the honor of going out to the town to buy his cigarettes. Or maybe it was because my father's store never charged him.

Through the cracks in the bricks we watched the last rays of daylight disappear. I moved the bricks in the entrance and crawled out. I stood up but still could not walk normally because of the pain when I bent my ankles. At least I could walk side-step holding my ankles stiff. I had to lead, for the area was unfamiliar to Szmul. Eventually we reached Podgórski's home in the suburbs of Izbica. I knocked hopefully on the door.

"Come in." It wasn't Podgórski, but a stranger. We felt uneasy. Podgórski was sitting by the oven. "Toivi," he said in surprise as he got up. He was still the same tall, dark-haired, skinny man. His wife came in and offered us bread and milk. They were good people. Later, they invited us to wash with warm water.

But we were still uneasy about the other man. And when the stranger spoke Ukrainian, we got panicky. Reading our faces, he tried to reassure us. "Boys, don't be afraid. I won't turn you in. I'm a good friend of Podgórski's." We relaxed a little. It was late when we got back to the brick factory. Side-step by side-step, it had been a long, laborious journey.

As days passed we tried another source of food—Podgórski's neighbor, Mr. Pasternak, who was head of the local post office. Late in the evening, we knocked on the door of Pasternak's house. This family, too, was surprised, but they let us in. There I met another classmate of mine, a girl named Wanda, who seemed friendly. Pasternak was warm toward us and not afraid to talk. He gave us bandages, water, and supper. We bought out his cupboard, including the smoked bacon and vodka, paying, as demanded, about twenty times the worth, and we made arrangements to buy food from him once a week. Passing the patio in the garden, I stole two old potato sacks to keep myself warm and a torn hat to cover my head, as a decent Jewish boy should, though I did not manage to have a bar mitzvah.

I was now eager to try Platto again. His home was near the train station, so we had to be careful, still suspecting that German railroad officers could be subleasing part of his house. Cautiously we crept into the yard, where a covered shed stood in the corner under a canopy. The door was closed with a wooden peg. We opened it, and our senses were greeted by the smell of warm manure.

There was my old acquaintance, Baśka the goat, in her stall. Even though we were intruders, she let us share her stall and milk her directly into our open mouths. Maybe she still remembered how, two years earlier, on Platto's insistence, I had taken her across town to find her a mate, and had successfully completed the mission.

Early in the morning, we decided to go out and lay down on the roof of the shed. Still covered by the canopy above us, we could observe the whole yard and maybe see someone friendly to call on.

Everyone was still asleep. The train station was just behind Platto's house, and we could see part of a military transport. German guards were standing on duty by the canvas-covered artillery.

Finally, Platto's seven-year-old niece came out. Following the sight of her bouncing a ball, she noticed us and immediately ran into the house. After a moment, the best soccer player for miles around, Mr. Kociuba, appeared. He put a ladder against the shed to reach us.

"Who are you? What are you looking for?"

"I'm Blatt, sir. Don't you recognize me?"

"Oh, yes, I recognize you now. You've changed."

"Mr. Kociuba, could you please tell Platto I'm here?"

"Listen, Blattchek, don't you know it's very dangerous to sit here so close to the train station, right under the noses of the German soldiers? Not only you—they will kill all of us if they find you here. And you know how many sons of bitches are after you. While it's still daylight, stay here and rest. But when it gets dark, go to Goldberg's sawmill at the edge of the forest and wait there."

When it was dark we went to that particular spot. Szmul was distrustful and suspicious. Maybe it was a trap, maybe they would kill us. He didn't have faith, but he waited with me.

About dusk we heard footsteps. Carefully, I looked out. I recognized Platto's brother-in-law, Heniek Królikowski, who had hidden me during one of Izbica's roundups. He was carrying a package in his hand. At that moment, Szmul lost his nerve and ran off into the forest, unwilling to risk the encounter. But I stepped out, and we greeted each other. He asked about my family and gave me two fresh loaves of bread.

"Toivi, be careful not to betray us if you are captured. I cut the baker's label off the loaves. If you don't tell, no one will know they're from my mother's bakery."

"Thanks, Mr. Heniek. Where's Platto? Could he possibly hide me?"

"I think you had better talk to him. Tonight you can't meet him, but tomorrow night at the same time be at the home of Mr. Haltuk, the sawmill guardian. Good-night. Keep your spirits up."

"Good-night."

Szmul was waiting for me in the bushes. We ate the bread and then moved on, afraid to stay in one area too long.

The next evening we went to the meeting place. The road to Haltuk's was even more dangerous because he lived directly opposite the train station. Nevertheless, we reached his home, but again Platto wasn't there. Probably he was too apprehensive.

Haltuk offered us food. The wound in my jaw didn't hurt, but I could swallow only with great difficulty because my lymph glands were badly swollen. Each swallow was extremely painful. Only with great difficulty was I able to sip the milk.

We decided to look on the opposite side of town for one more food source. During the night we moved through the fields and forest, Szmul patiently waiting for me as I slowly side-stepped, until we eventually bypassed the town and found ourselves on the northern side of Izbica. Ahead of us was an isolated farm. We had to take a chance. I knocked on the door, and it opened.

"Come in," the man said.

We entered. The kitchen was small. Next to the man stood a woman and child. Knowing that my father was well known in town, I introduced myself as Leon Blatt's son and asked if they would sell us food. They weren't frightened and showed interest in us. The farmer's wife invited us to a warm supper.

As we ate we told them about Sobibor, the revolt, and our escape—

careful to omit the Bojarski episode, for they shared the same parish in the village of Tarnógora. They showed no shock or revulsion at our mention of the gas chambers, asked no detailed questions; they just listened to our story.

The man sold us bread, vodka, cheese, and when I asked, a school notepad. We came to the agreement that we would pay him a certain amount to supply us with food each week, pork and bread, and vodka, to keep ourselves warm.

Stalked Prey

I began a new diary, this time consisting mostly of short notes without names or places. We decided the hideout in the brick factory was too risky. The building was not secure. Children were often playing there, as I had years before, so there was always the possibility of accidental discovery.

As night fell, we moved instead to the same mill where, a year earlier, I had tried to escape from the Nazi guard by luring him with the promise of gold.

We arrived safely at the mill. Now there was a big padlock on the gate. We didn't even attempt to break it. Instead, we went in through the wide, glassless windows; the iron bars, already slightly bent, did not block our emaciated bodies. We simply undressed, then smeared our bodies with bacon fat. Once our heads passed through the bars, the rest slipped easily inside. By moonlight we could see dismantled machines of some kind, and in a corner we saw a mound of straw. Happily, we burrowed into it, pleased with our new hiding place.

From here on, it wasn't too bad. We had a steady supply of food. On Sundays we went to the peasant on the north side, then concealed ourselves for three days in the mill. Next, we went to the postmaster, Pasternak, on the south side for the same order, and then back to the mill again for three days. Our menu consisted mainly of dark bread, raw bacon, and vodka. When we needed water, we squeezed through the bars and walked to the natural well adjacent to the mill.

We thought we would be able to hide there until the end of the war, but as it turned out, we had to leave this place, too. We soon learned that a man was using the mill for straw storage. We could hear him with his pitchfork as he took a little more straw every day. Slowly but steadily our mound diminished. One day the pitchfork accidentally smashed our water bottle. The man didn't suspect anything as he did not interrupt his work, but for us it was a sign to leave. The forest, now fully covered with green foliage, seemed a more secure place now. At times we hid in farmhouses abandoned by fleeing villagers, at times in haystacks. And so we lived, one day at a time.

One night, while visiting Podgórski's, I asked him to safeguard some notes of mine, and he agreed. We received some food and left. We stopped under the stairs on the side of his house to decide where we should go next. Then we heard voices. We hid behind some barrels. Time passed, and a silhouette appeared on the path to the main road. A few moments later we heard footsteps in the darkness and voices speaking in Polish.

"Password?"

"Rifle," came the answer.

"Your password?"

"Trigger."

On the road, barely discernible in the distance, a group of people were heading toward the train station. Soon we heard shooting and commands in German. The sky lit up for a few seconds with the flash of two flares. Heavy machine guns rattled. Bullets were exchanged across the road, and then, suddenly, the battle was over. Someone was groaning and cursing in Polish. We realized that by sheer accident we had come across a partisan operation attacking a German military transport at the nearby station.

We unexpectedly discovered the secret partisan password for that night, and now if the need arose we could use it. We weren't afraid of the Germans; we knew they now seldom moved at night. The main danger was the Polish partisans in the area. I had some idea of the political leanings of the various partisan groups. This particular group might be tolerant of Jews in hiding, but how could we know which group it was? We couldn't ask. The gamble was deadly serious; our lives were at stake.

Silhouettes moved in the darkness. The shooting started up again for another five minutes, then stopped. We waited a little longer before moving on.

A few days later we took a longer but safer route through the forest to Pasternak's home. "Look," whispered Szmul, pointing to a flickering moonlit shadow at the edge of the forest. We stopped to make sure it wasn't a figment of our imaginations. Was it a bush or a man? We stood still and strained our eyes. As we watched from behind, the figure moved. It was a man with a rifle! We were lucky we were heading through the forest instead of the fields, where we surely would have been spotted. We crawled back on our stomachs and reached Pasternak's by the main road.

As we picked up our food, I asked Pasternak if he could buy us some shoes. "Let's see," he said, "I've got a pair of wooden clogs for one of you." He brought them out. Szmul took them and handed him about one hundred dollars in American currency. "I'll get the other pair next week," he said, turning to me. He acted curt and uneasy. "Look," he said, "I'm worried. There are armed men who know you are in the area and are on the lookout. It doesn't look good."

This district was beginning to get too dangerous for us. But the final decision to leave was precipitated by another incident, this one again at Pasternak's.

It was June 1944, a Monday, eight months since our escape from Sobibor. It was Pasternak's turn to supply us with food. It was a dark evening, and we moved cautiously, sensitive to any noise. We were approaching his home from a meadow. Then, suddenly, the long ray of a flashlight from the edge of the forest had us spotted. "Stop, don't move!"

Our reactions were instantaneous. Szmul ran, but I knew I had no chance of escaping because of my legs, so I crouched helplessly in the thick bushes beside the fence. Two people appeared, running from the forest bordering the house; in the darkness they brushed by me without noticing. They were running after Szmul. Soon Pasternak came outside into the garden and I heard him talking to his wife. I rose from hiding.

"Mr. Pasternak."

"My God, they didn't get you?"

"No, they didn't see me. They're chasing Szmul."

"Wait in the garden until it quiets down. Maybe Szmul will be back." And Pasternak returned to his home, afraid to invite me inside. After a while, a couple of rifle shots were heard not far away. Pasternak showed up again in the garden.

"Did you hear that?" he asked me. "They got him for sure." In the same breath he added, "I have your food and shoes and a pistol. Now give me two hundred American dollars."

"Sorry," I told him, "I have no money now. Szmul has it all." Without a word Pasternak turned and went back into the house. I waited, but he did not come out.

It was freezing cold. I was miserable, my spirit broken, but no matter, I was determined to wait in the garden until morning. Maybe, by some miracle, Szmul would return. I still believed he was alive.

Dawn came, but no Szmul. Where should I go to find him? After some contemplation, I decided to go to our other pickup point on the other side of town, simply because there we had paid in advance. If Szmul were alive, I would likely find him there.

Resigned, I moved slowly and painfully through the meadow and forest, finally reaching our second provision point. The farmer, seeing me through the window, came out screaming.

"Run, you dirty Jew, do you want to kill me? In broad daylight you come? Run, or I'll bring the Germans myself."

That was enough to bring me to my senses. As fast as my swollen ankles allowed, I stumbled along sideways and hid in the forest. I didn't really believe he would deliver me to the Germans. I knew he threatened me because he was terrified the Nazis would punish him and his family. It was a stupid act on my part. I had lost my senses in my despair and loneliness, and so had committed this unforgivable deed, endangering his life.

As darkness fell, I intended to go back to the farmer, but upon hearing some shooting and suspicious commotion close by, I decided to stay put and sleep in the potato sacks that I had stolen. One sack I pulled over my head and the other I pulled up over my legs. Protected from the chill, I curled up like a dog and slept.

As always, even in my sleep my senses were alert. It was still dark, but the faint sounds of birds chirping told me that the sun would soon arise. Then again a familiar bird whistle came, and another. Then suddenly a false note intruded.

"TOI-VEE . . . TOI-VEE . . . TOI-VEE."

I awakened and sat up. Again I heard "TOI-VEE . . ."

No, that isn't a bird, I thought to myself. I know all the noises of the forest at this time of year by heart. I pulled the sack from my head to hear more clearly and waited. But all I heard were the chirping of early-morning birds. Was that Szmul?

After a few seconds I got up enough courage to call out halfheartedly, "Szmul! Szmul!"

No one answered. But I had a feeling that it was him.

I ran. Out of breath I reached the farmer's house and without knocking, I entered.

"Did he come?"

"He was here," the peasant answered impatiently, "and he told me that I should tell you, if you came, he would wait at the usual place."

Everything was clear now. In my mind I reconstructed everything that must have happened. Szmul escaped to the forest. The bandits shot at him and missed in the darkness. At the same time, he must have thought that I had been caught and so he did not look for me. The next evening, he went to the other food supplier. Then the farmer must have told him that I came by during the day, but I had left and gone to the forest. Apparently, Szmul waited through the night for me in the farmer's barn (where many times we slept without his knowledge), thinking I would come back. In the morning he went to the forest, logically thinking I would be sleeping there. Reaching the approximate area where he thought I might be, he called out my name, simulating a bird chirp. He had done this many times. Not getting a response, he quickly ran deep into the forest, as it was our strategy to move fast especially if we made any loud sound. I'm sure it must have been like that. However, by the time I had awakened and called to him, it was too late. He was already too far away.

I didn't know where to look for him. He had told the farmer that he would be waiting at the "the usual place." That could be any one of five places. The first was where I was right then; the second was in the Orlów forest; the third was in the abandoned flour mill; the fourth was an abandoned farmer's hut in a valley close to Bojarski's farm; and the fifth, Pasternak's, was eliminated as it was already discovered.

I decided to try the meadow in the middle of the Orlów forest first. I waited there a few hours, but no sign of him. Next, despite the terrible risk, I left in daylight through the fields to reach the mill.

I was so depressed I didn't care about anything. I felt an overwhelming fear of loneliness. More than anything I wanted to see Szmul. I couldn't wait. It's difficult to imagine or understand the loneliness I felt, alone day and night in the deserted mill, the fields, and forest, without a soul to talk to, with each shadow a possible enemy.

On the way leading to the mill I approached the Red Bridge, where I had gotten lost earlier that winter. I didn't want to pass over it. It was a very visible point in the landscape; I went down the slope to the valley below.

As I was crawling up the next slope, I noticed the uniformed Izbica railroad stationmaster observing me. With him was a girl my age. We recognized each other. We had met many times at the train station when I used to pick up the morning papers there for the newsstand. I sensed danger, but nonchalantly I went on. They were observing my every move.

The stationmaster below could observe me moving toward the barn on top of the hill overlooking the valley. He could see me entering the barn, but then I lay down flat on my stomach and, out of his vision, dragged myself out the other door. About eighty feet forward I could go no farther, as peasants were working in the field and could easily intercept me. Everywhere were the huge holes dug for clay to make bricks. I slid into one, intending to sit until nightfall. A short time later, I heard voices from near the barn.

"Hope to die if I didn't see him. I give you my word, I myself saw him go in!"

I hoped and prayed they would stop their search at the barn, but a few seconds later, my heart pounding, I was discovered.

"Hands up!"

I put up my hands and turned around. Next to the hole stood a sixteen- or seventeen-year-old boy with a gun.

"Get up!"

I crawled out of the hole and sat on the grass, surrounded by more youths.

"Get up and run to the forest!" he ordered.

"I can't. My feet are crippled." I remained sitting.

"Beat it," he said, "or I'll shoot."

"I can't run, and I don't care anymore."

He gave me a swift kick in the stomach. I gasped and groaned.

"Get up!"

I got up and slowly, painfully, side-stepped forward. I left the burlap potato sacks, which barely protected me from the cold, and a bottle of water. I was sure they would be of no more use to me. They took me to a meadow in the middle of the forest. Milling about were a group of young people, Polish partisans. One of them, apparently the leader, was a good acquaintance of mine, Tadek Nowosadzki, a Catholic Pole. He recognized me.

"Why so unhappy, Toivi?"

I answered the question with another question. "If you knew that you were going to die, would you be happy?"

"Relax, Toivi, don't be afraid. Everything will be all right. Sit down," he said kindly. "Tell me how you got to be here."

A fairly large group gathered around me. I knew everyone; some shook hands with me. I didn't tell them the Bojarski episode; I felt it could only hurt me. I assumed that if they knew the truth, they would shoot me if only to help Bojarski, a fellow Catholic. I lied and told them that I had run away from Sobibor to the Ukraine, where Poles had helped me. But I had to move back to this territory, I said, because the nationalistic Ukrainian bands, were wiping out the Polish population in the area. They believed me. I even thought I detected in some a sign of sorrow for me.

It was a long conversation. They were especially interested in what went on at Sobibor, which, though relatively close by, was shrouded by mystery. They already knew about the death camps for Jews, but firsthand information was something special and fascinated them. They expressed no sympathy for me or my family; they simply listened as though it were an exciting adventure story.

I suspected they were waiting for their orders regarding me. About two hours later, Tadek was called aside by someone who had just arrived from town. After a few minutes of whispering, Tadek ordered everyone to disperse. The partisans slowly disbanded. Lookouts in the trees climbed down and departed. Only Tadek and I were now left in the meadow.

Tadek was heavily armed. He proudly showed me his German army pistol. Under his belt were German grenades with long wooden handles and oval-shaped, carved Russian grenades. He confessed, not without pride, that though only eighteen years old, he was already a leader of a platoon of partisans.

"I'm sorry I can't take you in my unit of the A.K. [National Army].

You see, everyone knows you as a Jew, and as a rule, we don't take Jews."

"Why have you spared me?" I asked bluntly.

"A true member of the National Army," he answered, "will not kill a Jew, except when he is caught with a weapon.[6] But it's possible that some Poles posing as members of the A.K. are killing Jews while they rob them."

A chill went down my spine. How lucky I am that Mr. Pasternak denied me the pistol because I had no money left to pay for it. It would have been a death sentence for me now. I knew of cases in which the A.K. had killed innocent Jews, but I kept quiet and said no more.

Tadek got up and buttoned his coat, bulging from the weapons beneath. "Wait here. I'll bring you something to eat."

A few hours later he returned with his brother. He had brought me bread, bacon, and borscht in vodka bottles. I devoured the food. "Just keep away from this area," he said. "Go farther east, where the Soviet partisans are. They're more liberal in their membership—they're more likely to accept you." I listened attentively as he gave me a few tips on how to evade enemies. We shook hands, he wished me luck, and we said good-bye.

This scary episode shocked me back to reality. I had to be more careful. With extreme caution I made my way back to the area around the mill. There I sat in the bushes and waited for darkness.

I had a beautiful view of Izbica. On my right were the houses of friends and acquaintances, now occupied by strangers; on my left were green pastures.

With the onset of darkness, I made it to the mill. This time I slipped easily through the window bars without greasing myself. "Szmul," I called in a low voice. No answer. In the shallow straw, I found a bottle. I took it to the well and bent down to fill it with water.

Just then I looked up, and there stood a man I knew, Karaszczuk, peering at me. I was terrified. It was too late to run. He understood I was Jewish, but he didn't recognize me.

"What's your name?"

"Blatt. I'm Leon Blatt's son, Toivi."

"Oh, yes, Toivi. You must be hungry. Wait here, I'll bring you something."

Steady encounters with danger had sharpened my intuition to the point of knowing whom to trust. I waited, and soon he returned with bread and sugar. He mentioned that a Jewish boy had been hiding somewhere in the ruins of the brick factory. He probably was talking about me without realizing it.

I decided to try to find Szmul once more. I would go to the last place I could think of where Szmul might still be waiting. I headed south, and, after a long hike, was close to the local brewery. At this point I turned left and headed uphill. I came upon an abandoned farm hidden in the valley.

The yard gate was locked but I got over the fence and entered the attic with a ladder. Disappointed in not finding him there, I ended my search with a heavy heart and fell asleep there in the attic.

The next morning I made shoes by bandaging and tying my feet with the rags I found there. I imagined I looked like the star of *The Song of the Cossacks,* a movie about a Polish prisoner in Siberia, which I remembered seeing shortly before the war. I opened the attic door and looked out. The sun was shining and the countryside was abundantly green. I wanted so much to live.

Recovering from the previous day's turmoil, I tried to devise a plan for the future, taking into consideration my complete lack of money. Those who had until now steadily supplied me with ample food would not continue without pay. This made a bad situation even worse; I was desperate. I sat trying to think of possible choices. There were none. I was now forced to beg. For three days, water had been my only sustenance. But eventually I got too hungry. I knew that if I didn't eat I would soon lose even the strength necessary to get down from the loft.

At dusk I climbed down and went to the edge of town to try Mrs. Kowalczyk, one of my former teachers and a decent woman. I got safely to her house in the middle of a field and knocked. A tall skinny lady came out; it was my former teacher.

"Mrs. Kowalczyk, please, I haven't eaten for three days. Could I have some bread?"

She thought for a minute or so. "Toivi," she said, "I want to help you, but I'm afraid. The other day in the Germans caught the Jew Wang who went crazy and left his hiding place." Her voice was charged with emotion. "They tortured him, and he gave the names of the Polish people who helped him. And later the Germans arrested a woman who is sure to be executed . . . Toivi, I feel sorry for you, but I can't . . . you must understand." I had left already when I heard a voice. "Wait a minute." She was coming toward me with a big loaf of bread in her hand. She had overcome her fears to help me.

I returned to the loft. Very depressed, I decided to die by starvation. But the next day when I became hungry I changed my mind. I decided to take the gamble: I'd either get killed or get food. I climbed down the ladder, washed my face at the well, and was on my way.

If Not for Father . . .

I was near Podgórski's, but I didn't even consider going there in broad daylight. His house was situated conspicuously on the highway. My only choice was to go through the pasture to a little white hut, the home of the farmer Janeczek. A while back Podgórski had advised me never to enter that hut, but I figured they could either put me out of my misery or feed me. And either was fine with me at this point. But upon nearing the place, fear won out, so I turned in another direction.

It was too late. They had noticed me. A young boy, about twelve years old, had come out of the house and was riding his bike toward me. I was being watched; I couldn't disappear now. I turned again toward the hut and entered the yard. In the doorway stood Janeczek.

"May God help you," I said in the typical peasant greeting.

"For eternity, amen," came his reply.

Still uneasy about begging for food, I asked for a drink of water.

"Come in, I'll give you some."

I wanted to pass on this invitation. It sounded more like an order. But there was no turning back now. I entered.

A gaunt man handed me fresh milk and some cake. Intuition told me that I had somehow voluntarily gotten myself into another predicament. Meanwhile, a few strangers entered the room, observing me. At the table sat a young man with a bandaged leg.

Janeczek took off his slippers and put on boots. Then, nodding in my direction, he said to the wounded young man, "Take care, I'll soon be back."

I knew that escape was impossible now. I would have to wait it out. If I pretended to be stupid it might be easier to mislead him. The wounded man started conversing with me.

"Do you like to ride cycles?" he asked.

"Yes."

"Well, then, we'll give you a ride."

He smiled slyly. Little did he know that I realized that the ride he planned for me was one to heaven. With sadistic satisfaction, he continued speaking in this manner, hinting strongly about what was awaiting me and probably wondering at my stupidity for not being able to take an obvious hint. I could see he was deriving pleasure from his little game. I knew all too well what sort of man I was dealing with, but I continued to play the role of a gullible kid.

During the conversation he asked whether my father, known as a "rich" man in the vicinity, had any hidden valuables. Enter a faint ray of hope. I fortified his interest and admitted, "Yes, a whole bag of gold coins is hidden in an attic in town. If you would only help me, we could divide it." I was sure he'd take the bait and, if so, my chance of escape could be realized.

The gate squeaked loudly outside in the garden. It was Sunday, and the farmer's wife had just returned from church. At the first sight of me she froze, dumbfounded. When she regained her composure, she turned to the wounded one and asked, "Where did you pick him up?"

"He came in by himself."

The woman busied herself preparing food, shaking her head in disgust, murmuring, "For shame, so close to the end of the war. Pity the child, even if he is a Jew."

Shortly Janeczek returned. He immediately asked if I was still hungry and gave me some rolls. Was he joking? Was this the last meal for the doomed? What should I do? In my last hope I innocently asked to go relieve myself. My intention was to run when they let me go a little farther away from them.

He did not answer, but led me to the yard. "Get going," he said. "Head for the Biała Podlaska forest. There you'll find friendly Russian partisans who will take you in."

Against a tree nearby stood Podgórski. Where he had come from I don't know. Possibly he was there to show he was a witness to what they were doing to me and in this way protect me. I don't really know.

It looked like I was actually free. I thanked him for the food and slowly walked away.

These last two incidents and their fortunate outcomes were food for thought. I knew of specific cases where Jews were murdered by the dozens in this area. So why was I so lucky? Why didn't they kill me too?[7]

I didn't want to push my luck. Sooner or later the truth would come out about Bojarski, and then they would have no pity on me. Then they certainly would want to kill me for fear that I might someday take revenge on Bojarski. I knew I must vanish from this familiar area.

It was 1944. The German war machine was weakening. The Nazis, once so cocky, now hadn't the guts to show themselves in the villages of eastern Poland. When they did, it was only in convoys. My legs slowly healed, but I needed shoes and, feeling lightheaded, decided to go to Izbica to Heniek Królikowski for help.

As I had earlier, I sneaked through the town, around houses, and through the ruins of former Jewish homes, finally arriving near my destination. I had only to cross the main street. At that point the street was straight, lined with houses on both sides, and someone could easily notice me. I looked suspicious. Besides, every little child knew me here, knew that I was a Jew. It's no use, I thought, I must go. Up till now luck had been with me. So I again began to believe in my lucky star, Jewish though it was. It was twilight, and I walked nonchalantly in the street.

Soon I was at the door of Królikowski's bakery. However, upon hearing the voice of Piasecki, the baker's helper, I was afraid to enter. Instead, I went into the hallway and knocked on the door of Heniek Królikowski's apartment.

The door opened. "Toivi! Come in." It was Heniek's mother. The elderly woman wasn't frightened and wanted to help me. It was dangerous to sit in the room, so as soon as Piasecki left work she hid me in the bakery behind the oven. It was warm and dry there. I soon fell asleep. At dawn Heniek's mother shook me awake.

"Toivi, get up. It's late. In a moment the workers will come in. They mustn't see you here. You must go."

"Mrs. Królikowski, could you give me some clothes? I can't leave like this."

"I don't have anything that will fit you," she said. Then, looking down, "But I see you are barefoot and your feet are swollen. Maybe I can give you Heniek's sandals."

Now I was the owner of shoes! I had waited for this moment since I had escaped from Bojarski! Now my feet would be protected from the morning dew and would heal! I thanked her, said good-bye, and left.

Instead of going to the forest, I simply hid in the shed of the good woman's house and remained there till dusk. Then I stole up to the attic and stayed there a few days, right in the heart of the little town, which for some time now had been officially Judenrein.

Each evening I went to elderly Mrs. Królikowski for food. She didn't ask where I slept, but I could tell she understood. I had won a few extra days of life, and my ankles had healed a great deal. I could now walk normally, though still painfully. However, I couldn't go very far. If someone saw me, I'd be trapped. It was dangerous here. Mrs. Królikowski became nervous and impatient. It was time to leave this place as well.

Early in the morning, being careful to avoid people and open spaces, I set out. Using shortcuts and paths I knew well, I managed to cross the guarded railroad tracks that cut through the town. Now a very dangerous three hundred yards were ahead of me. On the right side was the police station, on the left the mayor's office and the local jail. So I turned to the right and made a big circle around the police station by cutting through the soccer field.

I reached my destination, the home of my former school principal, Mr. Sztajndel. I still remembered him lowering his head when he witnessed us being taken to Sobibor. I decided to ask him for help.

He opened the door, surprised to see me, "Come in, sit down!" He gave me food, and asked about my parents and brother and what had happened to us all. I told him of Sobibor, the revolt, and how I survived afterward. I could feel he cared, that he felt compassion for me. Sztajndel's son had been taken to Auschwitz, but neither of us spoke of it. His wife, who had been ill for many years, lay paralyzed in bed observing me, friendly but motionless. She had made an effort to reach my hand and tried to talk to me, but her words were unintelligible. "I'm sorry, Toivi, I can't help you. I wish I could hide you, but I can't," he explained sadly.

Ahead of me lay the village of Tarnogóra, along the Wieprz River. To the west were the villages of Ostrzyca, Mchy, and others. I only vaguely remembered the road leading to them. Once or twice before the war, my father had taken me with him on business trips to this area. I was about to cross the bridge to the other side of the river when I noticed a German soldier. He was standing guard at the gate of Count Smorczewski's estate, now the German military headquarters. He spotted me and called out after me. I jumped into the riverbank reeds, then swam until I crossed the river. I wandered on. Going through the fields, suntanned, in overalls and rolled-up sleeves, one wouldn't think I was a Jew in hiding, but rather a Polish youngster from town going to the village to purchase food or look for work. But I lost my way, and instead of arriving in the village of Ostrzyca I wound up in some pasture. To the right and left of me were deep marshes where one could sink right in, and in front of me was a herd of cows. There was only one way to go. I went over to the man tending the cows and casually asked for milk. I was hungry. Next to hiding, this was my biggest problem. The cowhand, a kind older man, immediately understood I was Jew. He handed me the milk and, after a short wary conversation, I moved on. It was broad daylight and there were only cornfields ahead. I turned into the field, delicately putting the cornstalks back in place so as not to leave a trail. I sat there in the corn a whole day. The sun was unbearable and the sweat was pouring from me. Exhausted and hungry, I made it until sundown and then fell asleep.

Early in the morning, after a long search, I found Ostrzyca. I remembered from childhood that my father's friend, Mr. Nizioł, lived there, but I didn't know in which house. There were some people moving about the village, but I was afraid to ask them, afraid they would recognize me as a stranger and a Jew. Finally I spotted a little boy about five years old.

"Hey, do you know where Nizioł lives?" I called out.

"Over there," he said, pointing to the third house on the street.

Mr. Nizioł and his wife opened the door. Recognizing me, they nervously looked right and left down the street. "No one has seen me," I said, "don't worry." They let me enter.

The woman hurried to get me food. "What happened to your family, your father and mother, your brother?" I told them my whole story. They were not surprised about Sobibor. They had known about it, but this was the first time they had a firsthand report, and they listened with cool interest. I concluded by asking them to hide me.

For the rest of the day and night they had me stay in the barn. I fell asleep, but was awakened a few hours later by many footsteps passing by the barn. I dug deeper in the straw and fell asleep again.

In the morning the farmer's wife called me for breakfast. I could see in her eyes that she was somehow nervous and frightened. Finally, her husband broke the silence.

"Toivi, you've got to leave. I am sorry. During the night a formation of Germans and Ukrainians passed through our village on the way to the next one. There they carted off farmers to concentration camps. You see, everyone in the area was supposed to deliver a certain number of food crops to the Germans, and some farmers held back. Yesterday the special Nazi penal expedition burned the village down."

I said nothing.

"Toivi, we were just lucky," said his wife, breaking in. "They could have discovered you here. Just thinking about it, I could faint. You must go now. There's another friend of your father's, Mr. Petla, living in the village of Mchy. Maybe he'll help you."

I thanked them and left. It took me some time, but one mile farther away I found the place. Petla was an efficient farmer. One could tell by his prosperous-looking house. The gate leading to the yard was open, and I stepped in. The furious barking of a dog brought the farmer out of his house.

I recognized Petla immediately. He had been a guest in our home many times. I introduced myself, told him my story, and asked for help. He accepted me warmly, and without hesitation I became his cowhand.

I always hated to get up early. Before the war my favorite days were Saturdays, Sundays, and holidays, when there was no school and I could sleep late. But that was the past. Now, by five o'clock I was up, putting the cows out to pasture.

This particular village, Mchy, and the area around it, was exceptionally helpful to Jews. Besides me, there were three other Jewish men and two Jewish women. They were the tailor Dawid Berend and his wife Baiła; Chuna Lipszyc; and saddlemaker Stefan Akerman and his relative Syma Unach. The tailor was the best off, for there was always a peasant who wanted his services. They even fought over him, vying to shelter him.

Also, two Jewish brothers from Piaski, who were hiding somewhere nearby, would drop into the village from time to time at night. They would pick up food from peasants and then disappear for a few days. I talked to them once when they came to Petla's farm. They were in bad shape. I could see they were jealous of my steady place. The Petlas had helped other Jews as well, giving as much as they could—advice, extra food and clothing, or whatever was needed.

Chuda, My Savior

Petla had only three cows: Łaciata (Patches), because of her red and white patches; Czarnula (Blackie); and Chuda (Skinny One). They were all good-natured and gave me no trouble. But I felt sorry for Chuda. For some reason she had lost her appetite, and the farmer, to make her eat, had a heavy piece of wood suspended from her neck with a rope. The weight forced her head close to the grass, but still she did not feed. It was hard on her, and she could only move slowly.

The field of view leading from the nearest town was wide open for about a mile. I'd be able to see danger in time, and on the east was a forest I could flee to if necessary. At the moment life was peaceful and serene, and I yearned for a book to read. All I had was the New Testament, which the farmer had lent me. I knew it by heart almost, yet it felt alien to me. It was their book, the book of my persecutors.

It wasn't long before boys tending cows in neighboring pastures came over to me. They befriended the ragged stranger, and accepted his story of being a Pole, a refugee from eastern Poland. And when Petla's son Romek told them secretly that I was a relative of the butler of former Polish president Ignacy Mościcki, they looked at me with respect. They ranged in age from eight to sixteen, and I blended in without suspicion. I took part in their storytelling, their "confessions," and games. Like all children, we played different games, but also, as a sign of the times, we played Szukaj Zyda (Catch a Jew).

In this game, a few boys would pick on one particular fellow and yell, "Jude! Jude Kaput!" The accused, knowing what came next, would try to escape but was usually caught. Here the ritual began. "Jude?" he was asked in a stern voice, simulating German authority. When the prisoner confessed to being a Jew, he was made to sit on the ground while his friends ran around him, aiming their cow sticks as if they were rifles, yelling "Jude! Christ killer! Bang! Bang! Jude! Christ killer! Bang! Bang! Bang!" The "Jew" fell "dead," and the game was over.

Sometimes, however, if the "Jew" did not admit to being Jewish, then there was the ultimate proof—the proof of circumcision. First he had to be wrestled to the ground. It ended with the bruised prisoner lying on his back with his pants pulled down, his indisputable proof of "pure Aryan blood" plainly visible. Then he was set free.

This innocent child's play was for me an absolute nightmare. I was constantly on my guard. When would it be my turn? When would Franek point to me and say, "Catch the Jew"? It was only a matter of time, it was inevitable. And one afternoon, while the cows were slow and lazy, with stomachs full, the game began.

"Szukaj Zyda!" The finger was pointing at me. My heart pounded. I had a choice. I could immediately admit to being a Jew. I would be thrown on the grass, spat upon, called "Jude," and finally "shot." But I no longer saw children, I saw Nazis. Their sticks were real guns, and their calls of "Jude" were real to me. I looked around, desperate to escape. There was still an opening in the tightening ring of boys, I dashed through.

The chase was on. Barefoot, I ran like a football player, tricking my pursuers. I knew I mustn't abandon the cows; my safe place depended on it. But I knew also that I mustn't get caught; my life might depend on it. While running I made a knot in the string that held up my pants, my farmer's gift.

Suddenly, the only girl in the group, Kasia, appeared out of nowhere and, standing in my path, neatly tripped me with her foot. In fast succession, the boys swarmed over me. "We've got him! Let's see if he's a Jew!" they yelled gleefully. Hands tore at the rope belt that held up my pants.

"Let go! I'm a Jew! Please believe me! Shoot me! Shoot me!" I screamed, pretending that I was deadly shy. God, why don't they stop! The more frantically I held onto my pants, the more they laughed and the more they pulled. If they saw my circumcision, they would know my dangerous secret—I was a Jew, a real one.

My admission didn't help. "Don't believe him!" shrieked Kasia. "He's not a Jew! Take his pants down, you'll see!" In revenge for my stubborn escape, they pounced on me. Suddenly there was the sound of cloth tearing. My shirt sleeve was ripped off. They stopped for a moment, scared. Shirts were precious, costly. This was enough for me to jump to my feet and run.

Again they were after me. I slipped on Chuda's cow pie and made a splash landing. Everyone stopped and burst into laughter. I was too dirty to touch, so they left me in peace. Thank you, Chuda.

The Exceptional German

June 1944. Petla had given me half a day off. I left for the village where Stefan Akerman, the saddlemaker, was hiding fixing horse gear for the peasants in exchange for food and shelter. The village was two miles away, and I walked openly. Nobody knew me, and I easily passed for a village boy. I found Stefan in the yard. He was sitting on a special saddler's seat with a wooden vise in front of him to clamp the leather together for sewing.

"Hi, Tomek."

"Good morning, Stefan."

We called ourselves by the Polish equivalents of our Jewish names, as did most Jews in hiding.

"How is Syma, Tomek?" He was referring to his relative who worked as a maid for one of Rosoliński's brothers in my village.

I lowered my voice to a whisper and came right to the point. "Stefan, the peasant is pestering her, and on top of that his wife is jealous."

Actually, this was my reason for going to see Stefan. Knowing that her relative was himself in a precarious situation, Syma had begged me to present her predicament to him in the best possible light. In reality, she was in a terrible situation. She needed to leave her place and had nowhere else to go. The farmer was trying to take advantage of her, and there had already been a fight about it in the family. The situation would not last long.

It was time for me to return. "I'll walk you partway back so we can talk more freely." We left the yard and took the straight sandy road to my village. We discussed the problem, not noticing three men on bikes riding in our direction. There was no reason to be alarmed. It was Sunday, and the only transportation to church was on foot or bicycle. By the time we noticed the green uniforms of several German military police, it was already too late to run. We pretended not to care and kept walking. My heart beat faster and my lips silently begged God to have pity. They passed us, and I sighed with relief.

"Halt!" We stopped frozen in our tracks and waited. The order had come from behind. They passed us, turned, and faced us with outstretched rifles.

"Partisans?" one of them asked in Polish.

"No, we are not partisans," I answered.

"Jews?"

"No."

Could someone have betrayed to the Germans that Jews were hiding in this village, or was it chance? They patted our trousers for hidden weapons and asked for papers. We were close to the pasture.

My cowhand friends, curious now, were closing in. I was terrified. Then, when I least expected it, help came. It was Kasia.

"Panie Niemiec [Sir German], this is our boy, from here, a Pole. Let him go." The soldiers ignored me, and I stepped aside to the group of boys who herded cows. But nobody vouched for Stefan. Kasia looked at Stefan. It was just like in the game Catch a Jew. "Take his pants down," she said to the Nazis, "and you will know for sure who he is."

"Take your pants down," ordered a soldier. When Stefan pretended he didn't understand German, (which every Jew in our region did), the soldier pulled down his pants for him. There was no doubt; it was clear he was Jewish. I was angry and scared. But I didn't show it. I had to be careful not to betray myself. I had learned a lesson on the train to Hungary. I must look secure, look my fellow cowhands in the face, and pretend I'm one of them. Yet I felt terribly for Stefan. An invisible wall separated us. I'm sure Stefan understood.

The Nazi turned to us now. "Would you like to shoot him?" he said. "Here is the gun. He's yours." The boys stared. This was real, no longer the wooden stick. We shook our heads and scattered. From farther on we could see them standing and talking. Then the eldest one took Stefan by the collar and led him toward the bushes nearby. The other Germans held their comrades' bike on the road. The one who spoke in Polish called to us.

"Do you know where any more Jews are hiding?"

"No!" we yelled.

Two shots echoed from nearby. Our heads instinctively turned in that direction. Moments later we saw the German come out of the bushes, push his pistol into the holster, pick up his bike, and, without a word, leave with his comrades.

"Let's go!" said Wojtek as he ran toward the bushes where Stefan was last seen.

"Come on!" yelled another. "Jews have money. He was wearing good shoes, too!"

I ran with them. I had to keep up the act. We searched. We looked all over the area. Darkness was approaching, and we couldn't find his body.

Stefan's death still shocked me, and I was anxious to hide alone in a stack of hay, where nobody could see me. Once in the hay, I felt a terrible heaviness in my heart. For Kasia it was only a minor incident; she probably didn't even think about it anymore. I felt responsible for Stefan's death. If not for me, he would be alive; he would not have gone on the road. Now what would I tell Syma? I fell asleep exhausted.

Half-awake, I heard a man's voice. "Tomek, where are you? Food is waiting." I had slept past mealtime. But the farmer had never looked for me before. Why now? I crawled out from the stack. "I'm coming, Mr. Petla!"

Petla was agitated. The news of Stefan's death had already reached him. Earlier, the same Germans had arrived in the village to buy eggs and butter. They could return. He was afraid.

"You must leave, Tomek. But I won't let you down," he said. "I'll arrange another place for you."

I hated to leave. In Petla's house I was a member of the family. We all sat around the wooden table, in the middle of which was placed a wooden dish of hot mashed potatoes with pig fat and another with sour cream. Everybody scooped as much as he wanted. At Petla's I felt like a person; I was treated as a person. I sat at the table with the others, and it meant more to me than food. It gave me the greatest happiness and the hope that another kind of world was possible.

"Mr. Petla, I'm going to sleep. I'm tired. Good-night." Outside the fresh air and the quiet of the village were relaxing, and I felt secure.

"Pssst . . . Tomek!" I heard a faint whisper. A dark silhouette was standing in the chicken coop. I recognized him immediately.

"Stefan, you're alive! It's impossible! Is it really you?"

"Tomek, quiet!" The chickens, awakened from their sleep, squawked and fluttered.

"Stefan, are you wounded? Come to the barn. I have a blanket. Sleep here. Early in the morning you will leave, before my farmer sees you."

"Toivi," he called me now by my Jewish name, "I have *meyer masel ve sechel* [more luck than brains]." He sat down. "You saw the German take me to the bushes. He had a good hold on me, and I was sure it was the end. Then he asked me if I smoked. I nodded, and he gave me a cigarette. I had heard about the last cigarette before the execution, and I was terrified. But he said, 'Boy, don't shake, I won't kill you.' Then he lit my cigarette and told me to run. He lifted his rifle and shot in the air. 'Run!' he repeated. It's a dream, I kept thinking, it's a dream. Then I realized I was still standing in the same spot. The German had disappeared. I had just enough strength to make it to the next field and collapse in the corn."

Kasia

The next day, earlier than ever, we both left, I with the cows to the pasture, and Stefan, by shortcut, to his old place in the next village. Soon, the rest of my friends arrived. The whole day Kasia eluded me. But at the end of the day she was waiting for me, and we left the pasture together. Something was bothering her.

"Tomek, do you think it was my fault they killed that Jew?"

I didn't answer.

She continued, "You know the Jews crucified Christ?"

"The Jews didn't kill Christ," I answered by reflex, as if to defend myself.

"So who killed him?"

"The Romans. The cross was their way of execution." I had heard this in a discussion in my parents' home, but wasn't sure it was true.

"How do you know? So why do they kill the Jews?" She threw out two questions at once.

She stepped in front of me. "Tomek, why are you defending them?"

I said nothing, but moved her aside.

"Wait, Tomek. Tell me, where did you learn to read?" She pointed to a newspaper stuffed in my pants.

"What do you mean?"

"You know. You read everything, even pieces of paper you find on the road. When you shit, you read, too. I've seen you."

Did she suspect? Was she playing a game? She was a peasant girl with perhaps three years of public schooling. She had typical Slavic features, blond with round rosy cheeks. Though not exactly pretty, she had a certain charm and was well-developed for fifteen. And she was bold, a real tomboy, exercising considerable authority in our circle of cowhands, the opposite of me with my rather shy nature. She never talked to me about sex. Only once when one cow mounted another, she called out to me, "Look at that stupid cow pretending to be a bull." My face had flushed red, and I went back to the cows.

"Tomek, I'll be waiting in the tobacco-drying shed in the evening. I will bring you a book. Will you read it to me?"

"Kasia, it's too dark there to read. I can't."

"You better come," she said, and was gone.

Back at the farm, Petla was waiting. "Tomek, after supper I will introduce you to your new boss."

We ate in silence. I knew they liked me. I was a conscientious worker and earned my bread. Romek, their son, who was my age, was especially fond of me, the boy from the "big city" who knew everything and could tell such interesting stories. They were good Christian people, and I felt comfortable with them. We were still eating when Mr. Stryjek entered.

"God bless you."

"To eternity, amen," we answered.

He seated himself on a bench and pulled out half a liter of *samogon* (moonshine vodka made from sugar beets), the way most peasants conclude a deal. Pan Stryjek patted me on the back. Apparently the decision had already been made.

"Tomek, I've heard a lot about you. You are brave and a good worker. I need help. I have no children." Then, bringing his lips close to my ears, "I knew Leiba," he whispered my father's Jewish name. "He was a true patriot. Do not be afraid as long as you are with me."

"Now let's drink," Petla cut in.

"Na zdrowie [To health]."

"Na zdrowie."

We clanked our tall, half-full glasses and finished our vodka in one gulp. I had been drinking since my deals with the guards in Sobibor. I was used to drinking vodka in large glasses, as was the custom here. But this stuff took my breath away. My throat was on fire and tears came to my eyes. But I didn't cough, curse, or jump; I was in full control of myself. As was the custom in those parts, it was a test of manhood. Their eyes were on me. "He is our man," Pan Stryjek said simply. I had passed the test. I was "tough."

Suddenly I remembered the meeting with Kasia. She must be waiting for me! Kasia intrigued me. I was sixteen years old and had never kissed a girl, let alone embraced one. Even in Sobibor with the Dutch twins, even in the shadow of death, I couldn't free myself of obsessive shyness and let my feelings take over. Now, a year later, the shadow of death still hung over me. I wanted to know the warmth of love, the secrets of sex, but at the same time I was afraid of her. She didn't hesitate to deliver a Jew to certain death. Is she not my enemy? She was from another world, Aryan, and she wanted me. Although I was still naive, I intuitively understood the purpose of my invitation to the tobacco shack.

"Tomek, what are you dreaming about?" Romek asked.

I was on my feet. "Panie Stryjek, I must go. See you tomorrow, early in the morning."

The door to the drying shed was unbolted. Inside, strings of tobacco were hanging wall to wall and the air was warm. I liked the smell of tobacco. Kasia was sitting on a heap of leaves near the cutter. The only window, high on the wall, let in some moonlight. It was quiet, only the crickets chirped without stop.

"Tomek, come closer. I don't bite." I moved a few inches and stopped, still a distance away.

"Tomek, why are you not like other boys? You talk differently. You don't swear, never. Where are you from?"

I stood up defensively. "You know I come from the East. We talk differently there. We have different customs, that's all."

"Tomek, I don't want to hurt you. I do like you." She stretched out her hand as for a handshake, and unexpectedly pulled me down. I fell on her in the soft leaves. She brought her arms around my back and gently squeezed me against her. I felt the warmth of her body and the scent of laundry soap. She was prepared. My heart pounded. I never was so close to a girl. I let her take over, let her fondle me; she was experienced. Suddenly, a flash of reality. "Tomek . . . you are a Jew . . ." There was no anger in her voice. She pulled me even tighter against her. But my heart nearly stopped. I was back in the real world, on guard. Was this her version of Catch a Jew? I jumped up.

"Kasia, yes, I'm a Jew. Sorry. I will not touch you again. Forgive me." And I headed for the door.

As I crossed the threshold, her soft whisper reached my ears. "Tomek, don't be afraid. I won't betray you."

Mr. Krupa's Barn

Mr. Stryjek came and took me to his farm. Now I worked a tobacco plantation. Though I worked well and with enthusiasm, his wife was always complaining and called me "dirty Jew" for any reason. I didn't complain to her husband; he accidentally overheard it himself. He had an argument with her and apologized to me. Shortly afterward, afraid of his wife's revenge, I moved on. It was important to me that time was also moving: day by day, hour by hour, closer to the end of the war. I *will* survive, I thought.

At the next hamlet, a peasant, who was also a friend of my father's, was unloading straw from a wagon into his attic. I gave him the proper Polish greeting.

"May God help you."

"So be it," came the expected response.

"I'm Blatt's son. Is it possible to stay a while? I could help you in your work."

"Blatt? You're alive? What happened to your father?" he asked, interrupting his work.

"My family was gassed," I said matter-of-factly.

"Go to the house. I will finish work shortly, and we can talk."

I preferred to wait in the yard. When he finished his job we went in. On the table he laid bread, butter, and homemade vodka. "Help yourself," he invited.

I told him how I was taken to Sobibor, of the revolt and the escape, and he, like the other Poles who fed me and heard my account, listened in disbelief as I told him of the inside workings of the camp. Although all knew of the death camps and were not surprised that thousands were gassed there, they couldn't believe how systematic the process of extinction was.

I stayed there a whole week. Perhaps I would have been there longer, but I had the urge to repay him for his help by fixing a broken grandfather clock that stood in the dining room. I used to fix bicycles, so I thought, why not the clock?

That was a mistake. Apparently, the screwdriver, pliers, and heavy hammer I found with the farmer's tools weren't right for such a delicate job and I ruined it. He was angry, and soon I was on my way.

I asked another farmer for food and shelter in exchange for labor. He agreed. Sunday, before leaving for church, he asked me to take care of the animals. When I entered the barn to pick up straw for the cows, I noticed some cages with rabbits. In one there were only three rabbits, but in the other were triple the amount. I understood that the males were separated from the females.

I wasn't able to resist seeing what would happen if I let the male into the female cage for a few minutes. It didn't take me long to select the biggest male rabbit and place him inside the other cage. Immediately hysteria ensued. The male rabbit was at his best. It took me a while to grab the champ. By that time the damage was done.

Time passed. One evening at supper my farmer, glancing at me, wondered aloud about immaculately conceived rabbits. I shamefully looked downward. The next day I left again.

It seemed to me I wasn't able to stay in one place for too long. Probably that "destiny" protected me, keeping me aware and on the move.

It was warm, and for a time I slept in haystacks, helped with food by my friends, Baiła and Dawid Berend.

One evening I was approached by a farmer, Krupa, whom I knew to be friendly to me. He asked if I would mind talking with him for a while. He took me to his yard, where we sat down on the grass, leaning on the barn wall. We talked about Sobibor, the escape, happenings in other villages where I had been before, who of the Jews I knew to still be alive, my experiences with people, and the hopes I had. He asked me many questions. The conversation lasted about two hours before I went on my way.

This episode was of no special significance to me, and it undoubtedly would have been forgotten had I not been reminded of it fifteen years later. When I visited the Pelcs, people from my hometown, out of the blue Mr. Pelc asked if I recalled the incident. It took me a while to dig this episode out of my memory, but I did remember.

"Do you know why Krupa asked you for this talk?" Pelc asked.

"He was simply interested."

"No, we asked him to do it as a favor."

I didn't understand what Pelc had to do with it. How was he involved? He told me a story, which I listened to with mixed feelings of anger and understanding.

Krupa had been hiding four Jews from Izbica in his barn. He was paid a huge monthly fee as compensation for the danger of being discovered. When the Jews were told that Toivi Blatt was in the village, they asked the farmer to bring me close to the barn and talk to me, so that they could hear my voice and the news. And while I was talking they were glued to the wall of their hiding place.

Even though so many years had passed, anger surged in me for their insensitivity and lack of support. They were fairly secure in this hiding place, and I, despite my superficial freedom, was in constant danger of being betrayed or otherwise discovered by the Germans and killed. Why had they not asked the farmer to allow me into their hiding place? Maybe it would have cost a little more, but what was this compared to saving a life? On the other hand, in those times, each individual was fighting for his life, and I really don't know all the details of their situation then. Besides, who am I to judge? When I escaped from Sobibor, did I care for those I met in the forest, those too weak to run? So many years have passed, and now it's only a tale.

A Courier in the Polish Underground

The Rosoliński family was large. The older son was a friend of my father's. Before the war, he was one of the founders of the Christian cooperative Laczność in Izbica. I heard he lived close by and was one of the leaders of the local peasant Underground, B.Ch. (peasant battalions), in the Tarnógora district. I found him. He was very nice to me and offered to keep me for a while and let me rest.[8]

"The Germans don't come here anymore," he said. "It's safe."

About a week later, Rosoliński sent me to deliver a note in a sealed envelope to a peasant in the next village. He cautioned me, "Be careful. Don't tell anybody who you are."

By now the neighborhood was familiar, so it didn't take long to find the place and deliver the note. Instead of returning that evening, I slept in the barn. During the night I was awakened by the sound of feverish movement. Through the open gate I could see silhouettes of armed people entering. The newcomers lay down on the straw next to me without taking the slightest notice of me, and soon they were snoring! This was a partisan group resting before an undertaking against the Germans. In the morning they were all gone.

It was Sunday, and the farmer and his family insisted that I go with them to church. My religious identity was very strong, but not to arouse suspicion I agreed. I tried to lag behind a little so as to observe the customs, which were unknown to me. I imitated every movement of my Christian neighbors, but managed to avoid kneeling before the cross. My hat, too, was still on, as it is a sin for a Jew to uncover his head. I was almost relieved when the farmer knocked it from my head with a swift movement of his hand. Now *my* God would forgive me; it was not my fault that the hat was removed. Being in a church for the first time, I felt strange. I was afraid I would betray my Jewish identity. Pretending to pray with the rest, in hushed Yiddish I begged God and the souls of my murdered parents for forgiveness, and I repeated the words I remembered hearing as the tormented Jews in Sobibor passed down the "Road to the Heaven": "Shema Ysrael! Adonai Elohaynu! Adonai Echad!"

In the evening I returned to the village of Mchy and reported to Rosoliński, my mission accomplished. From then on I acted as an Underground courier and leaflet distributor for the B.Ch. I moved freely between neighboring villages with no mishaps. Often I would get together with Stefan. He told me he was in contact with a left-wing partisan group, the A.L. (Peoples Army), and that he was considering joining them in the forest. I told him I wanted to join, too, for I considered my situation in the present Underground too fragile and dangerous. In the leftist partisan group I believed I would be more secure. He promised me that if he did join them and saw that it was okay, he would let me know. That was the last I saw of him. Shortly afterward he was found dead in the forest.

It was becoming obvious that Germany was being defeated. The fighting came closer and closer, and Mchy was now occupied by frontline German troops. They brought with them a group of Soviet POWs, whom they locked up in a village barn. The final days of the German occupation approached.

By this time, most of the Polish Underground had split into two camps. Some were prepared to cooperate with the expected Communist regime; others went deeper into the forest to continue the fight for an independent Poland. My group, consisting mostly of local peasants, dissolved, and its members returned to their farms. Again I lost my base and was wandering alone in the area.

Soon the whole population was moving to underground hiding places in the fields to shelter themselves from the impending fighting, which was moving closer. But no one wanted to admit a stranger. Not to arouse suspicion by being alone in the open space, I went back to the village. I went to a barn, took out a cow, and led her toward the fields.

Nearby, a shirtless German tank crew was washing up beside a tank. One of the men threw me a cigarette. I lit up and continued on. I climbed a hillside and looked down on the village. Columns of military trucks were heading west. A few trucks were siphoning gasoline from nearby tanks and leaving. After a few minutes there was a flash, and immediately afterward the loud boom of exploding tanks. Apparently the Germans were dynamiting their own armored vehicles and abandoning them.

From the direction of Izbica, guns thundered and Soviet cannonballs fell close to us. They were trying to hit the enemy's position on a nearby hill. After a few tries, they were more accurate. It was good to see exploding metal shooting sky high. They had hit their target!

From the edge of the forest emerged a horseman in a dark cape. He pulled in the reins and the horse reared. Lifting binoculars to his eyes, he studied the area, turned around, and galloped away. He must have been the head of a Red Army patrol.

The cow! I had forgotten the cow! She had disappeared. Now I must hide, for I could look suspicious. But the only hiding places were stacks of wheat. I approached one, and a face peered out. The man beckoned me and asked in Russian if I could still see Germans. He explained he was a Russian officer who had escaped from the barn where he had been held prisoner with the others the night before. Somewhere nearby, a machine gun rattled. Another answered far away. The Soviet officer listened to the sound of explosions and excitedly explained, with a voice of authority, that the front had moved and the Soviet soldiers were now most likely passing on the left side of the village.

The shooting intensified. After about fifteen minutes we heard a machine-gun exchange again. High in the sky, planes were circling like wasps, making slight knocking sounds and giving off white puffs of smoke. A dogfight was in progress. From the ground the planes looked like toys—some with new, unfamiliar contours and double tails. Then the action moved slowly westward and disappeared from view.

I walked down a village trail. No one was around. Peasants were still afraid to step outside. The village itself, as I could observe, was also empty. I reported back to the Red Army officer, and he concluded that the Germans had evacuated Mchy. At first I couldn't see how. But he explained to me that probably the main front simply bypassed us and the Germans escaped.

We reentered the village together. The officer went into a house to wash himself, and I wandered about, looking around in bewilderment. I still did not believe that the miraculous moment of liberation was here.

In the distance I could see a bicyclist. I recognized his green Soviet soldier's uniform. I started toward him. He turned his bike in my direction. Coming closer he stopped, lifted his leg over the seat, and quietly asked in Russian, "Germantzuv nyet [No Germans]?"

"Nyet, ushle [No, they left]."

The soldier turned around and continued in the direction from which he had come. A second later it struck me that this unbelievable moment was the moment I had waited for through many difficult years, thought of so often in jail, dreamed of in the death factory, built up in my imagination a thousand times, lived for in Bojarski's hideout . . . and now this moment had actually come! I was finally free. I should have been ecstatic, I should have jumped for joy. So why did I feel such sadness, such tremendous sorrow, such emptiness in my soul?

What my survival instincts had suppressed now hit me with full force. My loved ones were gone, my world was gone. I felt empty, sad, and alone.

A Free Man

I was free. I knew that my family was dead, and I had nowhere to go. Shortly thereafter the regular Red Army rolled into Mchy. A tank column stopped in the middle of the village. I started a friendly conversation with a tank commander, telling him my story. That afternoon the tank column received an order to move on. For the first time I felt secure and asked to be allowed to go with them. The commander declined, but I refused to step down from the body of the tank. He called two soldiers, who removed me by force and left me in the middle of the road. Sad and disheartened, I started to walk slowly toward Izbica.

After an hour's walk, I entered the shtetl and soon realized I was a stranger in my own birthplace and had nowhere to turn. I visited Mrs. Królikowski. The old lady greeted me happily. We talked until late in the night, and she tried to convince me to stop following the "Jewish ways" of earning a living through bartering. She said I should learn a useful trade, which she was ready to teach me in the bakery she owned. She gave me a blanket and directed me to a warm sleeping place on top of the oven.

At two o'clock in the morning, I was awakened by the baker, Mr. Piasecki, when his work began. I soon learned how to prepare bagels and pretzels and how to clean the oven. I received the same food as the other workers—soup and plenty of bagels. Tired, I went to sleep at six in the morning.

About two weeks later, in the middle of the night, someone knocked on the bakery door, demanding entry. Mrs. Królikowski came down, her hair unkempt. "Toivi," she said, breathing heavily, "run to the attic." Being used to such emergencies, I did not ask questions, and in a minute was hiding in the darkest corner of the attic. I heard the door open and some conversation, and then the door closed again. Time passed, and Mrs. Królikowski called me back to work.

By intuition I understood the danger I was in. They were looking for me. Since I had been working at the bakery I never ventured outside, but the word had probably spread that a Jew was there.

As soon as Królikowski disappeared, Piasecki called me aside and said, "Toivi, run from here and don't wait, because it will be too late." He told me that there were no more Jews in Izbica. Their property now belonged to strangers, who did not want to return it. In small places like Izbica, the few returning Jews were unprotected and often killed. "They are looking for you, they are looking. Run, run today to Lublin, before it is too late," he repeated.

I was shocked. Now liberated, was I still in danger? I took a few rolls wrapped in newspaper and went outside to catch a bus to Lublin, the big city, where I would be safe. It was afternoon, people were walking in the street, and many still recognized me. I soon discovered there was no regular transportation; the only way out was to hitch a ride. Solitary Soviet military vehicles passed by fairly often but did not dare to stop, even though I flagged them down. After a few hours of futile effort, I noticed some men following my every move. Coming closer, I recognized one as my executioner in Bojarski's barn. Izbica was a small place; word had probably reached them that Blatt was on the street.

I understood my predicament immediately and knew that they were only waiting for dusk to close in. When hiding in the forest I was always a step ahead of those looking for me, and now, like a fool, I had walked right into their arms. Bojarski knew very well that if I survived he would need to go into hiding.[9]

In despair, I told myself that, no matter what, I would stop the next passing truck. And so, when I noticed a heavy army vehicle coming down the road, I jumped in front of it, waving my hands. The horn shrieked and shrieked, but I did not move. It was my only way out. Behind me was certain death.

At the last minute the truck halted, hitting the brakes just a few feet from me. Out came a Soviet officer, gun in hand, yelling at me to get out of the way.

Trembling, in a quiet voice, I tried to make him understand. "I'm not an enemy," I said. "I'm only a Jew in terrible danger. Please, I beg you, take me with you!"

THE AUTHOR AFTER THE LIBERATION — AGE 17

"I'm sorry," he said roughly. "This is an army vehicle, not to be used for civilians. Besides, there is no room in the truck."

"Then you might as well run me over," I said. "I will not move. Please," I implored him, "take pity on me."

He stared at me intently for a few moments. "OK," he said resignedly. "Get in the back."

I jumped up. The bed of the truck held an anti-aircraft machine gun with a metal seat similar to that on a tractor. There I sat, holding onto the grips of the heavy gun handle. I looked down to see the few Poles below me, standing there, disappointed. I continued to look as the truck noisily moved on. Their figures gradually receded, becoming smaller and smaller until they disappeared altogether, as in bad dream.

Notes

Foreword

1. *Trials of the Major War Criminals before the International Military Tribunal,* vol. 30, p. 95 (2278-PS: Seyss-Inquart report on trip to Poland, November 17-22, 1939).

2. *Faschimus, Getto, Massenmord* (East Berlin, 1960), 46 (Frank speech in Radom, November 25, 1939).

3. *The Goebbels Diaries, 1942-1943,* ed. and trans. Louis Lochner (New York: Doubleday, 1948), 175-76.

4. Gitta Sereny, *Into That Darkness: From Mercy Killing to Mass Murder* (London: André Deutsch, 1974), 112.

Preface

1. Sobibor was one of three death camps built in rapid succession under the code name Operation Reinhard, named in honor of Reinhard Heydrich, chairman of the infamous January 1942 Wannsee Conference on the "Final Solution of the Jewish Question," who was assassinated by Czech patriots on June 5, 1942. Bełżec was completed in March 1942; Sobibor was built in March and April; Treblinka was finished in July. Referred to as *Durchsgangslagers* (transit camps), they worked assembly-line fashion to produce only one product: death. Of the nearly six million Jews annihilated in the Holocaust, between 1.5 million and 1.7 million were killed in the three Operation Reinhard facilities; the exact number will never be known (figures based on the Hagen Court proceedings).

2. At that time, the full story of Sobibor remained hidden from history. Sobibor was the most secretive of the extermination camps,

and very little official documentation survives. Most of what was written in the camp or by the Operation Reinhard staff in Lublin was destroyed. Only two contemporary documents referring to Sobibor were ever found. One, an entry in Emmanuel Ringelblum's Warsaw ghetto diary (June 17, 1942), refers to the Jewish "resettlements" and the Sobibor gas ovens (in *Yad Vashem Studies* 7 [1968]: 177-80). The other was a report by the Polish Underground, printed in the Underground press in July 1942 (Archive, Central Committee of the Polish United Workers' Party, Warsaw, Information for the Polish Government-in-Exile in London; see "Informacja Biezaca," #38).

The Beginning

1. Kapo: Possibly taken from the German *Kamaraden-polizei* (comrade police) or from the Italian *capo* (first). Trustee in charge of a detachment of prisoners. Drawn from the prisoners, Kapos enjoyed some privileges. Most of them were very cruel.

2. According to archival documents (RGL Adm. 643,k.59), Izbica, a town on the eastern bank of the Wieprz River, was established as a Jewish settlement in the seventeenth century by King August III of Poland.

3. *Yerishe* (Yiddish): An inherited family household.

4. Kohn's son survived and lives in Holon, Israel. When I visited him in 1957, he remembered sending this letter to his father.

5. After the war, Engels was discovered to be an owner of the chic Café Engels in Hamburg. The day after I testified at the trial against Engels (December 29 and 30, 1958; Hamburg [(56) 6/57]), he committed suicide in his jail cell.

6. In 1978, Klemm was discovered living in Germany under the name Ludwig Jantz. He committed suicide in his jail cell in Limburg in May 1979.

7. *Volksdeutscher*: A person of German descent who lived outside Germany. Most descended from former German colonists who settled in Russia and Poland. Classified by the Nazis as Germans, they were encouraged to become part of a "greater Reich."

8. Because Izbica was not an enclosed ghetto, Jews and Christians were allowed to live next to each other.

9. Y.W.A.: An ironic acronym from the Yiddish *Yidden Willen Azoi* (Jews Want It So).

For a Lease on Life

1. Red Cross food supplements were delivered only to Christian prisoners.

2. The Bełżec camp stopped exterminating Jews at the end of 1942, but cremation of the bodies stored in huge graves continued for several months in 1943.

3. In fact, there was an official order from the Office of the General Government in Kraków designating Izbica and a few other ghettos as places where Jews could live legally (VB I GG. S. 5).

4. This was a sadistic allusion to rumors that the Nazis made soap from human fat.

5. He was later killed by the police at the Jewish cemetery.

Sobibor – Hell

1. The Sobibor camp was located three miles from the Bug River in a sparsely populated area in the eastern part of occupied Poland near the village of Sobibor, between the cities of Chełm and Włodawa. A special side rail led from the Sobibor train station directly into the camp.

2. The interior of the camp was divided into a Vorlager or garrison area and four main inner sections—Lagers I, II, III, and IV (Lager IV was constructed later)—each separated from the others by a barbed-wire fence. These were, in essence, cages within cages.

The garrison area included the main entrance gates, the extension rail from the Sobibor train station, and the railway platform where the victims were taken off the trains. The commandant's villa, Swallow's Nest, stood opposite the platform, flanked on the right by the guardhouse and on the left by the armory. The SS villa, known as The Happy Flea, as well as additional quarters, a garage, and a mess hall were nearby. The Ukrainian guards' barracks were located to the north, opposite the fence. Jewish slave labor made life comfortable for the Nazi staff. Although the Nuremberg laws of September 1935 made sexual contact between Germans and Jews a racial crime, some Nazis used young Jewish girls for their pleasure.

Lager I, built directly west of and behind the garrison area, was made escape-proof with extra barbed-wire fences and a deep trench filled with water. The only opening was a gate leading into the garrison area. This Lager was the living barracks for the Jewish prisoners and included the prisoners' kitchen and workshops that provided services for the Nazi staff. The barracks were built with materials taken from the homes of Jews deported from nearby ghettos and from material delivered by train from the SS warehouses in Chełm and Lublin. Additional barracks were constructed toward the end of September 1942 and again in July 1943. Each prisoner was given approximately twelve feet of sleeping space. Female prisoners slept in a separate barrack. Approximately fifty Jews were employed in Lager I, and they provided virtually every needed service: tailor and shoemaker shops (separate for Ukrainian and German staff), shops for carpentry, mechanical, and other maintenance needs. After work, Jewish prisoners from throughout the camp (except Lager III) were assembled in Lager I for roll call and night lockup.

Lager II was a larger section and included a variety of essential "services"—both for the killing process and the everyday operation of the camp. Worked by four hundred prisoners, including about a hundred women, Lager II contained the warehouses used for storing the articles taken from the victims—hair, clothing, food, gold, and all other valuables. Lager II also contained a small farm with stables for the Nazis' pleasure horses and where cows for fresh milk and pigs and geese for fresh meat could be found. This Lager also housed the main administration offices. A tall observation tower overlooked the entire area. It was in Lager II as well that the Jews were "greeted" and prepared for their death. Separated from the women and children, the men were ordered to undress and led immediately along the Himmelstrasse and into the gas chambers in Lager III. After undressing, the women and children were led into a special barrack on the Himmelstrasse, just steps away from the gas chambers and the crematorium, where the women's hair was cut. In the meantime, with assembly-line efficiency, the clothing was searched and sorted, and documents were destroyed.

Lager III was where the victims met their end. Located in the northwestern part of the camp, there were only two ways to enter Lager III from Lager II. The camp staff and personnel entered through a small, nondescript gate. The entrance for victims was also the place of their earthly exit: it descended immediately into the gas chambers, which were decorated with flowers, a Star of David, and the inscription "Bathhouse." Security in Lager III was extremely tight, not only to prevent escape, but also to keep the curious and nonessential workers out. Barbed wire braided with tree branches prevented workers from others parts of the camp from looking in. Approximately 150 Jews worked in Lager III.

Lager IV or "North," as it was sometimes called, built in August 1943, was to be a depot and sorting place for arms taken from the Soviet army. It played no direct role in the extermination process, although many prisoners, especially Dutch Jews, lost their lives building it under torturous conditions.

3. Numbers indicate the location of Sobibor buildings. See the map on page xxiv.

4. SS Hauptsturmführer Franz Stangl, one of Sobibor's commandants, described the innocence and trust of the victims when he was interviewed in prison by Gitta Sereny, an English writer:

> When I was on a trip once, years later in Brazil, . . . my train stopped next to a slaughterhouse. The cattle in the pens, hearing the noise of the train, trotted up to the fence and stared at the train. They were very close to my window, one crowding the other, looking at me through that fence. I thought then, "Look at this; this reminds me of Poland; that's just how the people looked, trustingly, just before they went into the tins. . . ." . . . I couldn't eat tinned meat after that. Those big eyes . . . which looked at me . . . not knowing that in no time at all they'd all be dead.

(Sereny, *Into That Darkness: From Mercy Killing to Mass Murder* [London: André Deutsch, 1974], 201.)

5. I later found out that SS Oberscharführer Hermann Michel, dressed in a doctor's white coat, played this role of deception. The speech was designed to stall the group while the first group was gassed.

6. In the early days of the camp, approximately 85,000 corpses were buried in huge pits about 200 feet long, 50 feet wide, and 25 feet deep. In the second half of 1942, special cremation sites were built: huge roasting grills constructed of railroad ties set atop high concrete supports. Each device was able to consume two to three thousand

bodies at one time. Corpses from graves were burned together with bodies from incoming transports. The pyre was sometimes over three yards high when doused with kerosene and ignited.

7. The most conclusive evidence that something murderous was taking place in Lager III was the fact that no one ever came out alive, but such evidence was purely circumstantial. The Nazis made it difficult to collect any direct evidence of what was widely known throughout the camp. After the war, the only direct information came from former prisoners who had made contact with the Lager III workers and from limited observations from Lager II; testimony from Germans and Ukrainian guards filled in the remaining details.

8. Leon Feldhendler quoted these notes in his 1944 diary, deposited in the Jewish Historical Institute in Warsaw in 1945.

9. In his 1983 interview with me, SS Frenzel admitted that the Nazis were ready to liquidate all the prisoners if the camp perimeter was penetrated. See appendix.

10. This account comes from my interviews with Szlomo Podchlebnik, Josef Kopf, and others escapees who survived the war. Podchlebnik emigrated to the United States; Kopf was murdered when he went back to "friendly" Poles to pick up the belongings he had left with them for safekeeping.

11. Josef Duniec survived the war and lived in France. In 1965, a day before testifying against the captured Sobibor Nazis, he died of a heart attack.

12. Sasha was born in Kremenchug (Ukraine) in 1909. In 1915 his family moved to Rostov-on Don, where he earned a degree in music. Until the start of the war, he worked as an organizer and teacher of amateur drama and music groups. He was mobilized when the war started, and, in October 1941, was taken prisoner by the Germans and held in a POW camp. After an escape attempt in 1942, he was transferred to a punishment camp in Mińsk. Recognized there as a Jew, he was sent with other Jews to Sobibor.

13. The final accounting reveals how remarkable an achievement the revolt was. Out of approximately 550 prisoners, over half initially escaped.

Initially escaped Sobibor: 320
Jews remaining in camp, including 30 in Lager III: 150

Killed in combat and minefields: 80

Captured in dragnet and executed: approx. 170

Successfully escaped: 150

Killed in hiding, mostly by hostile local elements: 97

Killed fighting the Germans in partisan units or in the regular army: 5

Survived revolt to be liberated by the Allies: 48

All figures are approximate. See Hagen Court proceedings, Ks 54/76 LC; author's interview with Karl Frenzel, Hagen, Germany, April 1983 (see appendix); Zentralstelle Dortmund 45 Js 27/61 St. A. Additionally, eight Jews survived the July 20, 1943, Waldkommando escape and two survived individual escapes. A total of fifty-eight Sobibor Jews survived to be liberated.

Freedom – The Illusion

1. For the Jews who had escaped, the next few weeks were terrifying. They were hunted by a determined adversary that consisted of a company of over one hundred regular soldiers, one hundred mounted police, and an additional 150 Ukrainians and SS soldiers. On October 16 and 17, the Second and Third Squadron of mounted SS and police added five hundred more men to the manhunt. This force was formidable enough, but one must add to it the auxiliary units, regional police units, and local collaborators, aided by two Luftwaffe observation aircraft, to comprehend the odds against the Jews. The official search was finally ended on October 21 (author's interview with Karl Frenzel; see appendix). But escapees continued to be captured individually or in groups, and the police headquarters in Lublin continued to send cables to police headquarters in Kraków as escapees were caught (copies of these cables in author's files).

2. When I interviewed Sasha in Rostov in 1979, he told me why he did not come back:

My job was done. You were Polish Jews on your own terrain. I belonged in the Soviet Union and still considered myself a soldier. In my opinion the chances for survival were better in smaller units. To tell the people straight out "We must part" would not have worked. You know they would have followed every step of mine, and if that had happened, all of us would have perished.

On the night of October 19-20, with the help of a Polish peasant, Sasha and his group crossed the Bug River. Two days later they met Voroshilov partisans and fought the Germans behind the German lines by sabotaging their transports and annihilating small garrisons. Cybulski and Kali Mali were killed. Sasha soon joined the Red Army. After being severely wounded in the leg in August 1944, he received a medal for bravery and returned to civilian life. He died in 1990.

3. Most of the local Polish "intelligentsia" were taken to Auschwitz and killed.

4. After the war, I returned and talked to Platto about this incident. He said there were no Germans in his home at the time, and the dog belonged to him.

5. X rays taken after the war revealed a bullet lodged in my jaw, where it remains embedded today.

6. Carrying weapons was a danger for Jews because of order #116 issued by Polish Underground leader General Stefan Bor-Komorowski on September 15, 1943. The order implied that armed Jews are plunderers and murderers.

7. After the war, when I met Mr. Lewandowski, a friend of my father's, the riddle was solved. Since my father had been a volunteer legionnaire in World War I, he was considered a Polish patriot, a fighter for the freedom of Poland. So each time I was caught, the leaders in this area, former legionnaires and friends of my father, including Lewandowski, set me free.

8. The reader will wonder that I sometimes suggest that the nationalistic Polish Underground killed Jews and yet here the leaders in the local organization protected me and were, in regard to Jews at least, indifferent. In actuality, a great deal depended on the particular individual.

9. Bojarski and his family abandoned their farm and disappeared after the war. On a visit to Izbica in 1995, I learned that Bojarski died in Wrocław, Silesia, in 1993.

✤

Appendix

Translation from the German of an April 1983 interview between Thomas Toivi Blatt and Karl August Frenzel, a commandant at Sobibor. This interview was subsequently included in an article about Blatt and Frenzel, "Der Mörder und Sein Zeuge" by Ulrich Völklein, in *Stern* 13 (22 March 1984); reprinted here by permission. Blatt testified at several of Frenzel's trials. After one of these trials, Frenzel requested to speak with Blatt. They met in a hotel room in Hagen, Germany.

BLATT: *Here you are drinking beer. With that smile on your face you could be anybody's neighbor, anybody's fellow sporting-club member. But you are not anybody. You are Karl Frenzel, the SS commandant. You ranked third in the chain of command at the extermination camp of Sobibor. You were the commandant of Lager I. Do you remember me?*

FRENZEL: Not exactly. You were a small boy then.

BLATT: *I was fifteen years old. I survived because you made me your shoeshine boy. Besides me, nobody survived: not my father, not my mother, not my brother, none of the two thousand Jews from my town, Izbica.*

FRENZEL: That was terrible, just terrible . . .

BLATT: *. . . at least a quarter-million Jews were murdered at Sobibor. I survived. Why would you want to speak with me?*

FRENZEL: I would like to apologize to you.

BLATT: *You want to apologize to me?*

FRENZEL: I would like to apologize. Nothing can be done about the victims. What happened, happened. We can't change anything about that. But I would like to extend my personal apologies to you. I am not angry with you and the other witnesses, those who already testified and those who are still to come.

BLATT: *You would like to apologize?*

FRENZEL: I can only say it again in tears. Not only am I beside myself now, no, back then, too, I was greatly bothered by it all.

BLATT: *But you didn't prevent any of it from happening. You took part in it.*

FRENZEL: You don't know what went on inside of us. You don't understand the circumstances in which we found ourselves.

BLATT: *And we, and our circumstances?*

FRENZEL: I spent sixteen and a half years in prison. I suffered a lot and I thought long about justice and injustice.

BLATT: *Were you an anti-Semite or did you do these things because you were ordered to do them?*

FRENZEL: I was no anti-Semite, but we had to do our duty. For us, this was a bad time.

BLATT: *Duty. That's what it always comes down to, duty. Why did you club my father to the ground immediately upon arrival? Was that your duty too?*

FRENZEL: I don't remember.

BLATT: *Do you remember Cukerman?*

FRENZEL: Yes, he was the cook. At one time, five or eight kilograms of meat were missing. When we searched the kitchen, the meat was found. That's why I beat him . . .

BLATT: *. . . and the son.*

FRENZEL: He came to me and said, "My father didn't hide the meat, I did." I said, "Then you'll get twenty-five lashes with the whip too." I would like you to know, I was always fair. I never punished anyone who didn't do anything wrong.

BLATT: *So you were always fair. Philip Białowicz testified that you caught his fifteen-year-old friend stealing a can of sardines. You took him to Lager III, the crematorium, and shot him.*

FRENZEL: That wasn't me.

BLATT: *It wasn't you? And what happened to the Dutch Jews?*

FRENZEL: A Polish Kapo told me that several Dutch Jews were preparing a revolt and I reported it to Commandant Niemann. He ordered the execution of seventy-two Jews.

BLATT: *. . . and you were the one who took them to the gas chamber.*

FRENZEL: . . . no, not I.

BLATT: *Do you remember the little Kapo Berliner? Rumor had it that you gave permission to kill him. Is that true?*

FRENZEL: I remember it that way too. My Kapo at the train station command came to me and told me about Berliner. Then the Ukrainian guards said, "What shall we do with him?" Maybe I said, "Kill him" or something like that, the kind of thing one says at a moment when one is not alone.

BLATT: *You had children of your own. When you saw small children—*

*five years old, one year old, one week old—marked for death, didn't you
feel something inside?*

FRENZEL: I never touched any children, even though other witnesses
have accused me of it. I want you to know, there was a small child
and her mother. Wagner wanted to send them to the gas chamber. I
arranged it so they wouldn't have to go to the gas chamber. The
mother worked in the laundry. The girl was about ten years old.

BLATT: *Neither one survived the camp.*

FRENZEL: I don't know. But it is incomprehensible to me that I should
be accused of having killed children.

BLATT: *Tens of thousands of children were killed at Sobibor.*

FRENZEL: I condemn what happened to the Jews. I understand how
you must feel. You cannot forget; neither can I. I dream about it at
night; for sixteen years in prison. Just as you dream about it at night.

BLATT: *When did you join the party?*

FRENZEL: 1930. Before that I was a member of the communist carpenters' association. My father was a Social Democrat.

BLATT: *Why did you join the party?*

FRENZEL: Because of the unemployment.

BLATT: *What did your father say about this?*

FRENZEL: Well, we were adults and wouldn't have listened anyway.
Concerning unemployment, the situation then was just as it is today.
People join the Greens or the Rockers or whatnot. It was exactly like
that then. Only we were not as bad as they are today.

BLATT: *What was the situation like before the "seizure of power" at the
time when you joined the party?*

FRENZEL: I was apprenticed as a carpenter, and after taking the qualifying exam I was unemployed. And the party promised that there would be jobs after the seizure of power. Things actually did get better after 1933. But this whole problem which you are probably driving at, the anti-Jewish slogans, to that we didn't give much thought. When I got married in 1934, we bought our furniture from a Jewish furniture merchant.

BLATT: *Were you appalled by the first anti-Jewish measures?*

FRENZEL: I was appalled by that and so was my brother, who joined the party in 1929. I had nothing to do with Kristallnacht in 1938. There were no Jews in our immediate neighborhood. My first girlfriend was Jewish, at eighteen. The relationship dissolved when her father heard that I was a party member. Her father was the editor of the Social Democratic newspaper *Vorwärts*. In 1934, her family emigrated to America.

BLATT: *I guess everyone had their good Jews in those days. Did your girlfriend come from a religious family?*

FRENZEL: No. After all she was a Jew.

BLATT: *Did you go to church?*

FRENZEL: Yes, frequently.

BLATT: *Was there never a time when your religious views and your political views came into conflict with each other?*

FRENZEL: No. After all, we were German Christians [a sector of the Protestant Church close to the Nazi Party]. My children were all baptized. I was married in a church. My brother was a theology student. My wife and I went to church—if not every Sunday, at least every other or third Sunday—for the children's sake.

BLATT: *And even today, you, as a Christian, have no problem with that time.*

FRENZEL: I have nothing to hide, after all. I am sorry that I was part of that gang then.

BLATT: *Back then you had no regrets about it?*

FRENZEL: We found out about it when we arrived at Sobibor. When we received our orders, we were told that it was a work camp. What we had to do was guard the camp.

BLATT: *When you returned home on furlough, did you talk with your family about what was going on?*

FRENZEL: No. That was a state secret. It was forbidden to talk about it even with one's closest family on penalty of concentration camp or death.

BLATT: *Why didn't you just ask to be transferred—to the front, for example?*

FRENZEL: I wanted to get away. I asked my brother to effect my transfer. But it didn't work. So, all I could do was do my duty.

BLATT: *And you were not torn between your "duty" and your Christian faith?*

FRENZEL: Oh, yes, of course! Ever since 1945, I have been cursing the Nazis—for everything, for what they did, and everything they stood for. I fought against the devil. Since 1945 I have refrained from any involvement in politics.

BLATT: *Sobibor—the extermination of 250,000 Jews—that was your duty?*

FRENZEL: We had to do our duty. I am sorry about what happened there, but I cannot make what's done undone. I would like to ask the forgiveness of all of them. The things that have stayed with you have also stayed with me. And I, too, have often thought about it, about justice and injustice, and I have come to the conclusion that what happened then was an injustice. I condemn that time.

BLATT: *Duty and justice and injustice. What does that say about the death of a human being, a quarter-million human beings?*

FRENZEL: I can well sympathize. I do not despise you by any means. What you went through, you can never forget. And what we went through—I, too, cannot forget. Just as you dream about it at night, I dream about it at night.

BLATT: *What does your family, your children, say about it all today?*

FRENZEL: My wife is no longer alive. The Russians destroyed her in 1945. They raped her, then she had abdominal typhus, of which she died.

BLATT: *And your children?*

FRENZEL: The children detest it all and denounce it as a crime. But they still are on my side. They don't detest me. They condemn all that happened. They also saw the Holocaust film. We had a discussion then.

BLATT: *Do you think a film can recreate this . . . ?*

FRENZEL: . . . not recreate. No.

BLATT: *The reality was worse . . .*

FRENZEL: . . . much worse. Something like this cannot be recreated. I beg you to see me from a different perspective, other than Sobibor. I have much on my conscience, many human lives. Not one, no—100,000 human lives are on my conscience.

BLATT: *How do you respond when Germans say that it is not true, that it never happened?*

FRENZEL: When my children and friends ask me whether it is true, I tell them yes, it is true. And when they say, but this is impossible, then I tell them again, it is really true. It is wrong to say that it never happened.

BLATT: *Then why don't you go to the newspapers and tell them, I was there, I worked there, and it is true?*

FRENZEL: If I were to go there and tell them that I was part of it and that all of it is true—these five and a half million Jews were murdered—I would be afraid.

BLATT: *Of whom?*

FRENZEL: Of neo-Nazis.

BLATT: *Are they that strong?*

FRENZEL: No, they are weak and should be outlawed.

BLATT: *If they are that weak, why are you afraid of them? Why don't you tell? You have much to tell to the world.*

FRENZEL: They are here and there. If I went to the press—they have their connections.

BLATT: *Tell me again, why did you want to speak with me?*

FRENZEL: I wanted to apologize to you in person for all that happened then. If you would accept my apologies in the name of the victims, it would in some small measure be a comfort to me. I wanted to have a heart-to-heart talk between two human beings. I can understand how you feel and that you harbor a certain hatred against us. I don't hold that against you. I would feel the same way.

BLATT: *Do you want to ask me anything else?*

FRENZEL: That's all. It is, was, my heart's desire to have a heart-to-heart talk—and that you should see me in a different light, not as a member of the SS, but as a civilian, now forty years later.

TRANSLATED BY BRIGITTE M. GOLDSTEIN

✤

Jewish Lives